MOVING MOUNTAINS

or

The Art and Craft of Letting Others See Things Your Way

by

H. M. BOETTINGER

Collier Books
Macmillan Publishing Company
New York
Collier Macmillan Publishers
London

Collier Books
Macmillan Publishing Company
866 Third Avenue, New York, N.Y. 10022
Collier Macmillan Canada, Inc.

0-02-030660-1

Macmillan books are available at special discounts for bulk purchases for sales promotions, premiums, fund-raising, or educational use. For details, contact:

Special Sales Director
Macmillan Publishing Company
866 Third Avenue
New York, N.Y. 10022

First Collier Books Edition 1974 in rack-size, 1989 in trade paperback

10 9 8 7 6 5 4 3 2 1

Printed in the United States of America

For Shirley

CONTENTS

Moving Mountains

Background
or
Some Undistinguished Teachers I Have Known

We have played a nasty trick on generations of schoolchildren by telling them that "if a man builds a better mousetrap, the world will beat a path to his door." Later, when some of the gifted seize an opportunity for innovation, if they haven't seen the joke by then, they are headed for trouble. It comes in different sizes. Some wait like unrequited lovers for the assault on their doors which never comes. Others nurse grudges against a dense and stupid world which does not appreciate real talent, and the rest work off their bitterness by battering the ideas of others. Seldom do these good people find their source of failure in the faulty technique used to introduce their fragile infants to the rigors of critical opinion, prejudice, and human inertia.

This book is for those who have something to say, but who are dissatisfied or irritated by their inability to present their thoughts to others. As a boy I discovered Thomas Gray's *Elegy*, and several decades of observation and involvement have confirmed one of his insights:

1

> Full many a flower is born to blush unseen,
> And waste its sweetness on the desert air.

My own adult life has been spent in many areas of a large corporation, in a few universities, and as an enlisted man and junior officer in World War II. It is a life more typical than remarkable in our day. Like most of us, I have been involved in hundreds of situations where persons of diverse backgrounds and talents have tried to communicate what they thought, knew, or wanted to other minds. I have heard and watched practitioners in most areas of modern life in their attempts to persuade— lawyers, natural and social scientists, soldiers, civil servants, executives, physicians, engineers, foremen, politicians, mechanics, labor union leaders, shop stewards, artists, musicians, architects, philosophers, film makers, advertising men, accountants, college students, clubwomen, men of the cloth, sundry teachers, and lesser breeds without the law, to name a few. Some were eminent, most unknown. All were persons of intelligence, having something worthwhile to say, but the range of persuasive skill ran from embarrassing, painful failures (including cases of physical collapse) to skillful performers whose presentations were perfectly tuned to their audiences, and who made changing your mind an exhilarating experience. What makes the difference? Neither schooling, material, nor rank—of this I'm sure. Whether the audience was one or a thousand, success invariably attended only those who both understood and presented their ideas *from the viewpoint of the needs and characteristics of the persons in their audience.* This sounds like a useless cliché, but before rejecting it, recall incidents from your own experience and decide for yourself what determined success or failure.

> One ship drives east and another drives west
> With the selfsame winds that blow.
> 'Tis the set of the sails
> And not the gales
> Which tells us the way to go.[1]

[1] Ella Wheeler Wilcox.

The rest of this book tries to show how to "set your sails" if you want to achieve this viewpoint, for it is one observer's exploration of normal human nature and its reactions to ideas.

The skills, techniques, and "things to watch" are within the grasp of anyone who wants to acquire them. They do not require any special knowledge to learn, but desire and some effort are essential. Every reader can test the validity for himself, since he has been on both sides of conversations throughout his life. Presentation of ideas is conversation carried on at high voltage—at once more dangerous and more powerful. Good packaging will not gain acceptance for bad products (it really kills them faster). But a good package will at least give a good product a chance to make it on its own merits. Ideas are indeed quite fragile and need more "care in wrapping" than articles of commerce, but few realize it, and less practice it. If their number is increased by one, our world is better off.

Warning! Several well-intentioned friends have advised me to furnish voluminous footnotes, references, and learned texts to support the statements in this book. I appreciate their concern, but have rejected their advice for two reasons:

First, I assure the reader that I can produce some paraphernalia of scholarship to support and contradict nearly every thought set down here.

Second, but far more important, is the fact that if some of the ideas work for a specific reader and appeal to his taste, no amount of contradictory vacillation will—or should—deter him from their use. Conversely, if he finds others repellent or ineffective, he is unlikely to adopt them for his own use merely because some obscure research paper insists that he should.

Presentations are a very personal art form. The ideas expressed here are no more than the reflections and observations of two decades by one who desires the art to grow in better minds and hands.

I

Why Others
Welcome Your Ideas
And Why They Don't

Ideas are not truly alive if they remain locked in a single mind. Our need to transfer them to others forces us to consider why and where we want them to go, and how we want them to get there. This demands orientation toward the audience. "Audience" in its narrow sense, of course, assumes a *hearing* of the message. While the human voice is the most powerful method of communication, we will use "audience" in the broader sense, as the group aimed at regardless of the form used. Our objective is to get an idea accepted, and usually a mixture of methods—letters, memos, or reports as well as talks, conferences, and formal presentations—will be necessary if the idea is to have more than a trivial impact. The same principles and approaches are applicable to all forms, and the over-all plan should use whatever combination best does the job. We will go into the strategy and tactics involved in some depth later.

Ideas that call for drastic changes in the current handling of affairs, large amounts of money, or new allocations of manpower

5

are certain to require an oral presentation—usually at the highest level of approval. Requirements for this ultimate oral presentation should dominate the campaign from its earliest stages. At the other end of the range of human affairs, small changes or suggestions are handled almost entirely orally. Thus the crucial point in decisions—large and small—is an oral presentation, because the people who have the power and responsibility to say *yes* or *no* want a chance to consider and question the proposal in the flesh. Documents merely set up a meeting and record what the meeting decided. All the kings of yore listened, questioned, and judged (those wary of change or usurpers listened even more), but only a minority could read and write. Their lordly seals were devices to make up for missing clerical skill—which only clerics were expected to have. Old ways linger on. Garden clubs, faculty conferences, boards of directors, town meetings, and legislatures share a common origin in the councils of primitive tribes. A chief of the Sioux could grasp the idea of a city council meeting quickly, even though he'd find the furniture uncomfortable. Anyone serious about an idea welcomes the chance to present it himself—in person. We wisely discount proposals whose authors are unwilling to be present at the launching.

Audiences are not made up of homogeneous units. Every individual member of an audience brings his own unique mixture of background and temperament. As Alfred North Whitehead pointed out: "Each human being is a more complex structure than any social system to which he belongs."

What we call an "audience" is a group of individuals who at some moment have only one thing in common: They are listening to the same message. Each listens for a different reason, and each expects to carry away something different for his own purposes. A few years ago, the Metropolitan Museum acquired a Rembrandt painting, *Aristotle Contemplating the Bust of Homer*, at a cost exceeding two million dollars. On the first day of public showing, twenty-five thousand persons, after long waits, filed by its easel in the main hall with hushed, religious demeanor. For months the picture continued to attract enormous crowds. Busloads of school children, women's clubs, and fraternal groups made their pilgrimage to the Fifth Avenue shrine. Today, this painting hangs in a second floor gallery along with a dozen others from Rembrandt's hand. It is now viewed by the normal run of visitors, who distribute their attention about equally to each canvas in that Dutch-Flemish collection.

A painting is an idea involving peculiar and complex techniques for its own presentation. (These techniques offer many useful lessons for our purpose, and we will discuss them later.) But consider what was happening. A man's silent idea, conceived over three hundred years ago, was presented to hundreds of thousands of people, who went to a great deal of trouble to see what he had to say. Every one came for a different reason. Some to see what two million dollars worth of property that had dubious value to them looked like hung on a wall, others to enjoy a trip to town, but most were in search of an uplifting experience —though they'd probably be embarrassed if pressed to explain. Few came to reason why Aristotle was contemplating the bust of Homer; or why Rembrandt was compelled to immortalize this highly unlikely moment in Aristotle's life; or why he put him in the costume of a wealthy Dutchman. For some it was their first visit to any museum, and attitudes toward art began their growth in new minds. Some latent talent began its first stirrings in a schoolchild, and contemporary artists measured their own attainments with unaccustomed modesty. Not one will be exactly the same as before; not one took away the same message as the others. Other pictures of equal merit were there before, but crowds did not press to see them. Humans often do the right things for the wrong reason, and if publicity brought some who otherwise wouldn't go, we should be grateful, not patronizing.

This incident furnishes an accurate way to view an audience: as a long line of individuals who listen to your idea from their own point of view. Some see more than you meant, a few see exactly what you want, some are interested for the fleeting moment, and some couldn't care less. Only an unthinking spectator would lump them together as "that crowd at the Met on a culture kick," as one did to me.

Motivations of individuals are as varied as their number, and the experienced presenter knows and expects this. People voluntarily expose themselves to the stimulus of an idea either to damn it or to satisfy various needs: self-education, curiosity, social climbing, topics of conversation, erudite knowledge for future use, orders from superiors, ideas to spring on friends, milder forms of snobbery, or just to be "in on things."

Accept them on any terms they like, but how they feel when you've had your chance depends on your skill. Robert Ardrey in his book *The Territorial Imperative* says that all of us seek three things: identity, stimulus, and security. We avoid: anonymity, boredom, and anxiety. Success of an idea depends on how well it satisfies these drives.

At this point we may have a feeling of uneasiness, because we seem to be pandering to the baser motivations of an audience. Perhaps we feel that our integrity requires us to give the truth as we see it and let the audience take it or leave it on our terms. This attitude implies that we are absolutely certain our views are correct and inviolate, and that any deviation or negotiation on others' terms diminishes the purity or validity of our message.

Many have taken this attitude, and their failures litter the history of thought. Adherents of this self-righteous approach to their fellow man confuse certitude with certainty. Certitude is the *belief* that we are absolutely right; certainty is the eternal, unattainable truth, which has not the least possible chance of being proven wrong at any time, in the past or future. There is no room for any compromise or negotiation on something that is certain. It should only be communicated in edicts, orders, or pronouncements. There is no room for discussion or dissenting opinion, and there should be none. However, we are hard pressed to list even a few ideas that meet the tests of certainty—timeless, and equally true under every conceivable set of circumstances. The greatest minds have never felt certain in their fields of competence. Albert Einstein was congratulated on the results of an experiment predicted by his theory of relativity: "It must give you a great deal of satisfaction to have been proven right," an admirer said to him as they received the news. Einstein mused, "No amount of experimentation will ever prove me completely right, but one new fact can prove me completely wrong."

Humility of this order in the crystalline world of exact science suggests that a pose of certainty is even less appropriate in the inexact world of human affairs. We can only achieve half-truths. Unfortunately the rules of arithmetic do not apply; two halves do not equal the whole.

If we accept this, then we see why dialogue is needed on almost every subject. Exposure of ideas and proposals to other minds allows many other facets to be seen from different points of view. The total experience of an audience contributes insights denied you (since no two lives are exactly the same), and if a presentor is wise, he welcomes them for two reasons. First, the members of an audience have identified themselves with the idea enough to examine it through their own spectacles; and more important, you may even learn something new yourself. Hammer and anvil *both* shape the red-hot horseshoe—only the naïve believe the hammer does it all. The similar interaction between a teacher and his students underlies the old advice: "If you really want to learn a subject, teach it to others."

Teaching, discussion, or other methods of presenting an idea demand the use of symbols—words, letters, numbers, shapes, colors, sounds—by which our message is perceived through the senses of the audience. When we present an idea with such symbols we are engaged in art, and art is *not* nature in the fullness of its reality.

The essence of any art is *selection* of pieces of the real thing, and then putting the pieces selected in some new *order* or arrangement so that the imagination of the audience is stimulated to see what the artist saw. But no two people see the expression in exactly the same light. Consider the Mona Lisa and her smile. What is its inner meaning? What does the smile portray? Probably no two viewers have identical impressions. Some may contemplate and see in it unspoken or unspeakable gratification. Others see the smile that a palpably guilty poisoner might turn on the prosecuting attorney after hearing a "Not Guilty" verdict. Art puts nature in the form of a code, the audience receives the coded message, and if their experience and imagination are affected, their minds sense the original idea or uncoded message. There is plenty of room in this process for a number of things to go wrong. The final message in the audience's mind is always garbled to some extent, for it is distorted by one individual's reaction to another's mental vision. Selection, arrangement, or transmission may be faulty. The experience of the audience may not let them recognize the symbols (as in a foreign language), and if they do recognize the symbols, their imagination may be such that they cannot combine them in their minds in the same way as the man who worked out the new order or arrangement he calls his idea. Ideas do not really *begin* in the mind. We first collect a great deal of information through all of our senses and store it in the form of memory or sets of pictures. We began the selection process before we were born. We never *forget*, but often we cannot *remember* at a given time. By imagination we mean the rearrangement of these pictures in our minds in many ways—most of which never existed in what we saw originally. Sometimes we hit on a combination of old pictures which lets us see old things in new ways. We call this understanding or creativity. We have then created a new vision or idea of how things *can* be from what we found them *to* be. William Hazlitt, in *Lectures on the English Comic Writers*, said: "Man is the only animal that laughs and weeps; for he is the only animal that is struck with the difference between what things are and what they might have been."

If we shift slightly from "what might have been" to "what may be," we penetrate to the heart of what an idea is. It is a picture of what can be *made to exist* in the real world, or a different way to *interpret* the pictures we already have of the real world. The first we call "programs" or proposals, the second we call "theories" or explanations. If a man observed the Hudson River and saw that people on both sides had little to do with one another, he might get several ideas, if he felt things should be otherwise than as he saw them. His ideas could take the form of imagined pictures of ferries, bridges, tunnels, or cable cars. As he sat on the bank and examined the pictures of his mind, he would then imagine all the different things that would happen if the first idea of bridging the river came to pass. An engineer "sees" different ways of construction; a land speculator "sees" a fantasy of price changes; a conservationist "sees" a loss of natural beauty; a social worker "sees" new ways for relieving unbalanced population pressures; and so on and on. There are at least as many sets of ideas as individuals who "thought" about it. Yet the Hudson flows on, undisturbed by all the mental image-juggling going on at its bank. But some of the ideas, when accepted, can cause all sorts of activity in the real world—bond issues in Wall Street, orders to steel mills, ultimatums to utility companies, enrichment of lawyers, and protest meetings of nature lovers. Thus, the program or proposal type of idea acts as the igniting spark for explosion of human and material resources. It is generally related to that of someone who wants a hook on his wall to hang up his coat—a picture in his mind precedes the search for hammer and nails. The picture is often incomplete, like being oblivious of such possible side effects as mangled thumbs or irate neighbors.

The theory or explanation type of ideas are different. They take all sorts of observations by others and constantly rearrange them in the mind, relating them to one another until a new pattern or meaning is discovered.

Consider the two ideas of the "true" motion of the planets. Up to a few centuries ago most everyone believed that the earth stood still and all the other planets, the sun, and stars, went round it. This idea was a picture of whirling balls all going in circles. Why circles? Because everyone knew they were the only *perfect* figures. As observers became sharper eyed, little discrepancies came up, so Ptolemy of Alexandria placed little circles on top of big circles and had them all revolving like Ezekiel's wheels. But through all this whirling uproar, the earth still remained fixed in the mental picture of the universe.

Copernicus imagined a different picture. (Notice that the planets kept going as they had since their birth, in spite of what men thought about them.) He visualized the sun at the center of the whole arrangement, and then calculated what people should see if he were right. Galileo went out looking for what Copernicus said might be there—and found it (though he never convinced some powerful thought leaders of the day, and almost got burned for his trouble). But even Galileo's great mind still clung to the perfection of the circles. To continue the story, Kepler visualized the paths as ovals tied together by a force like the Holy Ghost, after a Dane named Tycho Brahe had already stirred up everything again with his set of observations. Newton finished the whole thing by showing that falling apples and moving planets were all part of the same great design. This picture satisfied everybody for a few hundred years, until Einstein questioned the fundamental relations between measurement, space, and time. But that is another story and is not yet settled.

Not one of these people ever touched the things he was explaining or met the other members of the great search party to compare their ideas. The phenomena explained remained untouched, even after the explanation filtered into everyday knowledge. In spite of all this work, it is interesting to hear our acquaintances say that the sun "comes up" and "goes down" as though all this never happened.

Thus, a theory differs from a program, but they share one common aspect: Both are ideas and live only in the mind. One triggers the search for new facts the theorist thinks exist, the other triggers the search for resources to turn a picture into reality.

We have singled out only two major types of ideas, but there are, of course, many more. A melody is a musical idea, a novel or play is an unfolding of ideas about human character, a philosophical system or religion is an idea for the conduct of life, a cooking recipe is an idea for taste and smell, and so on. All of these, like the program and theory types, start in the mind, perhaps as imaginary sounds and odors as well as pictures. Their variety is endless.

For our purposes it is only important to realize that every person's mind carries two basic types of material—old impressions and memories of events actually experienced, and imaginative rearrangements of parts of these actual experiences which never really existed. Recollections of incidents that took place during a vacation are of the first type; dreams, which are subconscious rearrangements of old incidents, are of the second; and remembrance of a character in a novel or movie is a mixture of both. These all exist at various depths of consciousness, like all sorts and sizes of fish in a deep pool. When you present an idea to someone, it causes effects similar to those produced by casting a baited hook into a pool. The hook causes some fish to scatter, attracts others, and is ignored by the rest, but it rearranges the total pool into new patterns. What happens depends on the place the cast is made, what's on the hook, and the style or skill used in placing it. The temperature, time of day, and season of the year also play a part, as well as how hungry the fish are. Each has its counterpart in the presentation of an idea.

Skilled presentation—like skillful fishing—requires a knowledge of what's in the mind, how to attract what you want, and how to reject what you don't. This brings us to the concept of resonance—the most powerful mechanism for transference of an idea from one mind to another. It is the basis for all advice and techniques of ideas communication.

In his autobiography, *From Immigrant to Inventor*, Michael Pupin tells how his early life as a herdsman in the hills of Serbia gave him the two ideas responsible for his scientific fame. Both involved an ear to the ground and an eye to the future. The first was the "loading coil," which made long distance telephoning possible before vacuum tubes, and the second was the concept of "tuning" electrical circuits, on which radio, television, and radar depend. Both are varieties of "resonance," which has its roots in Newton's law of action and reaction. (Pupin considered this the most important of nature's laws.) Serbian shepherd boys all carried identical long knives with wooden handles and used them to communicate with each other during the night. Each pushed his knife into the earth and, by striking the handle, sent messages to his colleagues who had stuck their own knives into the ground. By putting their ears to the "receiving" knives, they heard the taps of the "transmitting" knife over distances much greater than they could shout. A physicist today would say that the identical knives were in resonance, i.e., vibrations from one caused the other to move in sympathy. Its own natural vibration rate was triggered by waves just exactly right to produce maximum response.

Pupin's other boyhood experience came from hearing those

aristocrats of mountain music, the bagpipers (yes, in Serbia!) tune their pipes to one another, by adjusting each one until it vibrated in sympathy with the note sounded by another. (String instrumentalists still do this today.) When Pupin adjusted his electrical circuits to respond to certain incoming waves, he used the word "tuning" to describe the process. Every time we try to get a radio program, we say that we "tune it in." What we do is make our receiver resonate with a specific radio transmitter. As we move along different numbers on the dial, we make our receiver resonate differently, like hitting different keys on a piano. The "channel selector" on a TV set does the same thing. Many cases of resonance exist. Tenors shattering glasses with a certain note; a bridge vibrating so wildly that it crashes; stained glass church windows quivering at certain notes of the organ; pictures and china rattling from record players; an orchestra sounding its A; and the characteristic sounds of individual human voices all demonstrate resonance effects.

Everything in the physical world can be stimulated to excessive response if a disturbing force is "tuned" to it. Archimedes of Syracuse said that if he had a place to rest his lever (the fulcrum) he could move the world. If we know the natural vibration of an object, we can make it quiver without touching it. Resonance in the physical world is the way to get a maximum transfer of energy. In the world of the mind, it is the way to get a maximum transfer of idea content. What is the connection? It has its roots in sympathy. The word *sympathy* is derived from two Greek roots—*syn*, meaning "together"; and *pathos* meaning "feeling" . . . feeling together.

Sympathy, then, is the analogue in the world of feeling to resonance in the world of materials. Send out messages tuned to the feelings of the audience, and they will almost quiver with response. The analogy can be carried a little further. As people respond, they send back messages to the sender, setting up a kind of feedback which amplifies the original message. When carried to a high pitch, enthusiasm is generated, which later may be almost embarrassing to the participants. Veteran actors and concert performers are so sensitive to this two-way communication that they count on it to take them to their peak performance. They are often unable to do their best in the hollow environments of television and motion picture production, where audiences consist of preoccupied technicians. For the eminent, producers will often furnish a live audience, whose purpose and function are usually not perceived by the great mass of viewers, but who nevertheless play an essential, creative role in the performance. A cellist once told me when I congratulated him on an especially fine concert that, "This audience made me play better than I know how."

Those experienced in presentations, at some time in their careers make a profound and happy discovery: most audiences are eager to receive a message. Even when they disagree violently with its content, they like to see good temper and politeness shown to the speaker or performer by their fellow members in the audience, if the speaker has shown them himself. For the tiny fraction of presentations that must be made to audiences known in advance to be definitely hostile, there are many approaches, and we will treat them at some length later. But we have all been in groups where the hostile behavior of someone in the audience so irritated the rest that we eagerly awaited the boor's comeuppance, whether delivered by the speaker himself or by one of our more courageous colleagues. Often the greatest applause occurs at these times, and the energy expended acts as a purge of collective embarrassment. Many public performers have built their reputations around their ability to handle hecklers, and proposals have often been accepted with enhanced enthusiasm when they have been opposed vigorously by the wrong kind of people, or with the wrong kind of manners. As Maupassant pointed out, audiences cry to the message-givers: Comfort me, Amuse me, Touch me, Make me dream, Make me laugh, Make me weep, Make me shudder, Make me think. They still do so, and appreciate those who try—even those who fail in the trying.

Today, more than any time in the past, people of all conditions are eager for ideas. They are more willing than ever to listen to those who offer the slightest chance of satisfying their needs for change, education, amusement, inspiration or, at the least, relief from boredom.

Several factors have produced this hunger for intellectual stimulus. Perhaps the greatest of all is the shrinkage of our world —squeezed by the two forces of rapid communication and transportation.

Intellectual activity is now a universal phenomenon. It is the cliché of our time that the sum of facts and knowledge increases at a pace that leaves us out of breath if we try to keep up. We have had our era labeled without serious dissent as the Age of Anxiety, which is no more than the polite name for the Age of Floating Fears. And the mass media of printing, television, and radio continually deliver blows to the eyes and ears, clamoring for our attention to more and more facts, news, or problems. Our innate need to understand our changing environment demands that we form attitudes toward this overwhelming flood of information.

One aspect of the speedup in communications is that everything happening, however ephemeral or trivial in the long run, is presented to millions within hours of the event. We cannot comprehend the state of affairs where news of a military mutiny and massacre of British residents by the Sepoys in India took weeks to reach London. This occurred in 1857. Imagine the difference in reaction if it were on the TV news the evening it happened!

In the Western World the three unshakeable beliefs that allowed us to put new knowledge in its place have not only been shaken, they are in ruins. Nothing has taken their place. (At least nothing that enjoys universal acceptance.) The beliefs are national sovereignty; production geared to small-scale enterprise; and the idea that democratic discussion at all levels of government can administer to society's complex needs of today. They exist today only in the oratory of national holidays—a dying form of dubious art. Affairs are not guided by these principles any more, yet leaders dare not admit it publicly. We treat harshly those who strip away illusions, unless they substitute something else. The fairy tale of the *Emperor's New Clothes* does not record gratitude to the children who saw the king in his naked reality, and said so.

All of these stimuli—undifferentiated in importance—have

caused in many a sense of numbness toward any general information that is not directly applicable to the way they make their living, and an intensification of sensitivity to any knowledge and training that is.

Shifts in the age-groups of population, urbanization, minority groups, and increased levels of living have produced strains on traditional modes of thought and behavior.

While automatic progress as an evolutionary principle has been abandoned since World War I, everyone still seems to feel that he has an obligation to "improve" himself, his family, and their condition of life. Since it won't take place automatically anymore, he must intervene and exert efforts himself, or attach himself to some area of life that has already caught the escalator for a free ride.

In all this yeasty, confusing ferment, it is hard to separate the froth and scum from the wine. The pressures of time prevent reading for depth and foreclose guidance from schools. There is an almost nostalgic, primitive urge to trust our ears and eyes in discourse with a wise person—in person.

Yet for all our sophisticated pessimism, we vaguely feel that in order to cope with the fallout of past ideas, advances, and progress, we do need new ideas. We are eager to listen to someone who looks as if he might have one that will work.

In the last few centuries children could follow the paths of their parents, grab a little more education and advance a short distance beyond, and so on, generation after generation. They set down roots in specific places, accepted the same values, and gave similar loyalties to institutions that existed in childhood. Not so today. Both young and old want new answers to the new problems. The young eagerly, the old reluctantly.

This commingling of problems and opportunities is characteristic of those periods historians call Golden Ages. They are great periods to contemplate from a tranquil study, but they are, in many ways, hells to live through. Elizabethan England, Renaissance Italy, Revolutionary France, and Pioneer America still captivate our interest. Old modes of life and thought were crashing down, and ideas and thinkers found wonderfully manured fields for rapid growth of their various seeds. So it is today.

Listen to William H. McNeill in his conclusion to *The Rise of the West*, a comprehensive history of world civilization.

> The burden of present uncertainties and the drastic scope of alternative possibilities that have become apparent in our time oppress the minds of many sensitive people. Yet the unexampled plasticity of human affairs should also be exhilarating. Foresight, cautious resolution, sustained courage, never before had such opportunities to shape our lives and those of subsequent generations. Good and wise men in all parts of the world have seldom counted for more; for they can hope to bring the facts of life more nearly into accord with the generous ideals proclaimed by all—or almost all—the world's leaders.
>
> The fact that evil men and crass vices have precisely the same enhanced powers should not distract our minds. Rather we should recognize it as the inescapable complement of the enlarged scope for good. Great dangers alone produce great victories; and without the possibility of failure, all human achievement would be savorless. Our world assuredly lacks neither dangers nor the possibility of failure. It also offers a theater for heroism such as has seldom or never been seen before in all history.
>
> Men some centuries from now will surely look back upon our time as a golden age of unparalleled technical, intellectual, institutional, and perhaps even of artistic creativity. Life in Demosthenes' Athens, in Confucius' China, and in Mohammed's Arabia was violent, risky, and uncertain; hopes struggled with fears, greatness teetered perilously on the brim of disaster. We belong in this high company and should count ourselves fortunate to live in one of the great ages of the world.

The lyrical and sober tone of this excerpt encourages anyone who sees new ways either to arrange affairs or to interpret present phenomena. If you can relate your idea to the larger issues of our day, you will be guaranteed a hearing. People are ready and eager. However, they are easily bored, and while the temper of our time brings them to the theater, what they see and hear determines how long they stay and *what they tell their friends.*

If you are not to have your audience leave with a sense of having wasted its time, suitable care must be given to the manner and content of the presentation beforehand. Whether your audience includes the most powerful or the most humble, each considers his time worthwhile, for it is an irretrievable slice of his life.

In the higher courts of law and the lower houses of legislatures, rigid time limits, majestically enforced by venerable officials, are prescribed for making a presentation, or argument. (Alas, we cannot include that august body, the United States Senate.) University lectures take generally fifty minutes—strangely identical with the *Fifty Minute Hour* of the psychoanalysts. Plays run two to three hours, uninflated motion pictures a little less, and most TV shows get less than a full hour. Press conferences of world leaders (except those of newly emerging nations) rarely last beyond an hour, and sermons had better not. Thus, most of the ways in which important ideas are presented suffer the strictest constraint of all: time. Without constraint, there is no need for art. In fact one definition of art is that it is the method of presenting an idea under constraints. A painter has just so many square inches and just so many pigments. Sculptors must respect the limits of their material or it rebels. Musicians can play only a limited set of tones and in a narrow range of speeds and volumes. Poets confine their selection of words to a small fraction of a language's dictionary—for their appeal is through the ear. Books can be made only so thick, and even German philosophers produced a finite set of volumes. The recognition of limits is the beginning of real competence in any art—including that of presenting an idea. You must do the best you can with what you have. Ignorance of relevant limits—of material, time, and audience knowledge—accounts for more failures than any other single factor. Genius expands these limits, but only after mastery of existing possibilities. Advancement does not come by accident, nor by that random sloppiness which calls itself free inspiration. Remember, Shakespeare had only twenty-one thousand words from which to fashion his poetry and plays, but he fashioned them with immortal effect.

Trying to accomplish something when the things you need are

limited or unavailable stimulates a quest for efficiency. How can you get the most out for what you put in?

We feel that some kind of optimum is possible, but how to achieve it? Variables abound: the ideas themselves (existing as thoughts in the mind); their number, difficulty, and novelty; background required for full comprehension; characteristics and size of the audience; the over-all environment in which the idea is presented; action you want the members of the audience to take when you finish; your personal knowledge and character; and the time available to you. Judgments must be made to adjust those variables within your control to those which are not. Such judgments lead to the concept of *design*, which is the relationship of one variable to the others in creating an over-all effect. Like design in buildings, machines, paintings, utensils, tools, or interiors, a presentation can be clear and elegant, or confused and tasteless.

Again we encounter aspects of art, not science—certainly not mathematical theorems and proofs. Some of the worst presentations are designed like a lesson in geometry, and you can almost hear the QED at the end, if you are still awake. Other failures leave you with no idea of what action the advocate wants you to take. Inadequate attention to the physical environment and the hazards of irritating distractions dispose of some; and unskilled reading of text in monotone takes an even heavier toll. The inexperienced are also trapped by assuming that the audience is enthusiastic and convinced of the importance of their idea before the presentation. These unfortunates mistake the invitation for acceptance. Use of a style inappropriate to the subject creates effects ranging from low comedy to disgust, and inept use of visual aids enhances unintelligibility.

Presentation of an idea is similar in many ways to fighting a battle. Only fools underestimate an opponent and think they can give odds. First-class intelligence can make up for lesser numbers (witness the Arab-Israeli War of 1967). Clear objectives focus energy and give each part its job to do. Imaginative and unexpected deployment unbalances the opposition. Planning for contingencies absorbs counterattacks and makes for flexible ripostes. Appreciation of the mental habits and doctrine of the leaders of the other side lets their attacks be predicted and parried with a minimum of nail biting. There are, of course, rules of strategy and tactics that fill shelves of books, but mere knowledge of rules does not win wars. There are rules for painting, harmony, and architecture, but mere application of rules does not make an artist—or even a craftsman. The rules themselves come from studies of great battles, pictures, music, and buildings. Breakage of such rules by those *who have not mastered them* constitute the history of human failure.

Training teaches the rules, experience teaches the exceptions. In the remaining chapters we shall examine several aspects of the art of presentation of ideas and try to extract those guides, hints, and directions that lead to success through efficiency and design. We will, on the way, take note of the perils and snags that await the rash, unwary, or naïve. At the end, if your nerve is not equal to using this kit on real trips, it will at least set you up as a pretty fair critic—and many have made a good thing out of that.

We resent help from others if they either diminish our own sense of importance or show no sympathy for our problems.

Physicians prove this every day, as patients flee professionally good intentions when by indifference, irritation, impatience, or fatigue the doctor shows that he has no sympathy for them or their ailments. In dealing with many doctors, of course, this is the highest wisdom, for we sense in the most primitive part of our minds that if they have not taken the trouble to understand us and our conditions, then their suggestions and treatment are probably off the mark, and we had better run for our lives.

Faith in our sense of importance is the polite and quiet form of self-preservation. Insult it, and you send mobilizing messages for retaliation to every cell in your victim's body.

If wounded self-respect can drive a sick man away from the medicine he needs, imagine how much easier is the flight from suggestions of less importance.

When we say that we "have an idea" for something or other, we really mean that we want to change the world in some way. We call fanatics those who seize on an idea and who insist on lighting up the world with the blinding glow of their own vision.

They, of course, are pathological victims of their own particular brand of home-brew, but any reading of history shows that they produced some noteworthy events. Every sucessful fanatic had a first-rate grasp of human nature, and never diminished the sense of importance of his potential converts. Instead, the fanatics exaggerated it to wonderfully pleasant fantasy. Rather than showing no sympathy for the assorted miseries, doubts, and fears afflicting their followers, they evidenced such overwhelming compassion that millions stampeded for a chance to place their lives at the service of those who "understood" their problems.

Even the most cynical product of our own skeptical culture identifies with the handful at Thermopylae, Crusaders in Palestine, archers at Agincourt, or stonemasons at work on Notre Dame. How else explain our excitement as we share in the last charge of Napoleon's Old Guard at Waterloo, all grizzled, no-nonsense types, with every illusion gone, walking to music into a blizzard of flying iron, chanting "Long Live the Emperor" as they slog on to certain death?

Few of us would call these people stupid, but was their behavior rational? Probably not, but man is not only a rational animal. Emotions and beliefs are masters, reason their servant. Ignore emotion, and reason slumbers; trigger emotion, and reason comes rushing to help. At the least, reason excuses; at the most, it restrains its master. Examples from the past show how ideas have ruled the world. Ideas build, use, and destroy armies. Christianity, socialism, capitalism, imperialism, liberalism, democracy, and other creeds have their real life in the heads of their adherents, not in the real estate involved. Colored maps mislead us badly. Great institutions begin in the mind and are developed by other minds that embrace an idea at various stages. The fanatics of history are diseased cases of men whose ability to present ideas outstripped their capacity to control the forces set loose by their success. Santayana described a fanatic as someone who redoubles his efforts after he has forgotten his aim.

We are so repelled by the horrifying fallout of the fanatics that we often swing to the other extreme in our ceaseless quest for the proper conduct of life. "Hard facts and cold reason should be our only guides; scientific method our only instrument; utility our only measure." This is the path of a particularly virulent fanaticism and proceeds from the Inquisition, through the Terror and its guillotine, on to the totalitarian barbarities of our own time. Saint-Just, apologist for the French Revolution's terror, encapsulated this attitude in his remark: "We must impose the yoke of liberty on the necks of the people."

The neutrality of reason as to whom it serves was chillingly confirmed when the emotions of the people used Saint-Just's cold theory to put his own neck under the blade.

Reason operates by deciding (in some occult way) that a single aspect of an object, an event, or a person is truly representative of the entire thing itself. This accounts for our habit and need to put a label on everything. Since we feel that we know what other things or people with that label are like, we can then "logically" go on to the conclusion that the thing we have labeled shares the properties we "know" all other things of that kind and with that label have. Logicians and philosophers since Arisotle dignify this trinity of uncertain truth with the unlovely name of syllogism. For example: All Russians drink vodka; Ivan is a Russian; therefore, Ivan drinks vodka. Or as Saint-Just might have put it: All enemies of the Revolution must be killed; aristocrats are enemies of the Revolution; therefore, all aristocrats must be killed.

Notice the assumptions we have to make in reasoning. First, we must have a faith in our ability to detect a characteristic and label it. We then need to have a program ready-made to generate an attitude to things or people with that label. Once we have these, logic then merely connects our two statements. The trick is, of course, to select statements *ahead* of the logic, if we want to have it come out our way. We could just as easily have picked a more profound, if not a happier, property of Russians, as in: All Russians play chess; Ivan is a Russian, therefore, Ivan plays chess.

How do we initially select the property we want to reason on? We do it by picking those aspects of things that serve our purposes. We pick our purpose by what we want, and what we want has its roots in our own feelings and emotions—though we seldom tell ourselves so, and never tell others. We use reason in this way every day. All speeches, plays, trials, and arguments have a syllogism buried somewhere in their heart. They use many more words only because the logic breaks down if the hearer does not accept the first two statements, called the premises. The emotions must be addressed in every way possible within the limits of art available in order to get agreement on premises. Here, then, is the linkage of emotion to reason: Agreement, with the selection of properties pertinent to both our individual case (Ivan) and to the class to which we assign it (Russian), can only be relied on if the hearer *feels* them to be valid. If his feelings are on the other side—and perversely remain there —logic is useless. It cannot work without a set of agreed-on premises. Witness the reluctance of some juries to come to unanimous decisions in seemingly open and shut cases. This could be caused by boredom, indigestion, dislike of another juror, or disbelief in the whole jury system—especially if one resented being ordered to serve. If agreement on premises exists, and the ancient rules of logic are used to connect them, then the conclusion is valid—but only to those who accept the premises. They will all happily agree that "it stands to reason." A subversive Ivan, who drinks kvass but avoids vodka, could not possibly agree with the conclusion, regardless of immaculate logic. Disagreements, whether between nations or father and son, have their roots in premises—not in logic. As Justice Holmes said, "You cannot argue a man into liking a glass of beer," or, for those who remember their Latin, *De gustibus non est disputandum.*

What has all this to do with getting your ideas accepted? Simply this: Do not master textbooks on logic and then think that others are either ignorant or unreasonable if they do not agree with you. They may be just as reasonable as you are if *their* premises are correct. Sometimes, of course, they are not even aware of what their premises are (they could be prejudices imbibed with their mothers' milk), but if they resist your idea (conclusion) you can be certain that their premises (beliefs) don't jibe with yours. Ambrose Bierce put it neatly in his *Devil's Dictionary,* "Infidel: In New York, one who does not believe in the Christian religion; in Constantinople, one who does."

Once one sets up as an idea monger, it will not be long before he encounters those shrewd and practical opponents who fight under banners blazoned with the motto "Common Sense." These are tough customers. Men of genius over the centuries have met them and often lost. But when won over, your idea then enters the body of knowledge known as common sense, and opposition rapidly melts away. Victor Hugo had this kind of idea in mind when he said in *The History of a Crime* that "more powerful than armies is an idea whose time has come."

But it's up to you to get the idea, to know that its time has come, and to present it under *three* flags; Emotion, Reason, and Common Sense.

What is the nature of Common Sense? It is, first, all knowledge that floats in the public mind and requires no proof for it to be believed. Second, it is an appreciation of over-all causes and effects that agrees with everyone's everyday experience. The minute, detailed sequences between events which lead up to an over-all effect are considered unimportant. If ever thought of, the details are often wrong in a scientific sense, but common sense *does* somehow get the beginning and end straight! Consider the frozen surface of a lake. Everyone in its neighborhood knows that it freezes in winter. They have skated on it, known of drownings in the past as persons went through thin sections of ice, and so on. Countless generations observed it, walked on it in winter, and swam in it in summer. How many could tell you why it freezes on top, but not on the bottom? How many would know that water is heavier at 39 degrees than at 32 degrees when it freezes? How many ever heard of density or specific weight? And if they had, they would still cut a hole in the ice and go fishing in midwinter.

A physicist's answer to the question "Why does the top freeze first?" might need pages of formulas, and a thick book of explanation before he felt satisfied. Even if he spent a lifetime elaborating, testing, and patching up his theory, the inhabitants of the lake region would pay scant attention.

They might be amused at the foolish eccentric who put himself to such agony proving what everybody knows, but they would hardly change their daily lives after the book came out—and they probably shouldn't. It is enough to link events like this: Winter causes the lake to freeze; ice forms on the top; there's water below. That's common sense. Was Newton the first man to have an apple fall on his head? Of course not. Apples have fallen down since Eden. But because one particular apple fell on the head of one particular man, the incident has since been viewed with gravity.

If they see a cat in a dairy barn, most people can figure out that he's hungry. They do not need a deep knowledge of animal behavior to do it. People blessed with great common sense also tend to "reason backward," if they observe or are told something unusual or outside their range of experience. They trust the evidence of their eyes and ears more than deductive chains of formulae. "What I see is real; now what could account for it?" Primitive religions embodied the common sense of their time. Storms and lightning, seasons and earthquakes, day and night, sun and moon, birth and death, famine and plenty, were experienced first hand. "Effects" were everywhere—what was the cause? Nobody knew. So gods and myths were invented by "reasoning backward" from a world where the uncertain and the unpredictable were the only certainties, to a higher world where their lives were created and managed. Since the effects often appeared random and capricious, the angers and benefices of the gods were cut to fit, usually at the expense of some unfortunate goat. We are not so far removed from these ancestors that we have completely abandoned their ways. We still seek a scapegoat or two when things go awry.

In *Conversations with Wellington* the Duke told how he deployed his forces for an early victory in his career: "After dinner we talked of India. The Duke gave an account of his attack at Assaye and of his acting on the conclusion that there must be a ford at a particular point of the river because he there saw two villages on the opposite sides of it. 'That,' he added, 'is common sense. And when one is strongly intent on an object, common sense will usually direct one to the right means.' "

Imagine the difficulty of a staff officer trying to convince the Duke otherwise (he was not known as the Iron Duke for nothing), and you see why ideas that conflict with common sense enjoy a tough reception.

Common sense is the conservative force in human existence, for only the most time-honored knowledge is allowed in its corral. In fact, a good way to visualize it is like a corral, with each animal inside representing an accepted fact or idea. New animals are let in after they have been broken to service, and others die and are removed when they are either vanquished by a new animal or are no longer useful to the community. Hence, the odor of gasoline instead of horse manure around country churchyards on Sundays.

Also, antagonistic animals are tolerated for considerable periods. Every society has proverbs that can justify opposite courses of action in similar circumstances. Common sense does not insist on logical relations among its various pieces of wisdom. The body of common sense thus continues to change and is different for different groups. What is common sense to a farmer in Iowa is the most dangerous nonsense to a peasant in the Middle East—and vice versa.

If your idea strikes your audiences as in line with *their* common sense, you will experience a depressing reaction. First, they will agree much more readily, but this can degenerate to a boredom of "What's so new about this? Why waste our time with the obvious?" However, if the idea is generally of the order of "let things alone," "don't rock the boat," "let's wait until we know more," or other classic delaying remarks, the reaction will depend on the mood of the audience. If they are so anxious that any action is better than none, you lose; but if things are cloudy, and your idea has a respectable wrapping of reason, they will be grateful for an excuse to do nothing. If your idea clashes with common sense, you have both great advantage and a serious disadvantage. You will, of course, not be charged with being obvious, but slightly crazy. However, you will capture attention —at least temporarily—for you have triggered an emotional conflict. You have created a newsworthy event: "Man bites dog." Most newspaper stories have an element of the unexpected or unusual, and years of experience tell editors what grabs readers' attention. Ship sinking, yes; ship sailing, no.

Once you've got the attention, it is the highest wisdom to keep in the front of your mind that it is the attention of a challenge —with roots in hostility—and every eye and ear is alerted to catch the error in your proposal. Remember, if they do not find error, they must either live with a contradiction and its anxiety, or change their minds. If they change their minds, they must abandon a previous thought or prejudice, and that is like losing an old friend who has stood by you for a long time. We do not abandon friends without pain, but if proof of their faithlessness finally convinces us, we put them out of our mind faster than those to whom we are indifferent. There is no teetotaler like a reformed drunk.

If your proof fails, the anxiety and hostility produced turn back on you, the unsuccessful attack on the old friend reinforces the regard in which he's held (since there's now an element of guilt in that the attack was even temporarily tolerated), and you have made it a little harder for your idea to triumph if it gets a second chance in stronger hands. Your successor will encounter additional missiles labeled: "We've been through all this before, and it's no good."

Common sense is a society's survival kit—and it's value lies in knocking out bad ideas. It washes everything that violates it in skeptical acid to separate the base from noble metal. It enriches itself by taking the noble metal into its own treasury. Good ideas survive the acid—if presented properly. Common sense administers a rough justice, for it knows that the world changes, and it must also change, but it is wary. It prefers original ideas which have stood the test of time. The successful merchant of ideas must be uncommonly equipped with common sense, for it is potentially both his adversary and ally. Which it becomes is determined by his hands alone—their skill and the guiding knowledge beneath that skill.

Now that we have examined a few of the relations between reason, emotion, and common sense, we get a better fix on a familiar acquaintance—resistance to change. Unsuccessful idea-pushers throughout the ages have blamed their failures on the phlegmatic genius of sheer inertia that repelled their assaults on the established order, a sort of nonmilitant, ghostly Marshal Joffre. (Dinner was dinner to the Marshal, even though the Germans were breaking down the gates to Paris.)

In Vermont a few years ago one of its citizens attained his hundredth birthday, and reporters made a pilgrimage to his porch. They got an embarrassing, silent reception. One of the newsmen, unwilling to see the story melt away, tugged at his collar, cleared his throat, and tentatively began the interview on the safest note conceivable: "Sir, you have enjoyed an unusual experience. Your life has spanned the most remarkable century in history. You have seen countless changes in American life, marvelous inventions and progressive improvements brought to everyone. Our readers are interested in your views. Would you tell us what you think about all these changes?" After a great deal of silent rocking the old man shifted his tobacco, looked his questioner in the eye, and grunted: "I been agin 'em all." That worthy celebrity really valued resistance to change—and his dogged longevity was probably just his ornery way of resisting the greatest change awaiting each of us.

Fortunately, such types are not numerous, and his environment changed in spite of his desires. Ideas ultimately win—for good or evil. But let's remember that resistance to change can also be admirable if it is not, like justice, blindfolded.

What we call "the world"—or more modestly, "our world" —is the current sum of the ideas of our predecessors on this planet. Look about you. Your clothes, language, furniture, pictures, housing, neighborhood, city, and nation all began as visions in other minds. Your food, drink, vehicles, books, schools, entertainment, tools, and appliances all came from someone's dissatisfaction with his world as he found it, and also as he left it. What you work at, believe in, try to teach your children, and are ready to defend against attack are your personal selections from an immense antique market. It is stocked with the ideas of all human time. Some may be old and dusty, a few new and shiny, most are old and repainted, but each of us furnishes his home as best he can. A few believe in werewolves and witches, some in Yoga, others in DNA molecules, antimatter, or psychedelic vision. Our selections may be unconscious, impulsive, compulsive, whimsical, perverse, or rational, but we all have a full house, and seldom throw anything aside without grabbing something else to take its place.

Our time in the market is as long as we live. The centenarian in Vermont furnished his home early in life and thereafter never saw anything he wanted to substitute; but most of us are always on the lookout for something better. We have an itch to improve our condition. But the eminent vegetarian, George Bernard Shaw, prescribed the scratch appropriate for the itch: "Progress is impossible without change; and those who cannot change their minds cannot change anything." This is the side of man that makes him eager for new ideas. All lives unfold as a continuous contest between the inertial weight of not wanting to be disturbed and the desire to better their existence; between fear and hope, gloom and joy, resignation and rebellion, satisfaction or discontent. The tension of these opposing pulls underlies Alexander Pope's advice:

> Be not the first by whom the new is tried,
> Nor yet the last to lay the old aside.

Most people find this the behavior of prudence, and ignore the necessity for someone to start the game. When you present an idea to an individual you must see your act as an event in *his* life, as something that will *change* his life if he accepts it, approves it, or supports it. His decision is only one of thousands he will make. Yet if the idea is large and important, you may be asking him to risk his property, reputation, or even his life. Most trivial matters require him to risk at least his judgment. Every decision carries an element of irreversibility in it, for its failure or miscarriage leaves tracks in the memories of all who know about it. You really can't go back again and start over completely. Most know this instinctively. If you realize these implications of what you're about, you will take care to treat your conscience and audience with proper respect. This does not mean servility, but paying attention to their backgrounds and their capabilities, their weaknesses and restraints on their actions, their hopes and worries. When your audience senses this kind of respect in your presentation, you will receive respect in return. When they sense arrogance or obsequiousness, you will get what these deserve —and quickly.

Most of us truly admire intelligence, culture, and leadership when we meet them. But if they arrive wrapped in arrogance, we rightly suspect what we see is counterfeit, and later condemn those who tried to mislead us. There may be exceptions in the case of certain geniuses, but few of us ever meet them. It is possible that what they show is not really arrogance at all, but a frustrated, shy, oversensitivity to criticism which manifests itself in behavior akin to arrogance. Nonetheless, this luxury is paid for in deferred recognition—most likely far beyond the grave. Few of us have that kind of patience.

The man sincerely interested in the successful reception of his idea will not give it this handicap. If he doesn't know better, his proposal will be received as the product of one who's not very smart. If he sells it at all, he does so with a heavy discount on his intelligence. Audiences will often conclude that he stole the idea, especially if they embrace it in spite of the mutilation it suffered in his hands.

A melancholy choice faces a person with great egotism and thirst for personal recognition when he gets an idea: Is he interested more in the idea's success or in the chance it gives him to show off his talents? There is a seesaw effect; the more that personal propulsion dominates, the less energy is available for the idea, and vice versa. It is easy to sympathize with these people, for we often judge a person's worth by his presentations. After all, that is how he communicates to us with unusual concentration on mutual purpose. However, confusion of purposes creates confusion in the audience, and if a compromise is tried "half for me, half for the idea," all shots fall short. Both the idea and the quest for glory suffer. In a long enough run of association, appraisals of personal worth tend to become more accurate as judgment centers more on what the audience gets in the way of instruction, knowledge, or insight, and less on vague, over-all impressions.

There are legitimate times when the whole purpose of a presentation is to judge a person; then confusion disappears. The single idea is to display a personal product—the character, talent, and personality of the presenter—and the techniques of presentation are applicable. Auditions for the stage, orchestras, ballet, and opera occur every day. Interviews for other employment are their brothers, and oral examinations for advanced degrees are first cousins. All belong to the same family. But if acceptance of an *idea* is truly the main object, personal aggrandizement must take a back seat. Oddly enough, a successful idea carries its passenger to the same destination, but driving from the back seat is not the best way for either to get there. William James crystallized this effect in a little ratio:

$$\text{Self-Esteem} = \frac{\text{Success}}{\text{Pretensions}}$$

Most people see something admirable in self-esteem, but abhor pretensions. Basically, a mixed presentation goes off the rails by ignoring the needs of the audience. They pay attention only in return for a chance to learn something—excluding the learning of how fine a fellow you are. Confused aims violate an elementary rule of strategy—concentration on a single, ultimate objective. Diversions are useful, but they should be planned to support and relate to the final objective which must always stand at the front of your mind. We will elaborate this in several places and from different points of view later. It is enough here to state the point that *confusion of objectives* is the most frequent cause of failure to convince others of a good idea. Failures of this type occur everywhere—in scholarly journals and gregarious saloons, in drawing rooms and political conventions. Most failures in presentation are avoidable. I will try to show some ways to success in the following chapters.

2

Presentations *Are* Performances

or

Why There's No Business Without Show Business

Every renowned figure in history, famous or infamous, beloved or reviled, understood the power of drama. Churchill's speeches —uttered word for word by a phlegmatic predecessor—could not have inspired and rallied an entire free world. Sir Winston was a consummate, and not altogether unconscious, showman.

Thus, when you get an idea you must share with others, you will immediately face a hard question. The answer will depend on your character and past life; precepts absorbed from your models, teachers, and critics; development of your taste; your sense of etiquette; and painful memory of failures observed or experienced. As in questions of conscience, each man must fight through to his own answer. The question is simply: "To what extent are you willing to dramatize your idea in making it known to others?" Extremes of response can be: "To hell with all tricks —I'll use facts," or, "The sky's the limit—anything goes." If both extremes are absurd, as I think, there must be some place in-between which is best for a particular presentation and its associated circumstances.

Let's examine the position of the purist who wants nothing to do with anything except a flat statement of facts. He must first of all choose the *words* to use in his statements, and all words produce associations and impressions. Will he use hard-hitting verbs; should he qualify the nouns with various adjectives; should these be vivid or plain? Is the vocabulary to be elegant or vernacular? Should he use the passive mode ("It is believed," "It appears," etc.) or personal views ("I insist," "I believe that," etc.), or act as judge of the views of others? What demeanor will he assume—solemn or humorous, formal or informal, ebullient or dour—or what? If he does not *consciously* make these choices, his personality and lifetime habits will do it for him. He cannot escape creation of an impression once he begins.

In *The Greek Commonwealth*, Sir Alfred Zimmern discusses those aspects of environment taken for granted:

> Its influence is omnipresent, but it is seldom expressed. It is left to show itself, more spontaneously and truthfully, in the chance idiom or detail that slips out as the setting of a story, in what is implied or hinted rather than consciously stated, in the many little significant touches which to the careful observer, of nations as well of men, are always the surest and happiest revelation of character.

In fact, the intentional avoidance of all colorful or emotional words is itself a powerful dramatic choice—one of the oldest known. It is designed both to inspire automatic trust and to lend additional, unearned weight to every word uttered. As a device, it can usually be used effectively only by those whose previous reputation, rank, office, or position projects an aura of its own before they arrive.

Even Diogenes, the incorruptible Cynic, who preached the simple and virtuous life for all, maintained his unsuccessful quest for "one honest man" by stripping himself of every possession, except a tub in which he lived and a lantern carried lit during the day. Such is the drama of the undramatic and austere. Clothing, language, housing, furniture, and food preferences reflect the personality—real or desired—of each of us. Our choices are influenced to some degree by what we want others to infer from them as silent evidence of our taste and values. At the very least, the rejection of things we "wouldn't be caught dead with" has the same motivation. Our very word "person" has its origin in the Latin word for "mask" as applied to characters in a drama. The real "you" can never be known to others. They must arrive at their judgment by deductions from the varied impressions you present. There may even be irony in the advice "Know thyself" for those who aspire to the pinnacle of wisdom, for similar reasons. From childhood on we leave a stream of impressions, and if we have made the slightest effort to influence that stream, we have crossed the line which the naïve, plain, honest man thinks of as dividing truth from falsity. To be human, then, is to be engaged in a cosmic drama. Roles change, but there's a performance every day.

The other extreme attitude toward dramatization—the "anything goes" school—is equally foolish, for any substance in the original idea will be smothered in technique. So much mental effort will be lavished on methods and means that the objective of the original idea will fade from sight. Instead of the idea itself as a disciplining force—selecting, rejecting and arranging presentation elements—the urge to exploit devices for their own sake takes over, and we end with solutions in search of problems. They are like empty cabs prowling streets in the wee hours, hoping for a random customer. The wasteful methods that provided Macbeth his hollow crown were of this order: "A tale told by an idiot; full of sound and fury, signifying nothing."

Serious presentations (even of lighthearted subjects) must travel between two walls: tight-lipped Spartan roughness and irresponsible Bohemianism. Fortunately, the road is wide enough to have accommodated all of the great ideas of the past. Greek comedies and Voltaire's satires, Napoleon's orders of the day and Lincoln's inaugurals all negotiated the path without mishap. For our more prosaic messages, we need not even go close to the walls.

The greatest work of philosophical reason in Western history presents its ideas in the most dramatic of all forms. *The Dialogues of Plato* are supreme works of art, yet they sternly warn of the dangers of art in inflaming the passions. The passion for reason is evidently a tacit exception. Plato's pupil, Aristotle, emphasized moderation in all things in the conduct of life, yet he was said to be moderate in everything except in his insistence on moderation itself. If such minds and subjects needed the scaffolding of art and drama to support their ideas, can our lesser minds dispense with what they found indispensable? We must *honestly* recognize that some dramatic skill is absolutely essential—both complimentary to the audience and expected by them —if we are to prevent that niggling hesitancy that so often shatters performance. Surgeons with quivering hands do not inspire confidence. When a scalpel is slapped into the hand, there's no time to regret that cuts cause bleeding. When presenting an idea, there's no time to have doubts about the need to dramatize for easier and correct comprehension.

We should, then, agree that the desire to present any idea to others demands that we make many choices.

Those who have inborn dramatic talent will find this obvious, but they are few. Perhaps a slight digression on the nature of drama itself will make the advice and principles given later on in this chapter more understandable. Dramatic *talent* may be rare, but dramatic *sense* is universal. We can build on that.

Children learn by imitation. Their words, manners, and attitudes are, like their drawings, imperfect copies of those they have seen somewhere else. They also learn *over a span of time*. So do we all. Locked deep in our minds is the pattern by which we even conceive the idea of time. It is memory. We remember a past, live in a present (which we know will slide into the past), and by extension and faith, assume a future. To be human is to have this sense of time. We cannot imagine learning everything known about some field in one illuminating instant, and would be suspicious of someone who told us he had. We know that *understanding* takes time. Probably no one really knows why, but there are clues. Giovanni Battista Vico (1668-1744), an Italian philosopher, distills a lifetime of wisdom in a short statement on human temperament: "Men at first feel without observing; then they observe with a troubled and agitated spirit; finally they reflect with a clear mind." Notice the implication of time passing by the use of "at first," "then," and "finally." If Vico is right, as I think him to be, then by linking his insight to the concept of learning by imitation we have a key both to the nature of drama and to methods for the presentation of ideas.

In drama the actors imitate for us and allow us to see what happens to them all—from outside the action—as the story unfolds. But how does the story unfold? In all first-class work, it unfolds according to Vico! Analysis of great plays shows them to have three main parts: statement of a problem; development of inner implications; solution of the problem. These are sometimes put in this way: crisis, conflict, resolution. Often, our familiar division into three acts faithfully follows this plan. In homely terms, there must be a beginning, a middle, and an end.

It is curious how art forms, games and sports, humor and scientific method, all possess a similar structure. Musicians have their sonata form, which they say consists of statement, development, and recapitulation. Chess players describe opening, the middle game, and end game. Jokes involve description of a situation, placing two views of it in conflict, and a punch line. Scientific method uses Hypothesis, Inference, and Verification. It appears, then, that a trinity is important in many places besides theology. In fact, one could make a good case that the promulgation of the early Christian ideas enjoyed a tremendous enhancement by casting them in this form and structure, which is most congenial to human minds. (Additional force was realized by coupling its structure to one of the best methods for *maintaining* interest: The Trinity has been taught as a Mystery, i.e., its nature can never be *fully* known by human intelligence. By such means an idea can tantalize great minds forever.)

What is the lesson here for us with more limited ends in mind? Simply this. Present your idea in this structure and sequence: statement of the problem, development of its relevant aspects, and resolution of the problem and its development. Use this structure and you send your idea rolling down the well-worn grooves of the human mind. Ignore it and you send it into rocky, unknown canyons from which it may never return.

The rest of this book will relate in one way or another to this tripod of Statement, Development, and Resolution. Unlike the theological Trinity, it contains no mystery. But putting it under every idea, for maximum stable support, still allows full play for human ingenuity, from cookbook recipe to the heights of inspiration. At this point, reflect on the presentations you have experienced, both failures and successes. Did not every success satisfy this structure? Did the failures? If the failures met this test, did their ruin then lie in the *performance* skills employed?

By now I hope we have shown that presentation of an idea is an art—built on principles, yes, but still an art. A work of art has two parts: Composition and Performance, each complementary to and affecting the other. The previous concepts of structure dominate the *Composition* aspect of the presentation. In this part no audience is present, and design, selection, rejection, and sequence are decided. This is the homework, meditation or conference phase, where the form is hammered out by sketching in, erasing, destroying, reconstructing, testing, and regrouping. When one is engaged in this stage, he is companion to Brahms, alone with his piano, or Picasso, brush in hand, spattered with paints. As Ben Shahn says in *The Shape of Content*, no critic, however hostile, would ever defend the mutilation or destruction of a canvas presented for exhibition. The community of critics would fire a fearsome volley of moralistic essays condemning anyone who did so as a barbarian unfit for civilized society, even if some of them agreed with the taste that prompted the violence. And yet, Shahn points out, a painter continuously destroys the picture as he builds it. Shahn says that two sides of the character, constantly wrestling for supremacy, are engaged: the builder and the critic. The builder tries and suggests, the critic shakes or nods his head at every attempt or result. Few of us can carry on this kind of internal battle with the intensity of great artists, but the same process is set going once one sets out to present an idea. Our critic sits on a stool with three legs labeled statement, development, and resolution. However, this internal critical process is often so exhausting that it gives rise to this piece of wisdom: "Great works of art are never finished, they are abandoned." Critics have more endurance than builders, inside ones most of all.

Assuming, then, that out of this struggle finally comes a *composition* of the presentation for our idea, what next? At this point we have only an architect's plan, a messy score, a copy of the play, a sketch of what is to be done. Now comes *performance*. Here we set down a principle: Performance can never *add* to the intrinsic merit of a composition; the most it can do is to harm it as little as possible. However, bad performance can take a first-class composition and turn it into rubbish. The shrewd reader may now sense a false note in that he has often read reviews where it is said that the performer triumphed over his material. These are usually in connection with plays or music. True; but the composer or playwright is not very happy with such a review, for *he has not succeeded in presenting his idea*. The critic has commented on the skills of the actor or performer, probably out of kindness to him. He is applying a set of standards, not to the idea presented, but to the skill used to do it. This kind of review is the epitaph of failure. It is similar to remarks heard when a lovable man has tried to present an idea too demanding for his performance skills: "I didn't understand what he was getting at, but he sure is a warm human being." Those satisfied with that accolade should not read on.

Performance skill available will, or should, exercise a powerful constraint on composition. In presenting an idea, the level available is often your own, your superior's, your subordinate's, or at least someone else's who will be doing the job, presumably someone known to you. You do not enjoy the freedom of the musical composer who writes for the ages, or the playwright who expects only experienced stars to speak his immortal lines. Beethoven once replied to a complaint that his violin concerto was unplayable, "To hell with your damned fiddle!" (in German, of course). Presentation of an idea must keep an uneasy but vital three-way balance between content, composition, and performance. (We will discuss the subsidiary balance between *style* and content in a later chapter.) Consider these illustrations.

A beginning piano pupil, playing a piece geared to his level, produces murmurs of approval, even from a virtuoso present. But what happens if his beaming parents then set before him something for the concert hall? Parents keep beaming, perhaps even hold hands, but the child perspires and guests remember other appointments. When a fine actor makes records of classic children's stories, he gives them new meaning for adults, for he brings out more of their intrinsic merit than we had recognized before. But if he lavishes talent on the trivial, boredom soars, and we question his judgment or, at least, his agent's.

To sum up, the performance can be no better than the material, but good material can be ruined by bad performance. Old vaudevillians knew this in their bones, but to judge from many current presentations, this awareness declined at about the same pace as vaudeville itself.

There may be a social mechanism at work. In the past, when most knew less, emphasis went to craft and performance. For example, Greek sophists concentrated almost entirely on method. Today we emphasize ingestion and absorption of knowledge, and neglect disciplined expression. We have tried to tap the creative potential of the multitude by encouraging the formation of opinion, and giving everyone a chance to express it. But we seem to have set in motion, like the Volstead Act, a furious concoction of home-brew. Few knew how to bottle it properly for use by more than their circle of friends. Ideas *are* home-made, but even good ones need good bottling to stand rough use. Opportunity knocks.

Statement of the Problem

One of the clichés of our time holds that it is far easier to come up with solutions than it is to "define the problem." Unkind cynics satirize eager enthusiasts for new tools and techniques as people frantic to find a problem that fits their solution. Some of the most pitiful presentations are made by such enthusiasts. They delight in explaining the mystery of a technique, usually at great length, as though they were magicians showing how a trick is done. But they neglect to excite interest by performing the trick itself *first*. If the attention of the audience is not engaged by showing how the tool or method will benefit them *before* the loving explanation of how it was developed and operates, a gloomy cloud begins to fill the room, and written on it for all to see is the blunt statement of failure: "So what?" When these two violent words bob around on the listener's stream of consciousness, you'd better harness them as additional force for your presentation, or they will wreck the rest of your idea.

Skillful presentors know just how long to let these words float before resolving the tensions they produce in the minds of an audience. They answer the rude, but silent, question at just the right point. This advanced technique will be treated later in Chapter 4. I will only say here that it is related to mystery and suspense, and requires both deliberate design in the Composition stage, and steady nerves and sense of timing in the Performance stage. But when "So what?" is generated spontaneously by careless design or inept performance, your idea is on a suicide mission.

Rule 1: The *only* reason for the existence of a presentation of an idea is that it be an *answer to a problem.* This problem *must* be stated explicitly sometime early in the presentation.

If you think you can break this rule, you are better than the best essayists, novelists, and dramatists in history. So far, none of them has ever done so successfully. The statement of the problem is like a lighthouse. You may thrash around in a hurricane of thought, whip up storms of rhetoric or lie becalmed, but the rhythmic flash of the light allows the audience to keep their bearings. There are many ways to keep the problem flashing in the audience's mind, and the choice is yours, but it must be made. Restatement of the problem periodically throughout the presentation offers a great field for the play of ingenuity, for the restatement (except in revival meetings) should always be different in *form*, but not in content. This is especially true in a lengthy or complex presentation. The use of visual aids makes this quite easy, but it is a scandal how seldom it is done. Perhaps just because it *is* so easy, it's considered unnecessary. Like breathing air, we only notice the process when we feel in danger of asphyxiation. Taking things for granted is as hazardous in presentations as it is in personal relations.

Rule 2: Never overestimate the audience's information or

underestimate their intelligence. Repetition of the *sense* of the problem, but in different *words*, satisfies this rule. Repetition is related to *rhythm* in every form of art. Its appeal springs from that most primitive aspect of physiology—our pulse.

Let's assume that some constellation of forces has propelled you to the launching pad, and you must make a presentation. It doesn't matter what the forces are: divine revelation, an order from the boss, an attack on your previous position, a routine agenda, an invitation to address a group, just plain irritation at the way things are, or a genuinely creative insight, which must be expressed. In order to satisfy the requirements of drama and interest, you *must* find a way to state the problem plainly. Everything else in the presentation will be built on it. Variations of the plain statement will come easily to you later. Some arise in the Development stage; or, since it's more fun, when others volunteer ideas to help with the decoration. But the simple statement of the problem that caused you to stand before the audience is truly hard work. If it is done badly, the structure of the entire presentation will be shaky; if it is not done at all, you are well advised to catch a diplomatic virus or break a leg. Silence is still the best substitute for brains, though it is not yet an absolute replacement.

Just what do we mean by a problem? Think of some problems you know of right now: personal, family, career, business, community, national, or global. What do they all have in common? One thing, at least. All problems consist of a mismatch between two things: what *actually* exists and what we *want* to exist (in our desires and imagination). Since we also perceive events taking place in a stream of time, a problem's solution must be in the *future*. Some time, short or infinite, separates the present set of unsatisfactory circumstances from those we want to replace them with. These two aspects, *mismatch* between two conceptions, and their *separation in time*, furnish the clue to why other human minds can become interested when a problem is stated explicitly, and why they founder if they have to guess at what the problem is. A good way to visualize these qualities of a problem comes from a simple puzzle. Consider two nails, bent so that they can be linked or unlinked only by placing them in relation to each other in a special way.

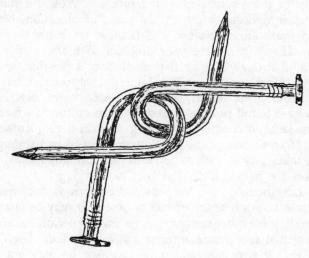

The puzzle, or "problem," is to separate the two bent nails.

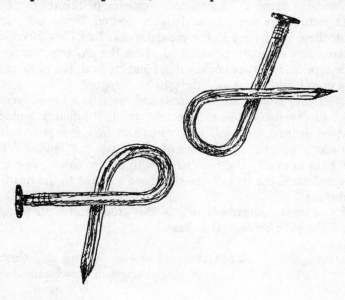

Note that two images are mismatched, the nails linked and the nails separated, and that we "see" the *desired* state because someone told us: "This is the problem—separate them," causing an image of them *separated* in the *future* to cross our mind.

Puzzles intrigue us, often to the point of obsession, because the two states are very clear, and because we know there is a solution. If you can state your problem with the clarity of a puzzle, and strongly suggest that a solution is possible, you can seize and focus that magnified interest that puzzles have extracted from great minds and small since prehistory. Archeologists have found puzzles in every human culture. In fact, one could make a good case for defining man as a problem-solving animal. It would seem to be a little more general and appropriate (if one takes a close look at some of our contemporaries) than adjectives like "rational," "social," or "tool-making."

Consider, though, what happens if the puzzle is not presented *as* a puzzle, but only as an artifact or object. It may be beautiful, or interesting for other reasons, but unless the person receiving it guesses that it *is* a puzzle, interest will quickly fade. Even if he guesses that it is one, should it be complex, he may not guess what the intended *objective* is. These circumstances of ignorance or confusion cause the subsequent behavior of the recipient to differ from what the puzzle designer desired. From our viewpoint, there is a failure in the presentation of an idea. Recollect presentations you have experienced where the problem was never made explicit. Did they not resemble putting forth the puzzle as a mere object, and not as something to be changed?

Select your favorite simple puzzle and use it as a handy mental gauge of problem-statement. Secretly recall it when a problem must be defined. You will be surprised at how few preliminary definitions meet the simple tests of: "What exists?" and: "What do I want to exist?" Used discreetly with others, these two razors have fashioned the reputations of "those who get to the heart of a problem."

If you do not already belong in this group and wish to join, here is the initiation fee: Use them.

Looking at the task of stating the problem in this way, we can glimpse its help in the two subsequent stages of Development and

Resolution. At every step we refer to the two pictures of *what is* and *what should be*. We can also see how conflict, the dramatists's form of development, flows out of good problem-statement. In those elegant solutions, which we call creative, two viewpoints, both correct in themselves, throw light on each other and illuminate our vision with new possibilities. Thus, dual pairs of opposites have been used in all works of powerful persuasion: love and hate; life and death; strength and weakness; fear and courage; disease and health; rise and fall; war and peace; right and wrong. Relating a problem to themes like these guarantees that your audience will grasp its association to their own lives, for we have all been there before. These pairs are really explosive code words for the two conditions mismatched in a problem. What we call our lives are probably tracks of careening from one problem to another through time, some solved and most postponed.

While mismatch is at the heart of every problem, clearness in describing the *desired* thing, state, or situation is vital. Without it, the vision dies. If your audience does not grasp the one situation in the future that is the objective of your idea, you will often see them exhibit symptoms that psychologists find in neurotics. Fidgeting, compulsion to flee, anger, hostility, daydreaming, indecisiveness, phony note-taking, and microscopic fingernail inspection are forms of self-defense when people are forced to consider *ambiguous objectives*. There are good reasons for the similarity of symptoms, for neurosis is that state where two conflicting desires remain equally strong. Energy, yearning to do one thing or the other, refuses to be kept bottled up by delay. It finds outlets in various ways, but unrelated to *both* of the warring objectives. Different persons use different outlets, but usually develop habitual responses. Everyone has seen these, but perhaps not observed them. Here are some I've experienced, and I submit them only as triggers for your memories.

One high corporate official always listened with great interest shown on his face, legs always crossed. As long as the presentation held his interest, his legs were steady. As the presentation became confused, his foot would begin moving, increasing in amplitude. The unlucky proponent either resolved the ambiguity, at which the foot would dampen its oscillation, drifting down to zero, or the official, unable to cope with his by now gyrating shoe, would stand up, thank the miserable character, and flee. Throughout, he never let his face betray his true feelings, and this probably subjected him to more frustration than those with less control could put up with. I knew him for many years and believe that he never realized how he had diverted the effects of emotion from normal facial reactions to his feet. If anyone had told him, the sharp-eyed would have lost a very useful telegraph, at least until the energy involved had found a new conducting path.

Another eminent man always carefully rolled a sheet of paper and peered through it as a boy does in playing sailor with a cardboard tube. Years of practice made the act one of polished elegance and often charmed visitors who did not understand its meaning. One engineer would move to a different chair. A brilliant attorney, known for his self-control and courtly manner, invariably sent a message (to those knowledgeable) that he had sustained a setback, or was about to object, by picking up his pencil, holding it in midair eight inches above his table for a few seconds, and then laying it down with scrupulous care and precision.

I have indulged in this little digression, not as a lesson in detective procedure, but to illustrate that a failure in problem-statement can be sensed even at the last minute if one knows what to look for. The failure may be caused in the performance, even though the composition had it well thought out. If you are prone to this kind of failure in problem-statement, there are several techniques to overcome it. (In those situations where visual aids are acceptable or customary, straightforward statement or representation is relatively easy. We will discuss the special techniques of visual aids in Chapter 6.)

Here are some approaches useful for getting the problem stated explicitly. These tag words are for convenience and brevity in later discussion, and the labels should not be thought of in their narrow dictionary sense. The examples, I trust, will make clear their over-all meaning. Remember, the two criteria they must serve are to show a *mismatch between the present and the future*, and *a difference in time span between the two images:*

Historical Narrative, Crisis, Disappointment, Opportunity, Crossroads, Challenge, Blowing the Whistle, Adventure, Response to an Order, Revolution, Evolution, The Great Dream, Confession.

HISTORICAL NARRATIVE

This is the method of the storyteller. By recounting a tale of what happened in the past, and bringing history up to the present, our inborn sense of continuity in stories—learned in the nursery—creates a momentum which projects the story into the future. To children, "They lived happily ever after" is a fine ending, but it is not too useful for idea presentation. As the narrative sweeps on, adults know that the "story" in the future can turn out in many different ways. Your idea must select one of these ways and show why the state it leads to is a good one for the audience.

Example: "Our town began as a trading post, grew to be an important manufacturing center, survived many disasters, and produced fine people. We must bequeath to our descendants and heirs better than we received. Therefore, I believe that we all want our town to . . ." (grow, become richer, be cultured, be cleaner, be beautiful, have better schools, or whatever other objective you want for the town).

By this projection, you have stated the problem, i.e., how to arrive at the state you desire from where you are now. The narrative approach offers rich possibilities for the development stage by drawing parallels to the past, remembrance of shared nostalgic values, adulation of previous outstanding contributors whose standards of achievement stimulate competitive instinct, and suggesting sad decline and an unhappy ending of the story unless your idea is accepted.

The generality of this example can be seen by substituting for "town," nation, family, club, business, church, school, or any other institution with some history. The historical narrative subtly suggests that the sucessful course was the result of personal decisions by men in the past, and that. *personal* decisions today by members of your audience can be equally effective.

(This personal element differentiates it from the approach I call Evolution. The assumption that the story has been one of success to be proud of differentiates it from Revolution.)

CRISIS

In Chinese, the ideographic character for crisis combines the two symbols for "danger" and "opportunity." The crisis method of stating a problem makes use of this ancient insight by sketching out the danger facing the audience, and showing that an opportunity exists to extricate the audience from the danger—if they accept your idea. This method should not lay blame for the crisis on the audience, as the Old Testament prophets did. (That method is covered under "Blowing the Whistle.") It is best done by showing the audience a quick succession of indisputable facts to establish that a danger exists. Only after that is done are they in the frame of mind to examine the array of facts to find a way out. Your idea should come as a well-thought-out response to the facts. If your proposal is appealing, the anxiety caused by the gloomy recitation will be transformed into support. The greater the danger described, the more potential energy is available for support.

This method carries a hazard in that neither selection of the facts nor their cumulative effect must create so much anxiety that the audience is unable to think because of panic. That is the point where inciting to riot begins. Excessive anxiety will also lead to contradiction, or charges that omission of contrary elements has caused the crisis to be exaggerated. In this situation the audience will seek immediate relief by embracing these contradictory views, and your idea will seem unnecessary. You may even hear nervous laughter—a physiological form of relief from the intolerable tension you have unwisely built. Experienced debunkers wait for such excesses to launch their attacks; they are generous with rope and always give more than enough.

Example: "We have just received the results of our operations for last month. They're not good—in fact, they're bad. Our products are not even holding their own. A large firm has entered our market with a brand new division, staffed with their best men. They are selling substitutes for our line of high-profit items at 10 percent below ours. The union is demanding a 5 percent increase in wages. Our stock is being sold short very heavily. Bank loans are due in three months, and we have large tax payments to make in five. Our product inventory is rising, even though we have cut back production substantially. We cannot ignore this crisis any longer. We must formulate a program for every area of our company so that everyone will know what we intend to do about it, and what we expect them to do. At stake is the very survival of this enterprise. Here is how I propose we cope with this most difficult period in our history."

Then comes your idea. If pessimistic, retrenchment and drastic cost-cutting may appeal to you. If optimistic, here is where those development projects get their chance, or increased sales effort and imaginative, radical marketing methods are embraced.

The crisis method, if skillfully used, announces that every part of the institution will be called on for its ideas and contribution. Some of the great ideas in every institution's history have had to lie in wait for a crisis in order to get a hearing. These are high points in human affairs. However, if the crisis is exaggerated, disbelief rushes in. Backfire can also come from too much repetition. Good people will hunt for other allegiances. Leaders, surprised and delighted at the teamwork and enthusiastic drive produced by a crisis presentation, can become addicted to it quite easily. Followers never like it more than once or twice in a lifetime. Before using this method, be sure to find out the last time it was used. Someone in your audience is bound to remember, and will often point up embarrassing parallels at an unfortunate moment in your presentation.

DISAPPOINTMENT

This method of problem-statement is required when some plan in the past has miscarried. If the plan was well known and generally approved by the audience, they are extremely sensitive to any possible blame and are anxious about their faulty judgment in agreeing to the plan in the first place. Wisdom counsels that you reassure them that neither of these two fears are appropriate before you present your idea as a response to the disappointment. Recapitulation of the assumptions they had to make when authorizing the original plan allows you to show how they did the only thing possible with the facts then available, and that no one could possibly have known of facts that only came to light after things were underway. Once the audience senses that you are not going to blame anybody *there*, they will be emotionally receptive to an objective statement of the mismatch between what they hoped would come about and what actually did—i.e., the source of the problem that caused the presentation to take place.

If the objective of the past plan is still good, it is well to state why, for then the failure was one of methods used, and your idea goes to them. However, if the original objective must be abandoned as either infeasible or no longer valid, this must be made explicit, or there will be confusion as to what you propose. If there were dissenters at the time of the original acceptance of the aborted plan, they will be basking in a feeling of "I told you so," and unless you draw their teeth early, their words will have inordinate weight when your own idea is discussed. It is usually best to recognize their previous positions, even by name, and subtly put them on notice that, instead of reiterating their previous views, they should apply their proven insight to the problems now at hand.

If your idea for coping with the general disappointment is well received, you will find an enthusiastic response far beyond what you have a right to expect. Its source is the gratitude and relief that: "We really did the best we could, and maybe everything will be all right after all."

Example: "It is my painful duty to report to you the results of changes we made last semester in the content of our course in English Literature II. You will remember that we completely reorganized both the approach and required reading because of complaints from students and our newer teachers. They felt that the existing course was too heavily weighted with obsolete works and lengthy classics whose meaning and relation to modern life were obscure. They felt this prevented a real appreciation of literature from developing. We appointed a committee of several in this room to reexamine the course, study complaints, investigate what others were doing, and then recommend a program for approval. This dedicated committee worked hard and long and produced a well-thought-out, if revolutionary, plan. You will recall the excitement and enthusiasm most of us experienced when it was presented last year. True, some of you, like George Draper there, warned us of some of the pitfalls ahead, and while we all respected his characteristically wise counsel, I'm afraid we outvoted him without realizing how correct his predictions were.

"From the point of view of satisfying the students and teachers we had great success, and English Literature II stimulated more interest and appreciation of good writing than ever before. But we underestimated one important hazard—the State Regents Examination. This year we received the lowest evaluation ever in the scores our students achieved, and we may even have harmed their chances for college selection. This is a grave responsibility. We know our action was good education, but we must also recognize that our results are judged by these allegedly impartial tests, which we do not compose or control. They still reward adherence to the old course. I'm afraid we were a little ahead of our time. I hate to see us lose the good we have produced with the new, but we must not create undue burdens for our students. I will propose one way we might cope with this dilemma, and this time, George, we will really listen to your advice and counsel."

The Disappointment type of problem-statement should always face the problem squarely, but look forward in its emphasis to hope, rather than backward to blame. Its danger lies in attributing blame to those not present to defend their position. True fairness to them is the best course, for they may get a chance for rebuttal later, and you might have to eat your words. This counsels that the blame be placed on unexpected events, outworn traditions, or other impersonal forces.

OPPORTUNITY

The opportunity problem-statement springs from the existence of possibility heretofore not available. A mismatch essential for a problem to exist lies in a new image of the future—one never imagined or presented before—compared with what presently exists. External events, inventions, new knowledge, discoveries, and techniques alter our view of what we could previously plan for before the opportunity arose. The audience can appreciate what the new opportunity means only if it is related to the past and present frustrations, limitations, and barriers to progress that the opportunity promises to remove. These hindrances must be presented and accepted as true before the proposal can have any appeal.

Once these are out on the table, the nature of the opportunity must be quickly sketched in, demonstrating how it overcomes these previous constraints. Then one must describe what life will be like if the opportunity is seized, and some of the consequences if it is not. However, the possibility that "others will take it if we don't" always carries a threat that must be deftly used, or the audience may get a whiff of blackmail. Such an impression can poison subsequent digestion of your idea. (This point is often much better left for cross examination.) It is advisable to delay the discussion of what is needed to seize the opportunity until you are certain that the image of the future described is an appealing one for the audience. They will have been worrying about paying the piper right from the start.

Opportunities are always open-ended. Since no one really knows where they will lead, it is wise to indicate only roughly the more distant possibilities that the opportunity at hand opens up. If you get too specific, you may find the audience homing in on these secondary images, where you are bound to be short on evidence and long on shaky speculation. Specificity and certainty about these far-off possibilities marks you as too visionary, or a fanatic. The audience will discount your present proposal and avoid future ones. Practical men know there is many a slip 'twixt the cup and the lip. They are often willing to settle if they can just be sure to get the cup off the table and let things go from there; but they justifiably resent the babying or condescending hand that insists on guiding the cup right on up to their teeth. Claims for panaceas are outlawed by the Food and Drug people. They should also be banned from presentations as strictly as they are from medicine cabinets, for they are purchased only by the ignorant.

Example: "I have never come to a meeting with more enthusiasm, and I am glad that you are all here for what may be a historic moment in the history of our industry. You know how hard we have worked to lower the costs and improve the quality of the steel we make, and how meager and disappointing our progress has been.

"Every time we got some new chemical discovery, it cost too much; and every time we tried to get more steel from existing plant, the quality went sour. On top of this we have had to raise our prices just to stay in business, and the public's impression of us has gone down every time prices went up. We have really been frustrated in our efforts to do a better job, and while we have achieved a plateau of development and built the industrial base of the country, our competitors in aluminum, glass, and especially plastics, have cream-skimmed markets once entirely ours. We have also experienced unfair competition from those abroad who have the very latest equipment financed by foreign aid programs.

"If ever an industry needed and deserved a breakthrough, ours is that industry; and, gentlemen, it is my happy duty to report one. Many people have been working on processes using high pressure oxygen in various ways and have had little success. Keeping alert for any possibility, we heard rumors recently that a small firm in England, extending a process developed in Austria, had licked the problems. We immediately sent off several of our best scientists and engineers for on-the-spot investigation. I received their final reports late yesterday, and the results are fantastic. We must quickly make up our minds about this opportunity—the greatest since the Bessemer converter—because the plans we agreed to last month will be affected in many ways, depending on how you react.

"One of the most surprising aspects is that a new plant can be justified economically at one-tenth the capacity and size we experience today! It also handles a larger range of mixes, and cheaply delivers quality tolerances better than we can hold today. The ultimate implications for steelmaking throughout the world can't even be imagined yet, and I won't waste your valuable time by speculating on them. But this process seems to be the answer we've been hoping for to solve *today's* problems —and yesterday's—and we have plenty to do just to insure that we don't miss the boat. We have many ways we can react, and after the technical people here describe the process and its benefits, I will present my view of the choices we have and their consequences for all of us here."

Notice that the opportunity method constantly suggests that *action* will be required by the audience, even in recounting the present. Interest can be sustained in the Development stage by means discussed later, but the *onwardness* of movement should never stop. The audience must become convinced that the opportunity is *theirs*, not yours. If an opportunity type presentation stops after merely a description of the event that produced it, the audience is left up in the air, and your idea joins the trash pile of lost opportunities.

CROSSROADS

Problems of the "crossroads" type result from a past sucess or achievement. One can picture them as that place on a journey where, if one wants to continue the trip, a choice must be made between two or more available routes. The old road behind has run out, and those ahead fork to right and left. Your presentation is not a plea for taking a specific road, but instead, attempts to establish that you are now at a point where a *choice must be made*.

Graduation from high school is a homely example. It is an instantaneous state and marks a success point. Here it is obvious that a choice for the future must be made as a result of the present success. It is not at all obvious in other problems of this type. Making an audience aware of the necessity for choice is more difficult than one would think, for situations involving a larger group of persons and circumstances are never as clear-cut as the graduation of an individual. There will always be some in the audience who believe that the momentum of the past achievement can best be continued by not touching anything and letting well enough alone. Your job is to show that this possibility does not exist. Crossroads presentations are sometimes mixed with an opportunity presentation, but in my experience this is a mistake. You are confusing the audience by statement of two problems simultaneously, and it will plague the entire development of both. A far better technique is to make *two* presentations with some time between, if possible. If not, then the crossroads problem must come first, and let the break be signaled by having two different people address themselves to the two different problems. The crossroads problem *demands* a change, the opportunity problem *allows* a change. This difference may appear subtle, but it is quite profound from the viewpoint of the audience.

Example: "After the acceptance last week of our report, plans, and specifications for the water pollution project, we must face the decision on what to do with the fine team we assembled for the job. All fifty of the people assigned were hand-picked experts in their fields and in the last year have learned to work together far better than we could have hoped. In fact, we did not expect to have to hold this meeting for another three months on our original schedule. We did expect to be asked to make many more adjustments and modifications to our plans, but the Commission's complete acceptance, while most gratifying, has caught us by surprise. You all know how difficult it was to recruit this organization, what a fine leader we developed in John Hustle, and it seems a shame to disband it. But we do not have any more jobs like that in the offing, and we've got to face it. The contractors would undoubtedly like to hire some of the engineers, and we have existing projects which could benefit from additional personnel. But their disposition in many different ways is not the problem here. We must decide very soon what we intend to do, so that we can allay the anxieties I know are building up, and deploy the people in both their best interests and ours. We have developed a few possibilities, and Clark will present them this afternoon, but before we discuss them, it is important for us all to agree that this project team must be redirected. Does anyone have anything to add at this time, before I go into more detailed consideration?"

While this sounds quite simple, you will generally be surprised at the tendency to maintain the existence of a successful entity. In fact, most institutions have many enclaves formed of the remnants of once successful groups. This is the result of never presenting the problem *as* a crossroads problem to higher authority. There are always some loose ends to every activity, and they can be woven into marvelous, if fantastic, designs. Unraveling them has made more than one consultant's reputation and fortune. Unrecognized crossroads problems, if left to breed, grow material for both comic and tragic plays.

CHALLENGE

A problem presented in the challenge format announces the call for a contest. The mismatch here is between the images of what exists and what *someone else* dares you to accomplish in the future. The idea of challenge rests on the existence of obvious obstacles to be overcome, much like the labors of Hercules.

Obstacles may be an assault or race against an impersonal force, like climbing a mountain or beating a speed record; achieving a level of quality or beauty never before experienced; or meeting a test for survival in the face of a hostile force.

The challenge triggers primitive emotions of rivalry, self-preservation, and the fear of being thought cowardly by those who know you have been "called out." The method has been used by every great captain and every good platoon leader since the Bronze Age. A game or contest gets its emotional impact from identification with the contestants by the spectators who share the challenge vicariously. The limits of the challenge form are that it be neither too easy nor too difficult. With too little challenge there is no image of real triumph offered as the goal; but a truly impossible challenge results in apathy, a refusal even to imagine a triumph. Both reactions prevent recognition of a problem. When used well, few methods of problem-statement can equal it as groundwork for colorful, emotional development. "Put up or shut up!" is its shortest form.

Example: "For years we have all complained that we do not have a good local theater. Well, now we have a chance to get one, but it will take every bit of effort we can muster. As you know, the State Arts Festival is scheduled in two years, and the Nord Foundation—out of the blue—has told us that they will match, dollar-for-dollar, any funds we can raise ourselves. We can't just sit on our hands and hope. We've got to acquire a site and have an approved architect's plan in their hands in nine months. Also, if we do not have the theater ready two months before the Festival, the deal's off. This is a tough challenge, but we are not likely to get another chance like it for a long time.

"We may fail and be the laughing stock of the state, but we also might succeed and show other donors what kind of people we are. The Foundation has put it to us fair and square, and now it's entirely up to us. Before you answer, let me take you through some of the important factors in this problem."

The challenge type problem is similar to an opportunity problem, but differs in that the emphasis is placed more on overcoming obstacles than exploiting an unexpected event. It also differs from most crisis problems as it is offensive rather than defensive in character, though of course a crisis is the pathological form of challenge.

BLOWING THE WHISTLE

A policeman discovering an unlawful act and then summoning help and attention exemplifies this type of problem-statement. Mismatch exists between behavior observed and behavior demanded. The image of what is demanded is embedded in a set of principles, laws, customs, orders, or conscience. Greek tragedies and plays of Shaw are the supreme examples of what can be done with this method, and the everyday dramas of magistrate's court use it in the less artistic way. The mismatch always implies that action is needed to bring the observed behavior in line with the code that has been violated. If this is not possible, punishment of some kind is to be dispensed, and steps taken to rectify the damage done.

It is essential that parts of the code be made explicit, either by quoting them directly or by reference to the pronouncements of authorities accepted by your audience. Facts concerning the actual behavior should be contrasted with the relevant citations. It is usually better to recite the facts first and the code provisions next. Though effective statement can interlace the parts of both, in ping-pong fashion, this sometimes leads to confusion in unskillful hands. You should also indicate quite early whether your idea goes either to *providing punishment* or to *rectifying damage* done. Mixture of these alternative objectives allows clever rebuttal and defense to show the audience that you are distracted and unclear, and that should they accept your idea, they will slide with you into an unwholesome state of confusion.

By selecting one or the other, cumulative, repetitive insistence on the need for future adherence to the violated code can build to a crescendo of feeling, like the bass drum in a funeral march. But refusal to make the choice will result in your audience not knowing what you want them to do. They hear simultaneous notes from piccolos and cymbals, sometimes interesting but never cumulative. When they do not know your objective, your chances of achieving it decrease with every word. If you must have both punishment and program, then split the story into *two* self-contained presentations. It is a rare or trivial institution in which the same people must take identical action for punishment as they must for programs of rectification or corrective action. Courts do not carry on the constructive work of society; neither do administrators sentence criminals. They are in two different games and play by different rules, yet both adhere to the same code of desired behavior. What makes them different is the different action expected of them when given the same problem.

Example: "In the past year the number of complaints about the fees charged by our physician members has increased alarmingly. We have tripled those of the previous year, and the press is getting interested. There also seems to be a pattern developing in the various specialities which some may infer as due to collusive practice. We have investigated thoroughly more than half of these complaints, and they seem justified. This disturbing development is completely contrary to the intent of the principles we agreed on last year, but the qualifying exceptions we put in to redress the unfavorable position of physicians in low-income areas seem to have been exploited by those for whom they were never intended. We need not discuss any action which our society should take against individuals. That's a matter for our special review board. But we must face up to what we need to do if we want to regain the trust and respect of the public at large. Not all are at fault, of course, but since we will all be judged by the actions of a considerable minority, we must develop programs and procedures to safeguard patients and physicians alike. These must be so explicit in detail, without clever escape clauses, that we can take a position before a hostile press conference. I will present my ideas for your consideration after we discuss the details of several cases and their violations of the code to illustrate the problem."

This method is not too effective if its entire thrust is based on altruism and moral force alone. You must always keep in mind the reason for the existence of the codes themselves: the preservation of the authority and position of the members of the institution to which it applies. If you can show the audience that the violations put them in peril, they quickly see the problem as important and requiring solution. A respectful hearing is then automatically guaranteed, whether the institution is a church, university, legislature, or industry.

ADVENTURE

A risky and uncertain image of the future is compared with the seeming safety of the present to produce a problem of the adventure type. Its appeal is based on lure of the unknown and a chance to test a person's or institution's mettle by engagement with hazardous, unpredictable forces. Enough information about the hazards is necessary both to establish the possibility of success and to stimulate the latent desire for excitement. Hints must be given about the gaps in knowledge or experience that the successful adventure will fill. The most difficult task in using the adventure type of approach is to establish why these gaps are important to eradicate, and what benefits will attend those who undertake, or underwrite, the search. Unless you secure this kind of momentum for your idea, it will screech to a halt when someone in the audience applies the peremptory brake: "Is this trip necessary?" You can visualize Thomas Jefferson persuading Congress to authorize funds for Lewis and Clark's proposed expedition as an elementary form of this statement type. If your taste runs to the classics, substitute Jason's proposal for the Golden Fleece recovery to the champions of Thessaly. This is the most exhilarating form of problem, but remember that the acceptance of your idea will depend almost entirely on the confidence you command with the audience. They must balance their fear of the unknown by faith in your leadership. If the scale comes down on the wrong side, no sale.

Example: "We have all heard complaints that the basic unit in our organization needs revision. We have listened to a dozen proposals for different rearrangements to improve customer service, optimize capital use, motivate employees, get a better technical job, and allow lower-level supervisors to take more responsibility. These ideas have all been well intentioned and ingenious. Yet their proponents have never been able to satisfy our fears that we will lose more than we will gain because of possible disrupted relationships, confusion, jurisdictional misunderstandings, employee resistance, loss of specialized knowledge, and customer irritation. Of course we will never have the kind of information and experience we want until we try, and we will be caught in this illogical circle of indecision forever.

"I propose that we set out to determine just what we need to know about these fuzzy areas so that we can settle, for at least the near-term future, what we should do. The trial I want will be a hazardous project and will require you to take chances that we are not accustomed to. We may fail or lose our nerve, but even then we will know much that we don't know now. We need not put the whole outfit on the line, but we must be willing to involve three entire districts, about two thousand people, in the experiment for two years.

"I am convinced this is the only way, and while I prefer less risky forms of tinkering with people's lives, that is just not possible. We can't test these ideas in a laboratory. We must see if they can stand the heat of combat in the real world. I feel they can, but can't be sure. Since the potential rewards of success are so great, I am willing to bet my reputation on them, and I know that many others feel the same way. The rest of our presentation is designed for one purpose: to convince you that we should have this chance. While we may conduct the operations, you must share in our triumph or defeat. We will not and cannot launch this without your support."

If you choose this method of problem-statement, abandon the ancient hedging maneuver of deploying a well-balanced list of "pros and cons." That is too often a subtle device for passing the buck to superiors and directly opposes the sense of adventure: a willingness to endure the slings and arrows of outrageous fortune for a higher goal. Adventure sounds a call to arms, not summations to the jury.

RESPONSE TO AN ORDER

The problem here is rooted in a comparison between the state of affairs someone else wants (a superior or other authority) and current conditions. Orders are usually resorted to after persuasion fails, and are most often unwelcome to their recipients. Stark statement is preferable to pussyfooting. The greatest difficulty is to get the audience away from a mood of "It's unfair, we don't deserve this, can't we fight?" and other forms of childish behavior. If you are really serious about resolving the problem, it is not advisable to identify with the sense of being wronged. The objective of this problem statement is to get all of the audience's irritation and anger diverted to constructive suggestion. Any castigation of the order-giver will plague you later, when you must defend the basis of your ideas for resolving the problem. More important, dissatisfied elements who disagree with *your* proposals may even use your opening remarks to quietly inform the order-giver that your solution is as bad as your stated opinion of his order. This can become embarrassing when you need his approval later for your program of response.

After stating the problem and indicating that it will not disappear in a cloud of wishful thinking, a factual description of the forces and considerations that caused the order to be given helps dissipate the emotional voltage, and channel it into mature reflection. If you can get the members of the audience to imagine that they would give the same kind of order were they in the order-giver's place, you are halfway home. Another positive step is to show that the order-giver has confidence in the audience's ability to deliver the goods, and that if successful solutions are forthcoming, his opinion of the group will rise.

If you cannot state these things as heard directly by you, the same effect, somewhat diminished, flows from a speculative explanation of "what must have been in his mind to give us this order." The final polish to an unpopular problem-statement comes by developing some variation of the belief that: "It's an ill wind that blows nobody some good." If a few in the audience come to believe that an opportunity lurks somewhere in the order, their mental energies can be brought to a hot focus. However, constructive response cannot occur if the audience "fights the problem" or refuses to come to grips. These attitudes must be demolished before development begins, or your idea will neither be heard nor understood.

Example: "Yesterday we received the final order from the city which forces us to put all of our pole lines inside the city limits underground. We have exhausted every appeal, but all we could do was to get the period to comply extended from the original one year to two. We can do nothing more. All of you have been working on the alternate approaches, but they must now be discarded. I'm sorry, as I know you must be, but we don't have a day to waste talking about it anymore.

"If we were in the City Council's place, I suppose we would have done the same thing sometime, but not as quickly. They don't seem to understand the difficulty of the job. One even told me, 'You people are real professionals—you'll work it out. We know you can do it.' We have talked about this amongst ourselves for some time, but now we have to do it. I know a few of you, particularly Jack Goodfellow, have tried to sell us on this for years. We will now see whether your arguments about lower repair costs and fewer interruptions in service are any good. You will have every chance to prove it. The public relations people also see this as not too bad, since it ought to cut out a lot of the complaints we've been getting recently. We must face the fact that a majority of citizens just don't like poles and wires cluttering up their view. So let's get on with it. We must have a complete program drawn up within the month if we are to obey the order."

This approach has another merit for the development stage. Since the order must be carried out, arguments for countermoves and delay can always be referred back to the necessity to comply. Once an audience decides that the order needs to be met, they are jealous of any time wasted on unnecessary discussion. Ready-made plans, in line with an order and loaded with detail, are impregnable to possibly better ideas, which are still only in the sketch or conceptual stage. This is where contingency planning pays off. Superior planning groups are those with a shelf full of ideas waiting for customers. Their effectiveness is best seen in problems of the order type.

REVOLUTION

Revolution-type problems find their mismatch between an unfavorable image of the future, which will occur if the present state is left undisturbed, and a better state, which is possible only if the historical and traditional inertia is arrested and cast down. Things must be turned over (revolved) by drastic intervention, or they will only get worse. Revolutionists for big issues see themselves as benefiting unborn generations, almost as engineers of future history. Their best appeal is to the latent rebel and maverick element in each of us, which is our counterbalance to boredom. Fear of the consequences is their greatest obstacle. Mismatch between the images must be so great that the will to "solve the problem" overcomes the fear of the consequences of failure. Weak problem-statement will not allow development of a strong program. The audience will keep hoping to have their cake and eat it if you don't show that the future demands scrapping most of the past—and much good along with it.

Revolution is akin to adventure, but with the hazards mostly known and predictable. Development uses these hazards as factors energizing the sense of self-preservation. Without them there is little need for the audience to submit to your leadership and gamble their destiny on the clarity of your particular vision. It appeals most to those with nothing to lose; least to those with much. Election speeches of the best type—by the "outs"—are polite forms of the revolutionary problem.

Example: "Our church loses vigorous members every month and gains only those tired of progress in their former congregations. Every day we act as though the great changes going on about us are unworthy of our concern. We keep looking backward, to a nostalgic day that really never was, hoping that all of our difficulties will disappear by magic. If we continue like this, we are headed for the ash heap, and our absence will be mourned by none except the hard-core reactionaries who have refused to see how sick we really are. We need a new look, a new mission, and a new management. Our present Council will keep reelecting themselves, holding things as they are, and treating us like a bunch of children. And yet under present rules they are the only ones who can make the changes required. We must reject them and establish a new order without them if we want this church to survive and to train our children properly. It will not be easy. We can expect the central authority to be prejudiced in their own favor. They are powerful men who can harass you and your families just for attending a meeting like this. They may try to expel us from membership. There may be bad publicity. But this tyranny must be ended if we want to be true to the ideals that built this congregation and made it, until recently, a force for good. The Council has betrayed our future by its petty and stubborn refusals to make even the slightest reforms required. It is up to us, the concerned and committed, to act on our own. Here is my idea."

Revolutions take nerve and are successfully prosecuted only by the ruthless. No halfway measures will work, and your opposition expects none. Never put a problem in this form unless you mean to live with the consequences of success as well as failure. A revolutionary idea is sometimes confused with a nihilistic idea, where mere destruction itself is the objective. Revolution is a means to an end: the vision of what life will be like after success. It is constructive in intent. Emphasis should always be on that. The uproar in-between is merely the vehicle to get there. Correction of injustice is its noblest aspect; simple spite, its meanest. Choose well.

EVOLUTION

An evolution type of problem arises when an institution or person, well adapted to its previous environment, is faced with a change in that environment that calls for further adaptation to remain viable. It has to "be out of touch," or "out of date," and dissatisfied with that condition. Mismatch lies between the present condition and the image of congruence with society desired in the future.

Emphasis should be placed on past success, and the adaptations successfully made to achieve that success. Then the change in environment should be sketched in ways that bring out the maladjustments calling for action. It is essential to show the positive results of future adaptation. You must also establish that the environmental change is not temporary or, at least, is not going to reverse itself to the previously happy state when all was right with your world. Intelligent resignation to overpowering forces is its mood, not belligerent obstruction.

Example: "Our efforts for conservation of the great wilderness areas have been the model for groups all over the nation. We have, to the credit of our previous leaders, a continuous record of successful battles against those who wanted to despoil our natural heritage. It was saved and developed by men of vision, who sensed the tendencies of their times, and who mobilized mass opinion to their cause. We can be proud of the large preserves now forever safe from the commercial axe and plow. Generations after us will benefit.

"However, our very success can endanger this great accomplishment, for social forces beyond our control require some alteration in our present policies. The state's population has doubled since we stabilized the wilderness acreage. All good recreational areas will have been developed to capacity in a few years, and the increasing population and urbanization will create pressures on the preserves. We can delay and fight scores of small legal actions, hoping to keep things as they are. But we will lose in the end, for one adverse ruling by the Supreme Court will destroy our position.

"We have always contended that our activity was for all the people against the exploiters, but in these cases, we will look as though we are against the people. We will appear to be out of touch with social problems and are bound to lose unless we adapt to the inevitable. We can anticipate and plan intelligently now, while we have time. We need to balance the interest between wilderness and recreational use, and shape viable programs. Otherwise we will be told what to do. We lack a grand design for orderly evolution. I propose one now."

Everyone feels safer with evolution than with revolution, and a calm demeanor can reassure the diehards no end. The tone to strive for is that of a duchess dedicating a new steel mill on one of her ancestral estates: progress with elegance.

THE GREAT DREAM

The only method of presenting a utopia, paradise, or hell-on-earth as an image of the future in contrast to the present is to rely heavily on fantasy. Fantasy, used seriously, can often be presented without being ridiculous by recounting a vision or a dream. Its structure is imaginative rearrangement of real things or facts in new ways. Dreams are unhampered by factors like time, gravity, or other restraints. Engineers like to say that dreams do not build bridges, but that no bridge is built without one. A dream-type setting is one that makes a tremendous leap from the present, beyond the imaginative capacity of most. The objective is to let others share its vision. Almost all religious problems are of this sort, Western or Oriental. If an audience's imagination can be extended to grasp the vision, then they see the problem and are willing to work on it. If they don't see it, you are put down as a visionary, and they leave the presentation undisturbed. The mood of a happy dream is hope; of an unhappy one, despair. You should think of yourself as leading the audience on a climb up a high hill for the first time. When they reach the top, show them the beautiful vista below. If you intend frightening them, substitute gaping chasms and boiling, sulphurous springs. Joseph in Egypt was a great practitioner of this method and was equally good on both sides on the street.

Example: "I have just returned from Bourneston, the once great center of our shipbuilding industry. It was a depressing visit. I saw the squalor and inactivity that have replaced the busy yards, prosperous streets, and happy children of my boyhood there. I came away with sad memories of broken windows, rusty cranes, dilapidated buildings, and yellowed paper blowing about in the offshore breeze. It is truly a ghost town.

"But as I climbed the hill in my melancholy mood, the sun was setting, and its light restored the scene below to its natural beauty. The whitecaps and rocks glistened, gulls circled, and the rhythm of the waves lifted my spirits. I had a vision of what might be, and all the way back my enthusiasm continued to mount. I became convinced that this poor victim of economic storms can rise again. The same coast, forests, inlets, and beaches that originally drew the industry can now draw others who want to enjoy, rather than to exploit, the advantages nature placed there. This forlorn place could become one of the great resort areas of this region. The time is ripe. Other resorts are overcrowded or honky-tonk, and fine boating harbors are rare indeed.

"If enough of you will entertain this dream for just a while today, I can give you some facts and ideas that might turn the vision into something of beauty, but alive and real instead of a dream. It may not be practical and will not be easy, but let's see what you think might be done. At best, you may be surprised; at worst, we will have done a little homage to a once lovely spot."

With this method, there should be an alternation of hard facts with aspects of the dream, like a photo of a junkyard, followed by an artist's colorful rendering of "what it's going to be like." Back to a photo, on to another drawing, and finally to costs, schedules, and the other paraphernalia of real projects. One must also show that the nucleus of the idea can spread and gather momentum. Use statements of influential movers and shakers who feel kindly—even if passively—toward the idea, and allude to similar successes elsewhere. The objective is always to strengthen a belief in *possibility*; but it must be approached indirectly by building on *desirability*.

CONFESSION

The mismatch here lies between what the audience *believes* exists and what really does. It is a tricky form of problem-statement, since all sorts of emotions are at work both in the audience and in the presentor. Use of this form calls for you to walk a high, narrow fence; one slip, and you're down. If your confession threatens to involve the personal reputations of members of your audience, they will usually greet the disclosure with silence at the outset. You should not be misled; they are feverishly thinking of ways to extricate themselves. Worry about the real problem, and your reputation is secondary.

If delivery is nervous and disconnected, you don't have a chance. The audience will see that you are in no shape to present an idea for the solution of the problem you've dumped in their laps and certainly are not the man to lead the way out. More than any other form of problem-statement, confession demands absolute concentration on the outcome you want. No matter how hot the recriminations or how violent the reactions, your personal resolve is the best lightning rod for the natural forces you have unleashed. They must be made to serve your idea, not to wreck it. As with all violent forces—like sea, fire, or wind—their control is difficult; but if harnessed to a specific purpose, they can amplify your own efforts.

Most people secretly and unconsciously enjoy hearing a problem of the confession sort, especially from one they considered above them in a hierarchical structure. In return for removing a previous invidious relationship, the audience will return sympathy, or at least pity, if their fears of being dragged down can be allayed. This is almost entirely emotional. Witness the public outcry at the disciplining of popular heroes whose clay feet are displayed when they make headlines from time to time.

Since Saint Augustine and Rousseau, the "Confession" has gripped the popular mind. This form ranges from the precincts of the highest literature to tiresome trash. Confession, while humble in expression, implies a manly act of honesty. It may be late, but it also bristles with silent pride. In confession's noblest form, there is always an element of self-sacrifice for some great cause. When coupled with development based on mystery, the audience sits expectantly, waiting for the answer to their inarticulate: "Why did you do it?" They can always identify with failure; not often with success.

In order to quiet their fear, it is essential that you take full responsibility, even if not deserved. After that, the audience will listen to the problem and your solution. Once their own personal anxiety is relieved, they will generally become constructive. If you can get the audience to imagine that each of them would have acted as you did, *were they in your circumstances*, you are on the downhill grade to home. This makes it necessary to describe these circumstances. Blame, if possible, unfortunate developments outside anyone's control, which you faced and tried to overcome for the good of others, especially for those in the audience. If your confession is one of having exceeded your authority, and success was gained because you took the risk, you may experience the heady reaction of applause and cheers. Disraeli, buying Egypt's portion of the Suez Canal, on his own hunch, is your example here. If failure develops, you at least get points for courage. Avoid the tone of guilt; embrace, instead, an air of responsibility and tragedy if things went awry. You must show the way out with all the passion you can muster. Without that, the presentation becomes only grist for the mills of gossips.

Example: "It is with a feeling of jubilation that we are gathered here to celebrate the success of our first School Fair. Many of you argued and pleaded for years that it would be a success; that it would bring the parents together; and that it would allow us to support some of the worthwhile activities desired by our teachers. But we were always deterred by fears of financial failure. Yet a few months ago we decided to go ahead.

"You will recall that I promised we would get the stands, lights, and carnival decorations from an anonymous donor. This was my own belief, but during the happy and hectic week before the Fair, I had a call from this gentleman—whom I still cannot name. He told me that financial reverses forced him to withdraw his promised support. I know that I should have told the committee, but as I saw all of you setting up displays, the children running errands, the husbands at work on a thousand projects, I simply could not do it. We had such a slim vote of confidence that I feared those who counseled us against the adventure would say, 'I told you so,' and stop the work we had so happily begun. I feared that if we did not go on, we would never get another chance. I believed so strongly we were right that I gambled with the good name of our association. I admit I had no right to do that, and submit no excuse except excessive emotional commitment.

"After hearing our treasurer's report and experiencing a sense of fellowship here tonight unique in the history of our association, I am deeply sorry at what I must tell you. We still have an unpaid bill which will take almost one-third of the total proceeds we have just cheered. I must ask you to honor this bill even though I exceeded my powers and imperiled the whole enterprise. There is no one to blame but myself, and I submit my resignation because of the danger in which I placed this association. I did it on my own responsibility, even though I knew I could not make it good if my judgment were wrong. I would not have missed the Fair for the world, and I must tell you in all honesty that I would do exactly the same thing again.

"Thank you for everything, especially for making a dream come true. I will try to answer any questions you may have and accept any blame you care to ascribe."

Notice that even in this saccharine scene, the problem of a mismatch between the treasurer's report and reality is stated for the audience. The suggested image of restored respectability *for the audience* must follow quickly, or their anxiety level will get out of control. This form of problem-statement can mislead you even when successful, for the initial identification of the audience with your act fades away quickly. You may find them looking at you a trifle uneasily when you are next on an assignment that carries discretionary powers. It is advisable to leave the premises as soon as you can, so that frank discussion of your disclosure can dissipate any emotional residue. If you've done a good job of problem-statement, those who saw your viewpoint will do a far better job of defending it than you possibly can. If no friends rise to this duty, then you are even better off by not remaining.

This form is akin to the "Disappointment" style, but here the disappointment comes though in an instant, like a clap of thunder. There is no time given to prepare for its effect. If a choice can be made between "Confession" and "Disappointment," choose the disappointment method for greater ease, and confession for greater drama. It is no accident that communist lawyers prefer a "confession style" trial to a "blowing the whistle" type. Such trials are designed as educational experiences and are put on for all other citizens who are watching or reading about them. "Confession" problems produce much more identification and emotional punch. They are consequently far more effective for such purposes of state than a tedious game of charge and denial.

Anyone can drum up his own list of pigeonholes to classify problems. It is a healthy exercise only if it impresses on him the nature of a mismatch between two images. There is something in each of us that is disturbed by a clash of conceptions or images. If we are geniuses, the resolution of the right kind of clash may win a Nobel Prize. If we are parents, we may try different approaches to bend a child's behavior toward our favored image. If we are leaders, we will try to get others to share our vision and put their efforts to our cause. If we are neurotic, we may get to enjoy the clash for its own sake, unable to decide which is the better. All attitudes, except the neurotic, lead to action; they attempt to achieve the better state. Merely *stating a problem* implies that some action is latent or about to happen, or you wouldn't state it. If you have none in mind, don't even begin.

To return to our triad of Problem, Development, and Resolution, the art and science of development rests on selecting aspects of *possible* action. Rearranging and relating them in different ways (so that ever new aspects appear) show that derivative problems flow from the original problem. After subtle logical and emotional repetitions, lead on to the resolution of the original problem. Finally, stress the favored image set forth in the original statement and leave the unfavorable one behind. In the analogy of an ocean voyage, the problem is to recognize that you are in Port A and want to go to Port B. The various difficulties and events on the trip furnish the development, and the anchoring in Port B is the resolution. This analogy makes it clear that everything that happens during the voyage is always referred to the objective of Port B, and grows out of the departure from Port A.

Presentations that do not keep their eyes, brains, and hearts on the anchorage at Port B can degenerate into random cruises. The passengers (your audience) who thought they had bought a ticket for some other place, even if unspecified, are usually exasperated if you return them to Port A. While this seems obvious, many presentations end in disaster because their proponents never knew where they wanted to go. These people are often perplexed and hurt at an audience's reaction. "After all," they think, "I know we came back to where we started, but it was really an interesting trip, wasn't it?" Just as cruises are a form of luxurious escape which appeal to a special class, such presentations are appreciated only by those who have nothing else to do. You have given them a vacation from boredom, nothing more. Audiences who like this sort of thing have no energy, power, or inclination to advance your idea. Serious members of an audience seek those with real insights and programs. They do not waste their time or resources on triflers.

In the next chapter we will explore various approaches to Development. This phase requires that you capture and sustain attention by playing variations on the clear and simple theme of your problem-statement.

3

How to Get
and Hold Attention

or

Creating Sleeplessness

With the problem-statement form selected, the next phase in development is how to generate interest in the path you want to take to get from one state of affairs to another. Your subsidiary objective here is to get attention—that subtle aspect of psychology whose underlying process is still in doubt. However, throughout history men have known how to do this. From their practice and the investigations of modern research, sufficient knowledge is available for the purposes of any presentation, even if the theory is shaky. Children still blow soap bubbles without encumbrances from the physics of surface tension or topology. Let me use a personal case to illustrate the point.

Over ten years ago a good friend of mine was invited to make a presentation of how electronic computers could be used in a large business. The audience was to be the president and all of the vice presidents of the company, and they were to assemble in an awesomely baroque room used by the board of directors for their meetings. His appearance was the result of the enthusiastic suggestion of only one of the vice presidents, who secured the resigned acceptance of his colleagues. My friend is an alert man and knew that he should expect less than passionate interest from this audience, whose greatest compliment would be attempts to suppress yawns. Still, he had the job to do and wanted to do it right. He was convinced that he had a good idea of real merit, but if he failed to excite real interest, he might kill the idea's chances for many months. If he muffed the attempt, even though under adverse circumstances, people would remember that: "They turned it down." Valuable time would be needed to fall back and regroup for counterattack. His problem: How to get the attention required for a fair understanding of his proposition?

Since the subject was known in advance by everyone to be technical, the attention had to be even greater than normal. My friend, a true expert, spent little time on the material itself, but instead concentrated constantly on the best method to rivet attention at the outset. He told me later that the idea came to him while raking leaves on the Saturday before the Monday meeting. It was such a startling solution that he did not chance telling anyone at all about it—including his sponsor. Convinced it was the only way, he immediately put down his rake and took off for the local antique shop.

On Monday he arrived in the board room, and things were even worse than he expected. As the members arrived, he experienced more heartiness than usual, probably as a compensation for what the audience really felt about their ordeal ahead. Fine, darkly luminous portraits of past presidents looked down on the proceedings as though alert for breaches of the traditions of great events that had taken place there. Doric columns, subdued lighting, the green-covered long table, and walnut paneling all hinted that only the best of taste and gentlemanly behavior would be welcome here. The total atmosphere nearly panicked my friend, but he decided to burn his bridges and blanked his mind to every signal that counseled decorum.

When everyone was settled in his chair, and the clublike banter fell off, the sponsoring vice president informed his colleagues that they were about to hear one of the world's experts, a man of probity and experience, who would initiate them in the mysteries of the arcane equipment that held such promise for all of their areas of responsibility. Amid a general shifting of position, every eye centered on my friend as he strode to the head of the table. Without a word, he opened his coat, reached down deep in his pocket and slowly extracted a Colt .45 revolver, the "Peacemaker" model, with its 8-inch barrel. He held it for a while pointed toward one of the more popular presidential portraits, and then brought it to rest on the table. Everyone in the room was aghast, but glued their eyes to the gun. Some sat bolt upright.

Before the inevitable reaction began, my friend said in quite a loud voice, "This, gentlemen, is a computer. Please examine it and pass it around." That done, he handed the pistol to the Treasurer with a courtly gesture.

He then went on to explain that the notches cut in the handle were a method of storing information (the number of persons who had stood in front of the gun with fatal results) in symbolic form. But, more importantly, the form was binary—a notch was either there or it wasn't. This is exactly the number system used in electronic computers. Instead of notches, they use things like light switches which can also be only "on" or "off." With this transition back to reality, everyone relaxed, and my friend delivered a first-class exposition to the most attentive audience he ever had.

A few months ago I was talking to one of the members of his audience, and computers entered the conversation. He stopped and said, "I never hear the word computer mentioned without thinking about a Colt revolver. You know, that was when Kelfer gave us our first presentation, and I always link up the two ideas. It's silly, but I just can't help thinking about the two together." This, after ten years, is high praise for any opening.

Here we get a clue to the method of arresting attention for an event: Create a clash between the background environment and the event. In this case with background of quiet elegance, a normal, courteous talk in good form insured a minimum of attention. Do something incongruous, like bringing symbols of violence into that environment, and no man on earth could resist the clash in his consciousness. Conversely, in an uproarious background of chaotic frenzy, a strong, calm statement, delivered with maximum gravity, is most effective.

Attention *attraction* is rooted almost entirely in the emotions. Reason is possible only *after* attention has been directed to the assumptions and logic used. Unless attention is secured, the audience will literally not hear the story. It becomes only another set of noises in the background. This is why some men, dragged to an opera by their music-loving wives, can sleep undisturbed through all the commotion at the end of a work by Wagner. At the other end of the scale, a mother can hear the whimpering of an infant through several walls as she sleeps in the dead of night; she will awake with a start at sounds so slight that no one else even hears them.

We can learn something about what attracts attention by examining its opposite, the art of camouflage, whose purpose is to minimize the chance that someone will notice some object. Animals represent evolution's greatest attainments in this art. Zebra stripes, giraffes' reticula, bird plumage, and insect colors have all evolved *in their natural surroundings* in ways that make them difficult to see in those surroundings; we often say that they "blend in" with them. During World War II the British developed a paint for ships which was reputed to make them invisible at dusk and dawn, favored hours for submarine attack. Its hue was a very light grayish white! (The familiar zig-zag, crazy quilt camouflage of World War I was designed to fool the eye of a man tracking a ship's movement for laying fire—not to hide the ship.) Soldiers putting twigs in their helmets or placing nets of foliage over artillery pieces have an origin that goes far back in time. In *Macbeth* Shakespeare arranges the usurper's downfall by having the opposing army advance under cover of a portable forest: "I will not be afraid of death or bane, till Birnam forest come to Dunsinane." Malcolm's forces met the specification by cutting their camouflage in Birnam Wood. If a pickpocket practices his profession during Mardi Gras, he had best buy an outlandish costume. But if his success then leads him to work Wall Street, that same outfit will not be very effective.

Zebras, giraffes, and tropical birds stand out in zoos because they clash with the city surroundings. A Chevrolet, anonomyous on a freeway, is transformed into a news event if found in the African bush. Recognition of your own state's license plate in a foreign country is the homely case.

We see then that attention depends on some kind of clash between an object and its environment. *Nothing has intrinsic attention-attraction power of itself.* Whether it is a thought, clothing, or word; a gesture, house, or rock, the measure of its attention-getting power is "How much is it out of kilter with its context?" In other words, attention is a *relation*, not a *quality*. Whether the attention developed produces a favorable or unfavorable subsequent reaction is another matter, which we will discuss later. But note the enormous difference between securing legitimate attention for an idea and crude exhibitionism of oneself. Few who saw it can forget Khrushchev's shoe-banging at the United Nations. How many remember what caused his outburst?

This digression on camouflage suggests why those presentations which are too closely tailored to the expectations of an audience turn out to be bland, with no bite and, most importantly, no impact. As one weary government official described a case he had to hear: "The same old tired answers to the same old tired questions." We see this sometimes in individuals who have such a compulsion to "fit in" a group or organization that they repress every aspect of their instincts or beliefs that clashes with their idea of what the group expects. These are the faceless men whose behavior is predictable, who don't make waves, and who are never looked to for an idea or opinion. They have developed camouflage as their perfect defense, like a mallard who prefers the safety of the swamp to a flight that silhouettes her against the sky. We need not waste time on their needs, for they are never concerned with presentations except as neutral members of an audience.

Securing attention for your idea compels you to risk the flight and its accompanying exposure. You must show your idea as a contrast to existing expectations, beliefs, feelings, or attitudes of the audience if you want them to notice it.

The key to getting and holding attention lies in having something *new* happen continually. This calls for a sense of *move-*

ment forward or backward, development, or the feeling of "something going on." Development suggests that what we are seeing *now* grew out of something before, and is going to turn into something else. Consider the difference between the attention a child gives to a basket of eggs on the kitchen table and his concentration on an egg that is being cracked from the inside by a chick straining to emerge.

Another illustration, probably old when the pyramids were under construction, is the attention given to workers and their machinery on a large building project by sidewalk superintendents. The same project on a Sunday morning will hold no interest from passing crowds, because "there is nothing going on." Yet the structure's design is clear, and all the machinery stands ready, but silent. Clearly, the sense of development is dead, and with it dies attention. The fundamental aspect of development derives from its continuity with the past and the future. This unfolding of your presentation must parallel nature. Even the most spectacular and dramatic event in the story must be related to what has gone before. A sunset so splendid that no painter would dare attempt it, still grows from the everyday path of the sun across the sky, even if the rest of the day has been rainy and gray. Clear problem-statement is important because it allows a development related constantly to both aspects of any problem: that which exists, and that which is desired.

Everyone subjected to a presentation brings with him several unseen retainers. Kipling called them his "six honest serving men": Who, What, Where, Why, How, and When?

Like six unruly children, each of these will tug at your audience's minds until they get satisfaction—or at least a lollipop. They are not nasty kids, but inquisitive, and their presence furnishes the basic structure of *any* presentation on *any* subject. The *order* in which they are answered depends on your own inclination, taste, and the style appropriate to the subject. They don't need equal time, but every one demands *some* recognition. Not one can be assumed safely asleep, no matter how sophisticated the audience. Persons listening want to know *your* answer to each one somewhere in your story.

Every successful presenter has his mind divided into the six compartments. They are used in the composition stage like six file folders for accumulating your basic ingredients: facts, opinions, and methods.

My nine-year-old daughter was once assigned the task of making a report on the Aztecs. Her teacher told her to "do research on it first."Since she was only nine, she lettered in a fine title on the cover sheet: "History of the Aztecs." Were she twenty-nine, and an expert on the subject, she would concoct a title like "Some Preliminary Notes on Aztec Grain Cultivation in the Period 1316-1319 A.D.," and take five-hundred pages to do it.

With the title inscribed and laid aside, she then enthusiastically accumulated a small pyramid of books and began to plough through them. Disillusionment set in fast after a couple of sessions. "Before I knew all this, I could have made a good report, but now all these things are buzzing around in my head, and I don't think I can unscramble them at all. What should I do?" she asked, with the soulfulness only girls her age possess.

I suggested she get her copy of Kipling's *Just So Stories* and read the page on which you meet his "honest serving men." After she understood the passage in new light, I asked her to write at the top of six separate sheets of paper each of the single question words. She then filled in a meaningful question behind each one, like "*Who*—were the Aztecs?"; "*Where*—did they come from?"; "*What*—did they do?"; "*When*—did they live," and so on.

Now her pile of books made sense, for what she had read let her answer each of the questions—or made her find out more for the ones she couldn't. All she had to do then was to shuffle the sheets about and place the precious title page on top. It is true that a definitive *History of the Aztecs* still needs to be written, but what her classmates got was a lot better for the help from Kipling.

A few months ago she was assigned another report, this time on "Primates." On this I was not consulted. As I saw her labeling six separate sheets with the same words, I thought how pleased the old Britisher would be if he could see his continued influence on young minds.

Once information has been accumulated in these bins, it is then arranged into a meaningful design, like a mosaic, or rather a necklace of different-colored beads, for the information must be presented in some order over the span of time available to you. What is the string that carries the beads? You can't just staple the sheets together and get away with it after the fourth grade. It is not wise merely to dump a pile of unstructured information into the laps of your audience. They will have the same reaction as if you take a watch apart, fling the pieces at them, and say "Here's all you need to make a watch." You may get high marks for research and energy, but that is a low-class consolation prize. By doing this you confess that you don't know what to do with all the stuff you've dug up. Audiences expect structure, not a happening.

Without structure, there can be no idea. It is easier to write sentences without verbs. Presentations all hold out the promise of some kind of *action*; without action, there can be no development. In fact, the word *development* itself comes from the Latin words for *unfold* or *unwrap*. Both meanings assume that something is there to unwrap, and that someone is doing the unwrapping. As each layer of material is removed, more and more aspects of the idea are laid before the audience. The process of unwrapping is the *style* of the presentation, and can range from the quick flick of the magician's cloak to the most involved and tricky angles of a mystery. (We will discuss various styles in Chapter 4.)

The dramatist presents his problem and develops its aspects for ultimate disclosure entirely through the conversation and movements of his characters. If the playwright wants to let you know that one of them is feeling or thinking things that he wouldn't tell the other characters, then he has to risk a soliloquy. This is a very high-powered, dangerous device, since it demands the greatest suspension of disbelief by the audience.

The novelist invents quite artificial and cut-down conversation for his characters. He supplements these fragments with narrative passages in which he tells you about things happening to them and around them, which they don't know about, but which will have a great effect on their behavior as he unfolds the story. The novelist also lets characters talk to themselves for your benefit.

Neither of these dramatic methods can be used effectively in a presentation of your ideas, except in unusual cases, where a skit or "role-playing" sequence is *part* of a presentation. These can never be the whole show, and cannot be used at all when the audience is small in size. All the background scenery and all aspects of the problem must be set forth by you alone, or by your colleagues in a multiple presentation. But you have great advantages over the playwright or novelist. You do not have to keep your remarks constrained to a character's personality or history; you can use all kinds of visual and audio aids; and you are not hampered by keeping all of the action tied to a specific place and time. You can also deal with future consequences of different hypotheses and courses of action, and present all kinds of information from a wide range of sources. Most importantly, you can tailor your message to take account of the backgrounds and experiences of the people in your audience.

But you *must* include one indispensable quality of a good novel or play: There must be some kind of conflict perceived by the audience, if you are to keep their interest.

What is a good way to do this? One of the best, and oldest, is the method of *opposites*. To understand its nature and to control its power requires a slight excursion to the fringes of philosophy. But as lawyers say, when the judge chides them for wandering, "We will link it up, your honor."

Every idea can be understood only by its relationship to other ideas or experiences. Whether the idea is about education, military strategy, furniture design, proper behavior of your friends, or an explanation of experiments in astrophysics, we grasp it only by relating the idea to our own previous thoughts and experience of its subject matter. These have been formed by the uneasy trio of reason, common sense, and emotion. This lists them in order of increasing importance.

For example, if you wish to know how you really feel about another person, imagine the feelings stirred on receiving an unopened letter from him, which you recognize only by his handwriting on the envelope. The attitude you have before you see the letter's contents is based entirely on emotions resulting from past experience with him. This has its parallel in the reactions members of your audience have when first being invited to a presentation by you, even before they know the subject. Sometimes this emotional reaction is so strong that they don't even come. Happily, these are often balanced by those who come even though they have had no previous interest in the proposed subject, but who always enjoy what you have to say.

Past experience puts an unconscious slant on what we hear or see. We sense the idea or proposition as fitting one of these slots: it is *similar* to something we already know or believe; it is *different* from everything we know or believe.

The more powerful relation for attention is that which is different; the more comfortable relation is that which is similar. Both are necessary in the development phase of a good presentation. The method of opposites (differences) is like the crashing wave; the method of analogy (similarities) is like the slack water between the crests. Together they produce a satisfying internal rhythm. We will hold the method of analogy for later, and concentrate now on the method of opposites.

Opposites

Attempts to understand how development takes place have occupied the best minds of every discipline over the last 2,500 years. I am not about to give the final answer. In fact, some theories of development hold that no final answer is ever possible. But there is one view that is extremely useful for anyone faced with the job of stringing together the various aspects of a problem in order to produce acceptance for his particular solution, i.e., the presentation of an idea. This is the method of the *dialectic*, as propounded by a great, but verbose, German philosopher, Georg Wilhelm Friedrich Hegel (1770–1831). The idea of the dialectic is one that has been known to every wise man since prehistory. Aristotle embodies it in his quest for "the Golden Mean," where he believes that truth lies between the extremes of viewpoints. Middle-of-the-road politicians sense that the bulk of voters are found there, and proverbs in every language counsel the wisdom of the Latin *Audi Alterem Partem,* i.e., "Listen to the other side." In Spanish it is: "He who has heard only one side has heard nothing." The idea permeates every court of law from Auckland to Zurich, for all men distrust with their most primitive instincts the one-sided story. Goethe found the basis in a peculiar quirk of the human mind: "Every word that is uttered evokes the idea of its opposite." A presentation that does not deal with the cumulative "evoking of opposites" finally founders on the shoals of disbelief. It is necessary to convince your audience that you see the contrary view better than they, and that in spite of its power, your proposal remains superior.

All development, whether of a child, a plant, an organization, a society, an economy, or a civilization takes place by a process that involves both additions of the new and rejection of the old. New cells form, old cells die; this process on a larger scale we call development. A tennis match is not a mere summation of the *individual* strokes played. Once the ball is served, the return has been influenced by the serve, the second response is determined by the initial return, and so on, until a stroke that violates the accepted limits of the net or boundaries produces points for the other player. The fascination of spectators springs from the observance of the *total process*, not from appreciation of individual swats. The dialectic is such a tennis match, but its action takes place in the mind. Its boundaries are fixed by the experience and imagination of the thinker and his audience; its net is the minimum logic needed for respectability, and its height varies with the players.

Hegel laid it out this way: Every statement about a person, organization, event, institution, doctrine, or phenomenon—anything in human experience—can give us knowledge about only one aspect of it. Since everything is much more complex in real life than words can describe, as soon as you select one aspect, the other unmentioned ones spring to mind. Of these, the ones most likely to get attention are those that appear to contradict the one you selected. But the contradiction itself is as faulty as the original statement, for the same reason of partial knowledge. However, the two statements combined *approach* the truth —but never achieve it absolutely.

This worries philosophers, but men of affairs acting in the

world as we see it, always act on imperfect knowledge. Uncertainty in human life begins with this fact of faulty knowledge, yet men *do* make decisions constantly. Alas, you can never make a presentation of an idea that contains the *whole* truth, for you can go only as far as time and knowledge permits. The great appeal of the method of opposites is its power to *suggest* the nature of the whole truth of an idea by showing the buildup of its various aspects. There is always the inference that one *could* go on to infinity, but that isn't advisable. (Many presentations give that hint quite quickly, and members of the audience then pray for any excuse to get away.)

There is a practical limit of the aspects that can be used, and that limit should be dominant in the design of the presentation. One should only go as far as necessary in order for the audience to make up its mind about the validity of your idea. You should settle for tipping the scale of *probability of belief* in your favor. When the balance goes your way, do not keep on adding extra burden to the material required for a judgment, or the method of opposition will turn back on you. Laborers on oil well rigs all know this injunction: "When you strike oil, stop the drill."

Philosophers will clap hands to heads in horror at this simplification of Hegel's life work, but we are attempting to apply his insight, grabbing only what we need. Before we leave him entirely, for examples, let's do him the justice of diagramming the core of his *system:* The first statement in the dialectical form is called the "thesis." The contradiction to the first statement is called the "antithesis" (anti-thesis). The combination of the "thesis" and "antithesis" is called the "synthesis" (syn-thesis, i.e., together-thesis). The syn-*thesis* calls forth a new antithesis, and so on to infinity, or as Hegel would say, to "the Absolute" or Pure Truth (see diagram page 85).

Here we see what wise folk in every walk of life call "the swing of the pendulum." They know in their bones that if any program, group, or idea goes too far, it will call into play opposing forces which will attempt to restore the balance. Leaders wish to retain both power and a reputation for probity. They unconsciously use the method of opposites in forming their judgments, though most of them would never expose their decisions

THE METHOD OF OPPOSITES

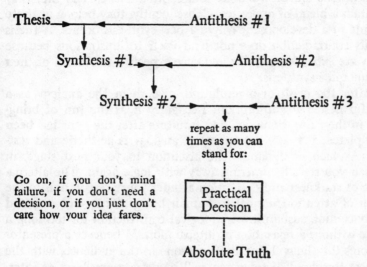

Thesis → ← Antithesis #1

Synthesis #1 → ← Antithesis #2

Synthesis #2 → ← Antithesis #3

repeat as many
times as you can
stand for:

Go on, if you don't mind
failure, if you don't need a
decision, or if you just don't
care how your idea fares.

Practical
Decision

Absolute Truth

in such analytical form. If you make a presentation to such leaders and synchronize with the rhythm of *their* thought, your idea is nearly irresistible. This, of course, is the ultimate in development. Few achieve it, but that's the target.

Analogy

Once we see the architecture of a development as a continuous welding of opposites, we can examine how and where analogy fits in the structure.

Analogy, anecdotes, examples, or illustrations are the ornaments and embellishments of a presentation. They appeal almost entirely to imagination, emotions, and common sense. As pure reason they are faulty, since no analogy ever fits an idea perfectly. Their great power is to link the similarities of the audience's experience with various *parts* of the development of your idea. An example brings an idea down to earth. It reinforces the truth of a specific part of the presentation, so that the next floor of development takes off from a firm base. Since examples and illustrations are drawn from similar situations in real life, they contain a blend of opposites. Consequently, they belong at those points in a development where a new synthesis occurs. A thesis or its contradiction does not lend itself to illustrations because they are extremes, and the audience expects a resolution of their conflict in a synthesis.

After the clash of a resolution, give them the analogy as a restful period for absorption. Recognize it as the fun of bringing in the paint, draperies, and furniture after the floor has been completed. Frankly, the appeal of analogy is aesthetic and restful. As such, it enhances the attention to your next stage, in which you start hammering away with logic again. The alternation of starkness and decoration attunes your presentation to the span of attention normal to human beings. They will not, and truly cannot, sustain involved logical construction for too long a time without a relaxation or interruption. Whenever a presentor ignores this, he will find that someone in the audience, with the lowest threshold of tolerance, will perpetrate any kind of interruption merely to get the relief everyone needs. It is extremely rare for an interruption of this type to be helpful. Most inflict fatal wounds, since presentors whose methods provoke this audience reaction are so rigid that they lack the flexibility to turn an irrelevant interruption to their advantage. (Handling of cross-examination is covered in Chapter 7.)

Another reason for alternating examples with hard propositions lies in the physiological connection of body and mind. There are two states of life that are unique to human beings: laughter and weeping. They both involve an imperfectly understood relation between the imagination of a person and his bodily reactions. During laughter or weeping, what takes place in the imagination affects what happens in the body, and what happens in the body affects, in turn, what happens in the imagination. There is a continuous and complex interplay until the heightened activity of both subsides to normal.

Compare some of the physical reactions (from a description by A. Koestler).

	LAUGHTER	WEEPING
Face	1. Eyes sparkle, corners wrinkled	1. Eyes blinded by tears, lose focus
	2. Brow and cheeks taut and smooth	2. All features crinkled and crumpled
	3. Expression radiant	3. Expression languid (even in joy or rapture)
	4. Lips parted, corners lifted	
Breathing	1. Expiratory puffs	1. Short, deep, gasping inspirations
	2. Long, deep intakes	2. Long, sighing expirations
Posture	1. Head thrown back	1. Head drooped
	2. Muscles contracted (slapping table or knees)	2. Muscles flabby, shoulders slumped
Sounds	1. Chuckling, giggling, or roaring	1. Laments, moans, appeals for sympathy

It is interesting that the specific physical reactions are almost complete reversals of each other, but this is not our main concern. The above table maps a physiological uproar. Both states are releases from unbearable tensions built up in the body by the imagination. As these tensions discharge they produce a feeling of relaxation. The safety valve pops. The application of this for making a presentation lies in two insights: No reasoning process can go on in the mind when it is occupied with laughter or weeping. During the relaxed period *immediately* following laughter or weeping, the critical faculty is at its lowest level.

We can connect these with our structure of development by this advice: 1. Use the example from real life, especially if humorous or emotionally moving, to reinforce the statement of a new synthesis. 2. Follow the example immediately with either the contradictory antithesis, or a restatement of the synthesis in a new way, if it makes the presentation of the next contradiction easier.

No human mind can resist taking in a statement made during the relaxed state following laughter or weeping. It will often be remembered for years afterward.

A word of warning is necessary. If your example or anecdote is not to the point of your synthesis, you will encounter both embarrassment and bafflement, for you have misled your audience. A few may be amused, but not those who have been following your development. Those previously interested will either resent the irrelevancy, or keep trying to fit it to your story. Both reactions distract their eyes from the ball and are disastrous for securing consent and acceptance of your idea.

Insertion of illustrations and anecdotes is a powerful device. But like all powerful forces, if not controlled and kept to their job, they become dangerous. Analogies must be selected with great care, for if they are too far off the mark, critical members of the audience will turn them back on you. I cannot overemphasize that every story from real life carries possibilities for drawing out differences as well as similarities. Hegel may have disappeared into a verbal swamp of his own making, but on this he is a trusty guide.

This diagrams the above:

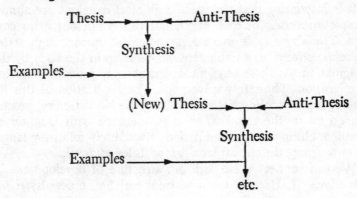

The preceding discussion has been somewhat arid and abstract. Structure is always so, and this perhaps accounts for its neglect. However, once the process is grasped, it can then safely be taken for granted, but not until then. An aspiring pianist must master the structure of keyboard and scales; an efficient typist must match the structure of her keyboard to hand and eye. Neither can become proficient if they continue to look at the keys instead of the copy or music. It is not an exaggeration to say that the overwhelming number of presentations that fail do so from structural deficiences, not from lack of content.

It is time now to follow my own advice and place some flesh on the dialectical skeleton.

A SITUATION: In the suburb where you live there has been increasing concern about recreational facilities. Population has risen, there have been more incidents of juvenile vandalism during the summer, and a new housing development and shopping center are planned for construction in the year ahead. A recent bond issue for the town park expansion has been defeated, and rezoning of a formerly residential area has been asked for by an industrial firm which wants to build a plant there.

In the past few weeks you and several of your friends have talked about what you should each do about these questions. Then one evening someone came up with the thought that perhaps all these things could be tied together in some way for everybody's benefit. In the heat and excitement of the discussion (by a process no one now remembers) you were selected to make a presentation to the town council for the great idea: the construction of a swimming pool and picnic ground.

How should you lay out the basic structure of the presentation?

Let's see how the application of the "six serving men," the method of opposites, and use of analogy might help. First, make up your questions to Who, What, Where, How, Why, and When, without regard to order. Just get them down. (One good method is to write them on 3" × 5", or 5" × 8" cards, one for each question. You can later move them about at will.)

FOR EXAMPLE: *Who*—will benefit? Later add population statistics, income groups, etc., for the "number-minded" on the council.

What? Swimming pool and picnic ground, accessory facilities; dimensions and acreage later.

Where—can it be placed? Start collecting alternatives; also ask your friends for some (they got you into this!).

How—can it be paid for? Here you must separate the initial cost and the operating expenses, the land and construction. List alternatives (more on this later).

Why—do we need it? Collect examples of the children going to neighboring towns or unsafe rivers, quarries, and lakes; get statements from physical education teachers, the Red Cross, church leaders, and other experts. Local newspapermen can often furnish hair-raising cases.

When—could it be completed? Here you need expert estimates. You can also use the experience of others who have faced similar problems. In extreme cases you can guess and let someone at the meeting give his correction.

Notice that this classification of the six questions sets up a natural *framework for factual information gathering*. You will certainly never use all of the details you gather, but it is better to have more than you need before you begin the arranging process. No artist ever finished a painting and then looked at his palette to find it completely empty. You will also find that the information you have gathered but don't use in the final presentation produces the subtle effect of building up your own confidence. It also plays its part as the reserve ammunition for fighting the battle of cross-examination (covered in Chapter 7).

Another value of the classification-by-question is its use in organizing the efforts of your helpers, whether volunteer or in a formal working group. You can give each person involved one of the cards, or questions, and he then knows fairly well what you expect of him. By concentrating on *what* you want and leaving the *how to do it* details to him, you tap wellsprings of human nature: personal involvement, creative contribution, and sense of achievement.

This is the way committed allies are born.

Now for the method of opposites. Before you lay out the sequence of presentation, you must have a clear answer in *your* mind to this question: "What do I want the council to *do* when I'm finished?" They are going to keep trying to figure this out as you go along. They can't keep from doing that, even if they want to. The whole setting and customs of their meetings tell them that you *want* something or you wouldn't be there. Let's look at some possible answers, but as you scan them, notice how each answer suggests a different development for your presentation. A presentor who hasn't picked *one* both confuses those who might be favorably inclined to his idea, and offers an easy target for those who want to shoot it down.

You may want the council to: 1. *Organize* a citizens' task force to study your specific proposal and submit a report to the council at some specified time. 2. *Approve* your idea on the spot. 3. *Submit* your proposal to a vote by all taxpayers. 4. *Instruct* the town manager to investigate the subject and report at the next meeting. 5. *Appoint* you as a recreation committee chairman.

Many presentations disappear in a muttered babble of: "He doesn't know what he wants." Without knowing where you want to go, it is impossible to lead others. A presentation, however much you may dislike the thought, *is* an exercise in leadership. At the very least, you are trying to lead the *opinion* of others; at the most, you are asking them to entrust their *fates* to your care.

In our example, let's assume you want the council to organize a citizens' task force to study the proposal. Now think of people you consider suitable, who enjoy the respect of the council, and who represent the various skills and interested groups. You will want to mention their names at certain places in your presentation, not as prospective members, but in the natural course of development point-by-point. Suggestion will do the rest. With your facts in front of you, begin to sketch in:

Possible structure: Problem-statement (historical narrative) —"We have taken pride in the growth of the town, but unless we face up to the neglected area of recreational facilities, we will find it a less and less desirable place to bring up our children."

Thesis 1: The town *has* grown (population statistics).

Antithesis 1: Growth has brought problems (mention some well-known irritations, e.g., traffic, parking, noise, etc.).

Synthesis 1: People who are now in town as a result of its growth have brought new energies, skills, and "know-how" equal to the problems. *Example 1:* Mention one of the council who is a new man, and the kind of contribution he has made in the past, due to a special skill.

Antithesis 2: Past success in coping with difficulties has attracted additional influx of new types; industry and housing development wish to capitalize on the town's reputation as a good place to live.

Synthesis 2: Recent defeat of the park bond issue shows that old solutions are not equal to the task today. Coupling of the town's problem with the desires of industry and home builders may offer the needed new solution, benefiting all. *Example 2:* Sketch in the requests of builder and industry.

Antithesis 3: But such a new solution may *not* be able to benefit all. There is increasing evidence of the youngsters' dissatisfaction.

Synthesis 3: This has produced parents' concern. The concern of citizens becomes a concern of the council. *Example 3:* Here use examples of children traveling outside the town for swimming; emphasize safety and diminution of loyalty to town.

Antithesis 4: This worry has created a new wave of interest in you and your friends who are loyal to the town. You believe there are many others who have become interested.

Synthesis 4: This has led you to come up with a possible solution. "Why not build a swimming pool and picnic ground?" *Example 4:* Mention the success of other communities.

Antithesis 5: There are many difficulties in the way: Where? How?

Synthesis 5: Yet recreational facilities are an important factor to industry (attracting workers and supervisors) and to home builders (make property more valuable). *Example 5:* Mention the opinion of a local real estate dealer, preferably one on the council.

Antithesis 6: If they know taxes will increase drastically, perhaps they will change their minds about locating here.

Synthesis 6: Therefore the proposal must be fair and offer a good balance of benefits versus cost to industry and home builders. *Example 6:* The industry is asking for a valuable right (rezoning) and will probably be willing to compensate the town in some way (other's experience), perhaps in a cash contribution to pool construction. The home builder has excess land for expansion; perhaps he may be willing to make over a suitable parcel for the area.

Antithesis 7: But no one knows for sure. The council can sit still and do nothing and see what happens.

Synthesis 7: The history of the town shows that whenever that has happened, the town has lost. *Example 7:* Name previous factories, roads, or housing construction. Mention council members who unsuccessfully fought those battles.

Antithesis 8: The council cannot let that happen now.

Synthesis 8: The need is urgent, there are many factors to investigate, and you realize that the council is overburdened. Suggest that the council organize a task force of people with requisite qualifications. *Example 8:* Allude to previous successes where the town benefited from this approach.

Antithesis 9: There is a danger that your idea may shove aside other worthwhile improvements.

Synthesis 9: You trust the wisdom of the council to decide, but this is all the more reason they should have a good fact-gathering job done, and alternatives to choose from. The right kind of task force would give them this. You would be happy to furnish the head of the task force the incomplete data you have assembled if he wants it to help get started.

You may then get cross-examined, but as we will point out in Chapter 7, that can be dangerous for your opposition at this time, *if you are well prepared.* They may try a test question or two merely to find out.

This is a severely simplified and somewhat artificial case, but it does illustrate how structure is necessary to development. A hundred variations will do just as well, and each allows different kinds of embellishment with visuals, recordings, handouts, etc. But unless embellishment be related to structure, it degenerates either to pedantry or to a bazaar of trinkets. Notice how your ultimate objective begins to influence the development quite early, and how the use of opposites disarms your potential antagonists by stating their points before they get a chance to do it for themselves.

Members of an audience sometimes pay this great compliment to a presentation, "It is well thought out." They really mean that you have taken account of all the possibilities, especially of the things that may miscarry. This causes their anxiety to decline. Their confidence in your idea goes up in proportion.

Another aspect of getting and holding attention, related to creating the feeling that "something is going on," is the concept of *progress*. I don't mean the idea of uplift, or a Victorian belief that things are always getting better, or faith in the automatic grand sweep of civilization, which was blown out of the water in the First World War. No, I have in mind the idea that something is continually developing: a sense of *motion*. Since most backgrounds are static and taken for granted, when something is *moving*, either physically or symbolically, we alert ourselves. This probably comes from our hunting ancestors who ambled about in skins, constantly alert for a disturbance to their environment, because disturbances spelled either trouble or a chance for food. In fact, there are animals, such as certain frogs, which see moving things with great clarity; but if an object is at rest, they literally do not see it at all. Audiences are much like these animals.

Progress is a tricky concept, for one can view it two ways: motion *away* from where you began, or motion *toward* a goal. Notice its parallel to the nature of a problem: a clash between the image of what exists, and the image of what you want to exist. When there is a difference between what you've *got* and what you *want*, you say, "I have a problem."

These two ideas of *progress* and *problem* lead to the most fundamental rule for successful persuasion. It is so important that I put it in italics:

Start where THEY are, not where YOU are. In order to start where an audience *is*, you must know something about them. Their familiarity with the subject, their present attitudes toward it, past views on similar subjects, what they are anxious about, limitations on their actions, and their goals in life all contribute to what they call their "position." The more precisely you get a fix on this position, the higher your probability of success. For this reason we tend to trust those who show that they understand us and our situation. The greater the understanding shown, the greater the trust we will risk, for trust *is* fundamentally risk in its most noble appearance. You must justify this risk, or it will not be taken.

Too many people with ideas are so eager to have others share their apocalyptic visions that they neglect this dictum. After they have suffered defeat, you can find them either staring into a flat beer, or backing luckless souls at random into corners of rooms, haranguing the trapped victims with laments on this theme: "Why can't *they* see what *I* see so clearly?" You can often escape by stating the rule above: Start where *they* are. It stuns the poor unfortunate long enough for you to shoot past him.

By stating, however briefly, your understanding of the current situation facing the audience, the mere fact of your presence in front of them silently shouts that you are going to *move away from that current situation*. This seizes their attention. You continue to hold attention by then showing where you are going, and how, using various methods. At the end of a really skillful presentation, the audience has a feeling that the route you took, from where they were to where you went, was an obvious one, now that they think about it. The most treasured remark is: "That makes so much sense and is so obvious, why didn't I think of it?" When you hear this, you can be sure that you started where he was!

Great teachers have always known that new knowledge can only build on old. The human mind cannot make great leaps across chasms of ignorance. This is the wisdom of the old aphorism: "There is no royal road to learning." While solemnly dispensed to students, its deeper meaning goes to those who would teach, and every presentation is a form of teaching. The presentor is presumed to know things the audience does not. A presentation gives a chance to bridge the difference.

The worst offenders against this view are those with special, expert, or technical knowledge. Narrowness of concentration, which is the fee exacted to become a specialist, often distorts the specialist's vision of his audience. Jargon, esoteric concepts, and arcane knowledge are flung at the audience as though they were also specialists in the field. Such presentations might just as well be given in Chinese, Swahili, or an unbreakable code, for all the conviction they produce. I mention this case here (even though how to cope with it is covered in Chapter 9) because it illustrates the contrary attitude to starting where the audience is. This is bad enough when the presentation is sincerely, if ineptly, designed to help the audience learn; but when obscure and unfamiliar terms are used merely to show off superiority in a speciality, they are worse than useless. They properly diminish the reputation of the presentor.

Distraction

With a variation of the method of opposites, we will conclude this chapter on holding attention. One can measure the height of a tree by the shadow it casts, or get information about someone's character by knowing who his enemies are. Knowledge of things that distract attention can help neutralize their disturbing effects on presentations. When eliminated, there is a reinforcement effect on your ability to hold attention.

Distraction possibility lurks constantly in the minds of the audience, and silently competes for attention with the presentation itself. Impressions from sight, hearing, touch, and smell continually assault the brain for primacy. Subconscious anxieties and desires are also on the prowl, waiting for an opening, and enjoy additional advantages when the audience is fatigued or preoccupied. Conducting a presentation is much like conducting a battle against a clever enemy: inattention. Only fools give odds, professionals never do. Persuasive presentations are difficult enough to run under perfect conditions; putting additional lead on the saddle by lack of preparation of the environment marks the amateur. Here are a few specific items which may appear trivial, but every one of them can derail fast trains of thought.

HEARING

Noises, especially vibration or hissing from projector fans, air-conditioning systems, workmen's power tools, leaking steam from radiators, or a whistling public address system are unnerving to an audience. With the advent of universal air conditioning, even archaic Broadway theaters are now equipped, some not too well from an aesthetic viewpoint. Their noise level is so high that directors insist on the system being shut down during crucial scenes. This has had a new dramatic effect all its own, since dozing critics now know that "something's up" when the fans stop!

Random noises are also ruinous. Banging in radiators, the clatter of dishes in an adjoining room, air hammers and pile drivers outside the building, or repairmen's hammers and chisels inside, upset the audience more than the presenter. Even though they may sympathize with your predicament, they cannot pay close attention to the unfolding of your ideas. In fact, their surge of sympathy distracts them even more. Skilled presentors usually have a person assigned to do the legwork necessary to fix those nuisances that can be fixed.

I once saw a very dignified executive negotiating with a hotel mechanic for the oiling of squeaky restaurant carts during his reconnaissance of the room where his boss was scheduled to speak. If you can get a man like that, you're lucky.

SIGHT

Sight distractions come from two sources: those that make it difficult for the audience to see what you want them to see, and those that suggest more pleasant activity than listening to you. Many rooms, especially those designed for other functions, have lighting fixtures that strain the eyes. Unshaded tiny bulbs or crystal chandeliers behind or in front of you will cause an audience to avoid the glare by averting their eyes from the lights and you. (If all else fails, remove the bulbs from their sockets.) Columns and pillars often require a degree of neck bending to see around, which few people tolerate for long. Also, when visuals are not scaled to the size of the audience, people quickly give up the effort (see Chapter 6). Wide changes in lighting intensity are actually painful to older people, and uncomfortable to all. Brainwashing psychologists use this technique to create anxiety on purpose, as it helps achieve the disorientation they primarily work for; but disorientation is the last thing you want in a serious presentation.

Visual *comfort* of the audience is your goal—and they resent being deprived of it.

Rooms with a splendid view have deadly distracting power. Few presentations can compete with the glories of nature for more than five minutes. If you have to use such a place, draw the draperies. Also, it is best to avoid locations with a great many works of art on the walls. These are powerful stimulants to the mind, even those whose content or style repels the audience. If you can't escape from such a room, refer to the art works as your development progresses. In this way, you enlist their stimulating power on your side, and impress the audience with your ability to turn potential obstacles to your advantage.

TOUCH

Uncomfortable chairs are tough opponents; they always win in the end, when the presentation is too long. This is so obvious, yet often neglected. It is a wise rule: The harder the chair, the shorter the presentation. Never forget: "The behind is oft persuader of the mind."

Temperatures too warm fertilize the ever-present tendency to doze; air too chilly creates an itch to move about. Outdoor revolutionists instinctively heat up their audiences with strong hints to shout, shake their fists, applaud, and wave their arms. But this kind of thing doesn't work too well in more sedate circumstances. It's much easier to get hold of the thermostat.

SMELL

This is the sense that really takes over, even though we do not compare as well as we once did with our animal cousins. Offensive odors will wreck the meeting and pleasant ones turn our minds to food. Both are undesirable. This kind of distraction is more common than one would think, especially where rooms are near eating facilities. The makings for coffee breaks should always be kept from the presentation area until you're finished. After-dinner speeches are the rule, rather than before-dinner ones, for similar reasons.

Attention to the above items may be odious to those who believe that the world is on tenterhooks awaiting their message, but emotions *are* influenced by the physical environment. Wisdom demands that you offset the adverse effects of the senses on emotion, for only then can your reason and common sense get a proper chance.

It is true that failure can occur even if the environment is perfect and the plan of development worthy of genius. Such possibility for miscarriage leads us to the next chapter, where we will consider the subtle relations between style and content.

4

Matching Style to Material

or

Don't Cut Meat with Scissors

None of us wears one suit of clothes for all occasions. Yet well-intentioned advisers to presentors of ideas unwittingly give dangerous counsel when they say "Don't pay any attention to style. Just be yourself." Which "self" should they use? Each of us is presenting many different "selves" to others throughout the course of a single day. Depending on the circumstances and mood of the moment, someone who has not known us previously will form his own judgment based on those of our expressions and actions that he personally experiences. The "self" he perceives will differ in many ways—some absolutely contradictory —from the "selves" we have shown to others at various times.

During the nostalgic period before World War I, known as the Edwardian age, English society would spend long weekends at each other's country estates. Their activities marked the high point of frenzied leisure on our planet. On Sunday, if you were a guest at one of these houses, you would be expected to change clothes completely at least four times during the day. A different outfit was required for church, luncheon, tea, and dinner! The same "self" had to be rewrapped every few hours if it wanted to take part in the action appropriate for that slice of the day.

Nowadays we find this ritual a bit excessive. But most of us don't wear the same clothes for business and shopping as we do for picnics, sports, or a formal dinner. Only an inverted snob turns up at the opera in jeans and sweatshirt; and if a neighbor cuts his hedge in white tie and tails, we think him a trifle eccentric. A tolerant, urbane acquaintance of mine nurses an almost murderous dislike of a homeowner on the same street who clears snow from his driveway with a war-surplus flamethrower. Most of us are annoyed when we see people dressed in shorts, with shirttails flapping, walking about a cathedral or museum. We would, however, be hard-pressed to explain our irritation on completely rational grounds. In fact, all of these people may be blindly following the advice: "Don't worry about what to wear. Just be yourself."

An inappropriate style used for presentation of an idea produces an almost identical, nonrational annoyance. Certain types of behavior disturb us because we sense violation of the essential "fitness of things." This feeling represents an aesthetic judgment, not scientific.

The word *style* itself derives from the Latin for *writing rod,* the pointed stick used to inscribe wax tablets. In other words, the stylus was the *means* used to express the *thought* written down. Likewise the style of a presentation is the means selected to express the thoughts involved in its central idea. Just as there are different kinds of outfits for the same person, depending on what kind of activity he is engaged in, so should there be several different presentation styles available for that same person. The choice of the best style depends on the kind of idea he has in hand. Styles exist only because choice is possible among various alternative modes of expression for the same thought. The idea itself is the "what" of the presentation; style is the "how."

Every presentation requires mingling of facts and inferences. In this it is like conversation. Shrewd observers and evaluators of other persons discern their character almost entirely from their conversation. How they express themselves, the words they use, how they react to events, the stimuli that affect their emotions, hints of their inner conflicts, and their opinions and judgments all add up to a composite we call their "personality." Reflections on this process caused the French naturalist Buffon to conclude that "Style is the man himself."

There are many (some in high places) who consider accomplishment in adapting various methods of expression to the nature of the material a useless ability. In fact, some go so far as to scorn any proficiency at all in adding force and color to a presentation. These people are most often completely ineffective themselves in this art. Whenever you hear such opinions, you usually get a distinct whiff of sour grapes. I mention this in order to warn those who aspire to increased skill that, if achieved, it will not necessarily be appreciated by everyone. Like the highly educated man, many admire him at a suitable distance, but don't like to be in the same room with him. However, skillful adjustment of your style to take account of such people's views can often disarm their potential harassment. This suggests a strange but valid concept: The apparent suppression of *all* style is itself a style, and sometimes quite powerful with certain audiences. The "old shoe" personality, the "I'm just an ignorant country boy," or "I don't know any way except plain talk to say what I mean" types, all extract enormous mileage from this styleless style. Don't be fooled by them. They know what they're up to, and so should you.

In the last chapter we said that the Development phase of a presentation was like unwrapping a package. Let's continue the analogy to see if it helps illuminate this idea of various styles. Assume you have something unknown to the audience wrapped in a large package. How many ways are there to open it in front of a group of people? Innumerable—and that's the point. You can create suspense by shaking it, saying, "I wonder what it is?" several times. You can heighten the suspense if the item itself is reached through a series of individually wrapped boxes of diminishing size, one inside the other. You can admire the wrapping paper and delicately try to preserve it as you carefully remove ribbons and seals. (If you take too long with this, the audience may begin to squirm.) You can rip the box apart with your bare hands, flinging debris everywhere, intent only on seizing the object wrapped. Or, you may use a hatchet or butcher knife to slice your way through to the prize. When you finally get hold of it, you can make loud exclamations, hold it up for all to see, choke with emotion, laugh uproariously, or pass it around for everyone's minute inspection.

If there are people in the audience who do not know you, they will form a long-lasting appraisal of your character solely from the way you carried out this simple task. Notice also how the style of unwrapping *should* be different for a retirement dinner, a bachelor party for the prospective groom, a booby prize at a golf tournament, a bridal shower, shipboard sailing, birthday party, or any other social event graced by gift-giving.

One of the best styles I remember for receiving a gift took place when a silver tray was presented to a well-liked, colorful man retiring from a company. Tradition called for the recipient to make a speech after the gift was handed to him. The large audience was eager to hear this one, for the man honored had a great reputation for humor. But the high official making the presentation became so carried away with his own reminiscent eulogy of the man standing beside him that twenty-five minutes elapsed. The official held out the tray several times, but pulled it back to his chest whenever the guest of honor made motions to accept it. The audience became uneasy, and the man honored quickly sensed their embarrassment. (He told me later that he threw away his speech after his fifth futile pass at the tray.)

Finally, the official paused for a deep breath, got caught with the tray extended, and the guest of honor grabbed it. With that he turned to the audience, held the tray triumphantly aloft, and said, "George played this tray as though I were about to play the deuce!" He sat down amid tumultuous applause and cheers. To this day, the official believes his presentation was a model of its kind. It was.

Thus, a simple act like receiving a present in public causes an audience to form judgments about character. Think how many more impressions they get when exposed to the presentation of an idea by the man who stands before them for an hour. He is constantly broadcasting signals about himself and his idea.

The first step in learning how to send clear signals instead of static requires honest recognition that every thought needs some adornment when presented to an audience. If you deplore this to the extent that you refuse to make the effort, you should not make oral presentations. It is far better for your mental and physical health to write out your stark facts and circulate them to your potential audience on paper. But remember that no important ideas are ever finally approved without someone facing an audience in person.

Why isn't the paper enough? For the simplest of reasons—and the most complex. You can never affect others if you yourself are not affected by the idea. Others cannot tell if you *are* affected by it except by your language and expression. The best novelist who ever lived cannot show the human passion behind an idea as well as one human being talking to a group of others. We were members of tribes before we learned to read, and we want to see proposals that carry the marks of a man's passion and soul. Only then do we feel that the idea will have a chance to withstand the passions and fears of its opponents. Cool, clinical men may analyze an idea until it lies dead in their hands like a dissected frog. But even Hegel, that most academic of philosophers, acknowledged: "Nothing great has been accomplished without passion." This does not mean abandoned wildness (which fizzles out quickly), but the disciplined harnessing of human will to that which you believe can and should be done, no matter what the obstacles. Once the will and belief exist, then the search for a proper vehicle to carry them narrows.

Scissors cut cloth by combining two sharp tools. No one can say which blade of a scissors does the cutting. The most you can say is that *both* do. Passion and reason likewise cut through the fabric woven of doubt, inertia, and fear, which stands between an idea and its realization in human affairs. Neither can cut it alone.

Other "scissors" of similar, opposing pairs are made of logic and style, drawing and color, and the tongue and the heart.

In harnessing the passions, we should recognize that certain talents remain only *possibilities* unless disciplined to an idea's service. They are like the sails of a ship; intellect is the rudder. These "sails" are nervous energy, a sense of harmony between opposites, a store of imagery, and richness of expression. Certainly we are not all equally gifted in these potential talents, but whether we merit praise or blame is not determined by the amount we *possess* of these gifts, but *how* we use them. A skillful sailor with a catboat can overtake an ineptly sailed yacht. When we see unrestrained impatience charge forth in an attempt to rush the barricade of others' viewpoints, we also see the evils of an unripe mind. The effects produced by this sort of rashness are obscurity, incoherence, and wild extravagance. While the wage of theological sin is death, these evils are paid for in neglect of an idea and, if grievous, in contempt for it. Every Greek dramatist illustrated this point: "Those whom the gods would destroy, they first make mad."

A presentor who has let his passion for an idea slip the reins of a disciplined style is easily spotted. He falls into agitated forms of speech. Every sentence is broken or crippled. He furnishes many minute pictures, but none are completed. He leaves mutilated expressions lying about the field of discourse, and tries to put a hundred things into one breath. He allows no interruptions from others, but constantly interrupts himself with exclamations, self-directed questions, doubts, and even profanity. He catches new trains of thought, which no one else even sees coming, in the middle of his exposition, and uses odd expressions to embellish them. Throughout his entire fever he creates the impression that he will never be able to say all that's on his mind—and is angry about it. He usually accompanies these oral phenomena with all kinds of body movements which add to the general pandemonium.

People who are prisoners of such uncontrolled passion should *never* be told: "Just be yourself." They are natural forces to be trained for meaningful contribution. The passionate men may be rampaging rivers, but the timid time-servers are stagnant, shallow pools. The work of a disciplined, but passionate man will always bear the stamp of his own personality. A working knowledge of various styles is the engineering needed to turn his powerful waters into constructive channels.

The truly great men in every field of human endeavor have accomplished the marriage of passion and discipline in just this way. It is probably from considerations like these that the late Sir Harold Nicolson gives his advice for successful negotiations. He spent his lifetime in diplomacy, politics, and literature. In his slim masterpiece, *Diplomacy*, he states that one should not send as negotiators on important matters three types of men: "missionaries, fanatics or lawyers." The missionary insists on actually converting his opposite number; the fanatic will not make the tiniest concession to the purity of his own idea; and the lawyer's admirable attempts to narrow issues do so at the risk of squeezing out all human juice and passion. The first two suffer from excess passion and deficient reason; the last, from just the reverse. (I am sure that Sir Harold knew, as I do, of outstanding exceptions to his dictum in the case of those lawyers who are men of broad and humane culture.) While Sir Harold singled out types of *practitioners*, what he really wants to avoid are certain *styles* of presentation for those ideas used in negotiations, where mutual concessions are expected.

Competent lawyers are usually excellent presentors in the special framework they must operate within; but in the larger area outside the halls of justice they face the same problems as other technical experts (covered in Chapter 9). Those who successfully translate their ideas in presentations to laymen alter their accustomed style. When they do this well, few presentors can top them in virtuosity. When done badly, their aridity makes the Sahara seem like a garden.

Logic may be the language of reason, but style adds to it life, sentiment, shading, and judgment.

Let's now attempt to get some light from heat. There is a complicated area of study known as thermodynamics which addresses itself to the phenomena and laws of heat. One of its most esoteric concepts tries to describe the tendency for all things of the universe to "run down." In other words, *if we leave things to themselves*, they cool off or become more and more disorganized. They never get hotter or more organized unless energy is brought from somewhere else and applied to the things previously left alone. Thermodynamicists describe this precisely with the term *Entropy*. They say that entropy increases as things get worse, and decreases when the right kind of energy is added. (They also call this the Second Law of Thermodynamics.) If you have a car and leave it alone, the engine will rust, the tires go flat, the paint flake off, and so on. To restore the car to a usable state, you must put some extra energy into its restoration. A car never gets better by itself. Likewise with a presentation. As you accumulate more and more information, make more and more inferences, add more and more examples, the whole thing tends to become more disorganized—its "entropy" rises. Audiences will not be able to relate one part to another, or to the whole idea. Style can thus be looked at as an *organizing force*, and it requires a great deal of mental energy to discipline an increasing mass of material. How can we use this insight?

Many subjects for presentation *are* complex and need, to be understood, some exposure to obscure facts, techniques, or inferences. Yet every presentation does address itself to some problem, the clash of two images: the state existing and the state desired. This clash may be an economic "problem," where uses are unlimited, and resources are not. Or it may be a theoretical "problem," where new phenomena observed do not "fit" the existing body of theory. Or we may face a "problem" in human behavior, where existing responses to stimuli are not the ones desired, and so on. The more knowledge we acquire about these problems, the more difficult they seem to solve. We find ourselves in a dilemma. If we don't know much about a problem, we find solutions simple; but these simple "solutions" usually create larger problems than the one faced in the first place! Violence is a more "simplified" solution to problems than diplomacy, but its use, after patience has run out, often produces worse problems than the original.

One of the wisest men I ever knew once told me that most of the troubles he had seen in a long life came from two perverse tendencies in human nature: 1. Treating as simple, things that are actually complicated. 2. Making too complicated, things that are actually simple. He also confessed that he was seldom able to decide in advance which one had caused a particular trouble; he needed postmortems for an accurate diagnosis.

So far, not much help. But assuming his observation on his

experience was correct, what does it tell us? If true, then it indicates that human beings yearn for a certain limited amount of complexity. They give in to their desire for this optimum complexity by *adding* it to some things, and *eliminating* it from others. Two examples can illustrate the extremes. A few years ago a psychologist investigating prison life told how jailed men, with no decisions to make about food, income, clothing, shelter, etc., manufactured situations that called for elaborate decisions. They measured with exquisite precision the space allocations in cells; they placed benches as though constructing watches, they took excruciating pains in making up file cards, and violent arguments erupted if a new man would not take these "problems" seriously. The psychologist concluded that: "When *nothing* is important, *everything* is important."

This may account for the increase in busyness and detail-mindedness often observed when men of action enter retirement. Their decision-making apparatus shouts for work, and if none exists, they create it out of thin air merely to keep interested. A captain of industry who never noticed a lawn in his heyday becomes the sworn enemy of every blade of crabgrass. The underlying driving force of Parkinson's Law (Work expands to fill the time available) and the Byzantine routines of minor officialdom seem related to this human quirk.

These foibles do not affect affairs except as a waste of valuable human energy. At the other extreme, treatment of truly complicated affairs as simple ones creates disasters. Jacob Burckhardt (1818–1897), the great historian of the Renaissance, became very gloomy toward the end of his life. He feared that the increasing complexities of the nineteenth century would call into action men whom he described as "terrible simplifiers." His prophecy was fulfilled in our time. As increasing multitudes became baffled and anxious by great social, economic, industrial, and political changes which they could not understand, they sought relief by embracing the "simple" solutions of charismatic messiahs. These "simplifiers" promised them a return to former happiness in exchange for acceptance of absolute leadership. This flight toward oversimplification is still strong. "Simple" solutions, ranging from anarchism to totalitarianism, are offered everywhere as escapes from a complicated reality. Responsible leaders are always targets for the radical revolutionist or the radical reactionary. So are responsible presentors of ideas.

If these extremes exist, they suggest two pieces of advice about the style selected for the presentation of an idea:

First, if the subject *is* a simple one, then embellish it to give interest, color, or significance. The best essayists and humorists are your masters here. Watch how skillful presentors can take the simplest event that "happened on the way to the dinner" and develop it into cosmic meaning or uproarious fun. Most after-dinner presentations of the highest type employ this technique to perfection. Also, notice the "simple" titles or themes of great poems, and see how the poet takes a commonplace observation yet extracts the most complicated ideas from it. Whether it's John Keats looking at an old Greek vase, or Robert Frost mending a broken wall, or Robert Burns watching a mouse, the events that apparently *start* their immense chains of thought and emotion were simple things which all of us can see ourselves doing. Great works like these *add* complexity in just the right amount to produce maximum effect. They also build up their complexity in a zig-zag fashion, like the method of opposites, and alternate the moods expressed—just as should be done in a good presentation. (More on alternation of mood later.)

However, most presentations of ideas involving human action, scientific work, or philosophical discourse face the inverse problem. Here is the second piece of advice from our consideration of extremes:

If the subject *is* complicated, it must somehow be simplified in order to reduce its inherent complexity to the optimum for a specific audience. But *don't go too far,* or you will overshoot the optimum and join the crazy band of Burckhardt's "terrible simplifiers." This requires a very high degree of sensitivity to your audience. If you overshoot, you may be fooled because of the welcome your idea receives. But you must realize that the acceptance is based solely on *relief,* not true understanding. You should start chewing your nails at this kind of success, for you have set in motion the production of more serious problems whenever an audience embraces an *oversimplified* solution.

I once heard an expert advise some business leaders about the benefits of a new technique by saying that its greatest benefit came from the reexamination of current methods required to apply the technique. The expert remarked, ironically, that one should probably act like he was going to use it, get his people to do all the reexamination, and after they had inevitably found many ways to improve the present systems, cancel the introduction of the new technique. But this was said so subtly that some of the audience missed the irony and took him literally. Later consequences were very awkward indeed. He had overshot the point of optimum simplification completely.

H. L. Mencken remarked that whoever named "Near Beer" was a poor judge of distance. Unlike the baptism of that dubious beverage, the quest for proper simplification of the complex requires a very good judge of distance; he must determine with nicety just how far to go. What are some approaches to organizing material in ways that simplify it, yet amplify an idea's impact? This is only another way of asking: What kinds of stylistic tools are available? One essential element is found in Chapter 2, where the merits of *clear problem-statement* are discussed; another is in Chapter 8, where the need for developing clear statements for the *finish* of the presentation is argued. These two stakes mark the beginning and end boundaries. All development takes place in between, and every aspect included must be related to them in some way. Sometimes you relate the points developed explicitly, more often by suggestion; but the link must be perceived.

Architects use a rule which has application for presentations: Form Follows Function. Before a good architect even makes a sketch, he needs to know what you intend to *do* inside the building and also the surroundings *outside* it. The differences in function and location of a skyscraper, a circus tent, a Victorian house, or a Moorish palace influence their differences in appearance. The same competent commander planning an engagement does his work differently for a massive offensive, a strategic retreat, a raid, or a counterattack, for similar reasons. *Purpose* is the greatest influence on form; inventiveness and taste come next. Experience and insight know no boundaries. Whether the field be art, science, management, or philosophy, good methods for communicating ideas to others are all blood brothers. Each uses many different styles to match its moods and purposes.

Now we will examine some attributes of style which can aid the idea when they are present, and harm it if not. Following this, we will show how they can be applied to various over-all plans of exposition.

When we say that someone is a "true professional" in some activity, we usually intend it as the highest compliment possible, this side of genius. Yet most of us find it difficult to describe what makes someone a professional in his field, as contrasted to an amateur. The naïve may suggest that, "the professional earns his living by his activity and the amateur does not," but this is not what we have in mind when we use "professional" as a mark of excellence. After many conversations directed to this question with persons in all sorts of work, I have found only three criteria that apply to *all* professionals in any field. The jobs covered ran from ballet teachers, journalists, salespeople, television directors, scientists, lawyers, sportsmen, managers, writers, surgeons, actors, to soldiers, teachers, plumbers, waiters, musicians, lecturers, and many more. Most had some difficulty articulating the qualities of a professional, but everyone agreed with the following criteria: 1. Given the same circumstances, the professional always does the job *more rapidly* than the amateur. 2. The professional can successfully do his job in unfavorable environments and under conditions so difficult that they keep the amateur from even trying. 3. The professional does his work competently even when not feeling well.

Why do I bring this up? Because the *way* things are done is only another way of describing style. To meet these three criteria for excellence in any field, two things are absolutely necessary: 1. Economy of means: Professionals all make a job look easy and don't waste their energy or time. 2. Intense pride in the quality of the work: It must meet the professional's *own* standards of skill, even if no one else is observing him directly. Effectiveness of the presentation of an idea can also be judged in this way. Let's look at a few ways to economize means, and to elevate quality in presentations.

BREVITY

Nothing gives an audience greater pleasure than the experience of quickly grasping a new idea. Lack of appropriate brevity denies them this experience, and they subconsciously resent the loss. The modern emphasis on scholarship and research creates an accompanying evil. It is the prejudice that an expression of an idea that does not exhaust the listener or reader has not been exhaustively treated.

The legacy of nineteenth-century German scholarship originally produced this false equality: The weight of documents and the length of time employed equal the weight and merit of thought. Modern universities that promote or retard their faculty members on the basis of column-inches published have spread this evil even further.

That most lovable and wise economist, Marcus Nadler, once told me of an incident in his early career which shows how even practical men of wide experience can fall into this trap. Young Nadler, even then an authentic expert in international finance, was called in by a high official of the central bank to prepare a position paper on a difficult problem involving international payments. Marcus had been studying and watching this development on his own for several months, and after a half-hour session with the official, returned to his desk. He feverishly set out to produce the document required. He passed up lunch, and by three o'clock had it finished. He immediately dashed over to the official's office and asked for an audience.

When he entered, the official smiled at his new, bright young man and said: "Well, I guess this problem was a bit more difficult than you thought, eh? What other advice do you need?"

Nadler said, "No, sir, I have the solution all worked out."

At this the official clouded up, frowned, and in a solemn voice gave this advice: "Young man, we do not make snap judgments here. We expect you to take a great deal of time to work on these important matters, so go back and do a first-class job. I won't even look at what you have in your hand. I don't want to embarrass you on your first mistake here. Come see me when you've got it in proper shape."

Nadler left, crestfallen, and after rereading his paper, knew he could not add anything to what he had already done. He put the paper in a drawer and went for a walk. One week later, he nervously brought back his same paper, with only the date changed. After twenty minutes of close study, the official beamed, reached out to shake Nadler's hand, and said, "An absolutely brilliant job! I hope you see now why I had to be so harsh with you last week. But I know you learned a valuable lesson. You have a great future and it should not be handicapped by inattention to quality."

Marcus *did* learn a great lesson, but not exactly the one his well-meaning mentor had in mind. He told me that one could only use high speed with high-speed minds, and adjustments had to be made to counteract the prejudiced who believe time spent and quality achieved are synonymous. I should add that never in his later life did Marcus Nadler ever behave like that official, for he prized the qualities of speed, insight, and brevity as signals of authentic excellence. They still are.

An elderly painter I knew was once asked by a visitor to his studio how long it took him to produce a picture just finished and drying on the wall: "Two hours to put on the paints, but forty years to learn *how*." That sums up the essence of true, professional brevity. How can one achieve this in presentations? Here are some devices which many find useful.

Be as ready to discard minor, involved, or irrelevant points, as you are to search for new evidence or better material. These kinds of thoughts should be prime candidates for the waste-basket: 1. all mean or malicious remarks, for they lower the dignity of the entire idea without contributing anything to its force; 2. gigantic ideas beyond your powers of expression or control; (these have a tendency to creep in almost unnoticed. In one case a legitimate idea for an improvement in agriculture was made the panacea for every ill affecting an entire underdeveloped country. When this sort of thing is not checked, it destroys credibility.) 3. trivial points which do not affect the rejection or acceptance of the idea itself, but which have some high personal interest for the presentor. (These create an insipid tone and take the audience for a tour in a fog. The listeners keep expecting the trivial point to turn out important in some way, and try to relate it to the idea, as a clue to a mystery. But when they find they've been fooled, curiosity degenerates into contempt.)

Other useful gambits are to use consent or cognizant omission to shorten and speed up the treatment of troublesome, controversial areas, if they threaten to divert the main thrust of the presentation. These two devices go down very hard with those stubborn presentors who insist on absolute agreement on every miniscule or obscure detail of their idea. The method of consent grants what you *might* deny to remove it as a source of contention or sidetracking. You do this in order to acquire control over the main line of argument. This also prevents someone who is sensitive to the previously unresolved question from being blinded to your idea because he holds strong opinions about it—even though the question may have only minute bearing on your own idea. One usually encounters this when people fear that your idea will cause a great deal of upset in an existing organization, doctrine, or public position previously taken. They are hypersensitive to any hint that *you may be about to attack something they hold dear*. Relieve the anxiety by flatly stating that you are *not* going to do so.

I once heard a tax specialist describe a new method which would improve the determination of property assessments. He wished to rebuild the archaic structure of a hundred years' patchwork, which fewer and fewer people understood. It was a well-thought-out plan, but as he effectively made point after point, the audience became restive. One visual aid had accidentally hinted at demands for funds in the future, and the presentor saw whispering behind hands and a general buzzing of disturbance. Through all their minds was flying the horrible thought: "He's going to raise all our taxes!"

The presentor was a true professional. He sensed the fear before it became articulate and quietly said, "A few of you may think that this is just a scheme to increase your taxes. That is simply not so. In fact, if we adopt this plan, we intend to implement it in ways that no one will pay more this year than last. Many of you will experience small reductions. Minimum disturbance to existing expectations has been a central feature of our planning, and I'll explain that in a few moments."

There was an audible sigh of relief. Everyone then refocused attention on *what* he had to say, rather than on what they thought he was *going* to say. He won unanimous approval twenty minutes later.

Another fear comes from the feeling that the idea is going to be rammed down the throats of the audience, whether they like it or not. One always gets further by admitting that, even if the audience rejects a proposal, the whole world will not collapse. Also, if you possibly can, advise them to reject your idea if they do not see long-range benefits to themselves or the people they represent—after giving you a fair hearing. This creates a much more relaxed atmosphere, and their minds can then safely open up to listen and imagine useful effects instead of digging in for shelter against hostile attack. After laying out a preliminary sketch of a presentation, search for every place that a minor concession can eliminate major potential trouble.

"Cognizant omission" offers another way to achieve brevity. It is very useful in complicated subjects where innumerable angles suggest themselves in advance before the audience has heard what you are going to say. The technique is simple and easy to use with a remark like this: "When we first began work on this problem, we listed everything we could think of that might influence a good solution. Some of these were: [Here list all of the angles or variables]. As we went further into the subject, we found that, while all of these did have some bearing, only three of them were really important. Ignoring the rest would not affect our answer to any appreciable degree. The rest of my story addresses itself to these three factors, and after I'm finished, if anyone wishes to discuss the ones we omitted, we can do so."

Finally, brevity is served by a crisp, well-chosen example or anecdote, which embodies the abstract principle in a concrete case. Such examples, coupled to a principle, can illuminate the entire scene like the flash of a searchlight, and remove the need for a thousand cumulative details.

Brevity, like all virtues, can become a vice if pushed to extremes. The qualities of style that keep it under control are the needs for:

CLARITY AND ELEGANCE

Elegance is an elusive quality, easier to recognize than describe. It should not be confused with fanciness or "dandyism," which create effects similar to the tinsel and cheesecloth sets of a vulgar Broadway show. Elegance exists when a great many aspects of a subject or person are expressed in the simplest *possible* way. If simplicity is carried *too* far, the thoughts of a presentation appear tortured and cramped; if not carried far enough, the effect is one of laxity and sloppiness. Neither produces elegance. The presentation must be put together methodically, but the method itself should not be obvious or perceivable. If it is, everything takes on an air of cold mechanism and predictability which strangles interest. Even Beethoven could not grab your imagination if he wrote a *Sonata for Snare Drum*, yet many overly methodical presentations set out on similar excursions to boredom.

Shakespeare suggests the opposite in Enobarbus's view of Cleopatra: "Age cannot wither her, nor custom stale her infinite variety." Such a magnet dragged Antony to disaster, but you can't fault the recipe for keeping someone interested. The kind of grace-with-strength seen in great athletes, performers, or certain machines also hints at the nature of elegance: no motion wasted, yet nothing essential missing, done hesitantly, or with jerkiness. The *Ole* roared at bullfights is always a tribute to elegance, not to nerve or strength alone. "What" is common; "How" is personal.

Extreme brevity leads to a cryptic style, which requires excessive work by the audience to decode your meaning. The whole purpose of a presentation is understanding. When the meaning of an idea must be *guessed* at, instead of being clear to the average eye and mind, mistakes, discord, disputes, and confusion result. The tests of whether an expression is clear and elegant are these: Is it ambiguous? Is it embarrassing? Are its images or examples farfetched? Is it difficult to relate to those thoughts of common sense that lie at the core of human nature? If the answer to any of these is *Yes*, it requires more work.

Sometimes the quest for elegance produces unintentional

comedy, embarrassment, or disgust. This occurs when dreary thoughts are dressed in gay diction; the effect is similar to a slattern in the dress of a countess. I cannot forget how a high-ranking government economist described his attitude to increased unemployment: "Up to now, I've found the unemployment figures extremely dull, but now that they're getting larger and affecting many different segments of the economy, I'm beginning to find them of considerable intellectual interest." He almost rubbed his hands in glee. This oaf's debonair approach to the human misery of joblessness nearly made me nauseous, and the little gasp that escaped the audience was completely lost on him.

Actuaries use an expression which shocks you on first hearing. If groups of people are living longer than the actuary's calculations assumed, he calls that "unfavorable experience." Both of these lapses fail to meet the test of the four questions above. Every presentor must be on guard against similar errors, especially if he is an expert in a field unfamiliar to the audience. His terms may suggest bizarre overtones for those unschooled in their technical meaning.

The opening phase of a presentation exerts major influence on its tone of elegance and clarity. Your demeanor as you take the podium, or rise to your feet in a meeting, communicates a great deal of information without saying a word. If you shoot up like a jack-in-the-box, or listlessly shuffle as though on your way to the block, your listeners form adverse opinions about your idea. A good form to follow is this: Give a polite nod of acknowledgment to the man who introduced you, calmly stride to your position, neither hurrying or dragging, take in the audience with a deliberate, panoramic sweep of your eyes, and return to a focus halfway back in the center of the room. *Do not look away from the audience at this instant.* Every eye is on you, for their curiosity is at its peak, and you haven't had a chance to bore them yet. Pause for a few seconds and begin. Choose your first sentence with more care than any other, for it will set the mood for all that follows. Here are some examples of opening lines from great presentations of the past:

"A new era of prosperity is about to blossom for the faculties of the sciences." [Pasteur]

"I am told that there is no danger because there are no riots; I am told that because there is no visible disorder on the surface of society, there is no revolution at hand." [Tocqueville]

"Fourscore and seven years ago, our fathers brought forth upon this continent a new nation, conceived in liberty and dedicated to the proposition that all men are created equal." [Lincoln]

"When, O Catiline, do you mean to cease abusing our patience?" [Cicero]

"Partisanship should only be a method of patriotism. He who is a partisan merely for the sake of spoils is a buccaneer." [Beveridge]

"I want to talk for a few minutes with the people of the United States about banking—with the comparatively few who understand the mechanics of banking, but more particularly with the overwhelming majority who use banks for the making of deposits and the drawing of checks." [F. D. Roosevelt]

"At long last I am able to say a few words of my own." [King Edward VIII]

"A shadow has fallen upon the scenes so lately lighted by the Allied victory." [Churchill]

Notice how every one of these hints of something important to come, shows respect for the audience, and uses simple, familiar words for maximum clarity. Even in cold black and white, without the richness of each author's emotional coloring, we sense the spirit of someone worth listening to. The men who used these could have had their audience's attention if they had recited the ABC's. But, instead, they obviously took a great deal of care with their opening sentence. Why? Because as expert presentors they would not throw away the best chance of all to set the tone and seize attention for their idea. Should anyone without their personal gifts do less?

Everyone's experience is unique. He can use it to develop the best opening for his particular idea; but it will not come by chance, or from following advice like, "Be yourself."

One example of the kind of latent ingenuity available occurred in a writing class a few years ago. The instructor stressed the necessity for a good opening line to seize attention. He said that the four surefire subjects for getting attention were Royalty, Religion, Sex, and Mystery. Get one of them in the first sentence and the reader was bound to continue. He asked for exercises which would illustrate their use. A bright student turned in this one which has all four in only nine words: "My God," said the Queen, "let go my leg!" It's not much good for a presentation, and it certainly fails in elegance, but you must admit that the author could go anywhere with that kind of opening. Most people would probably hang on for the next few lines, at least. Presentors should seek the same punch, but with more decorum.

VARIETY

Variety may not be the spice of life, but it certainly perks up a presentation like nothing else. Variety occurs when we experience a series of states that *contrast* with one another. Its presence marks the difference in interest between a river and a canal. The river is natural, with a surprise around every bend, with rapids and serene pools, gorges, forests and farms, continually appealing and making new suggestions to the mind. A canal is man-made, straight and dull except when its surveyor hit an obstacle he could not blast from his preferred path. Good presentations are like rivers; bad ones like canals. How can one inject variety into the presentation of an idea?

First, strive for a mixture of the lofty and the commonplace. Soar with the eagle, and crawl with the caterpillar, and you'll get a wider perspective of nature. If you produce a generalization, buttress it with a homely example. If you must use an esoteric aerodynamic equation, show how it's used by the bumble bee. If you are explaining a theory of aesthetics, show its expression in primitive pottery or a Vermeer interior. If you are developing an idea in metallurgy, show how sweating men labor at the hearths and foundries. Tether the intellect to human scale, and the humans before you will accompany you on the ascent to new mental heights. Let it run free, and they will allow you to disappear in mists of your own making.

Use words from different vocabularies, but always confine yourself to words understood by those before you. Here's a list of some categories to think about: standard contemporary, colloquial, dialect, formal literary, archaic, technical, foreign expressions, slang.

Another source of variety lies in the tone, mood, and outlook of the presentor himself. Augment these with a range of loudness and softness, or changes in tempo of delivery, and they increase the sense of variety produced. Here are some adjectives that suggest the enormous stylistic keyboard available to the average man. He can be described by every one of them sometime in his life: bold, witty, solemn, joyful, agreeable, phlegmatic, humorous, shrewd, delicate, flowery, melancholy, quick, energetic, gracious, blunt, deliberate. By making remarks that deserve such labels, the presentor can interweave them to keep the audience constantly on its toes. No one, of course, can use them all in any single presentation, but the various pieces must differ in color if they are to have any bite at all. At least don't have all thoughts come out in the same dull shade of gray. The ability to produce a "change of pace" is as important for a presentor as it is for a baseball pitcher. When both have only one good pitch, they are driven from the mound or podium, since they are completely predictable. One loses games, the other loses audiences.

MYSTERY AND SUSPENSE

Contrasted to predictability, mystery and suspense keep an audience on edge. Once interested, the members have an urge to see how the presentation will turn out. The essential quality for the use of mystery is that interest be captured immediately. This can often be done by letting the audience know in advance the subject to be discussed, preferably in the most colorless phrases possible. Whether the title is made known in a printed program, a typed announcement before the meeting, or an oral introduction, the audience should have in mind something fairly dull. This allows maximum contrast for an obscure or colorful opening statement. The audience feels that they knew what you were going to do, but they can't link up an odd or *seemingly* irrelevant incident. They will go along quite a distance, for they trust you to come through with an uncommon revelation. They keep wondering "How can he possibly relate this to his assigned topic?" In the hands of first-class men, the suspense developed can keep attention riveted until the key is produced to unlock the mystery.

There is danger in this method, for if obscurity is maintained beyond the audience's patience point, the whole presentation collapses and turns into a bore. Suspense should be used in all seriousness, never with blatant humor or "cuteness." Above all, the presentor himself should know *exactly* how he intends to uncover the connection. If he doesn't, he creates effects similar to an inept raconteur who tells a funny story with colorful detail and then forgets the punch line. Here are a few examples of the *title* of a talk, known beforehand, followed by the opening line of the presentation. They are actual cases, and all turned out extremely well:

TITLE: *A Proposal for International Finance.* "Come with me to an ancient English university on a sunny afternoon ten years ago. As we approach the Gothic buildings, a dignified, middle-aged man emerges from a portico, hands his academic gown to a servant, dons a leather helmet, adjusts his goggles, jumps on a motorcycle, and roars out of the peaceful quadrangle." (Ten minutes later the speaker linked this incident to Lord Keynes's suggestion for monetary stabilization.)

TITLE: *Cost Reduction Possibilities for Solid State Devices.* "At a remote village in the Libyan Desert, a camel train camped for the night. Mingled with sounds common to caravan life since the Pharaohs were the alien strains of popular music coming from a radio." (The presentor led on to a proposal for inexpensive transistor production to aid a developing country's communications.)

TITLE: *A New Approach to Factory Supervision.* "As young René Descartes prowled the streets of Paris, he clutched a copy of Thomas Aquinas's *Summa Theologica* under his arm." (Here followed a fascinating exposition of attempts through the centuries to reconcile man's ethical and economic needs, ending with a report of a recent experiment in management.)

These illustrate the character of mystery. A touch of the exotic, unexpected, literary, or historical contrasts to everyday occurrences and heightens attention to the real message. While most effective at the opening, the same idea can also be used during the development phase. Another way to create suspense is to keep a large visual aid or a demonstration model of a device covered by a cloth. At precisely the moment of reference the cloth is quickly flicked aside. This has an effect like unveiling a portrait or statue. Few in the audience can resist wanting to see what's under it. Ingenious minds invent all kinds of variations.

One rule must be observed in using mystery or suspense: Don't disappoint the expectation of the unexpected. When you select this style, you make a silent promise that it will be worthwhile for the audience to stay with you. Keep it.

We now turn to forms for the over-all presentation that affect its style. The philosopher C. S. Peirce discerned four ways to fix beliefs in a person's mind. He called them the methods of *tenacity*, *authority*, *apriority*, and *science*. Tenacity is related to habit. By constantly perceiving the same linkage of cause and effect, the brain sets up well-worn, automatic paths which don't require conscious thought after a while. Beliefs expressed by "It just isn't done," or, "Our success has been built on our liberal refund policy," or "There's only one way to make quince preserves" are formed by this method. The unquestioned, taken-for-granted ideas and the muscular motions we use to get through most of each day spring from such habits of thought and action. Without them, driving a car, adding a column of numbers, or eating a meal would be an exhausting task.

The method of *authority* uses the respect that someone holds for the knowledge, opinions, or power of another person or text. Since the person to be convinced defers to the mind or character of the authority put forth, he is inclined to embrace beliefs similar to the authority's. Sentences that begin with: "The Bible says . . .," "The president has often said . . .," "All osteopaths agree that . . .," or, "Brewmasters always use . . ." are forms of this approach.

The method of *apriority* assumes that the audience completely accepts certain premises without any doubt whatsoever. These premises are usually moral, ethical, religious, or political axioms. Statements based on apriority sound like this: "This plan places burdens unequally and is consequently unfair," "The majority decided on this action; it is thus the only right thing to do," or "An honorable man could not entertain that suggestion for one minute." Arguments from apriority veer closely toward prejudice and are beloved by demagogues. But they often have legitimate employment if used to save time of those audiences who do accept the axioms.

The method of *science* doubts everything not verified experimentally. It allows speculation on cause and effect in the form of working hypotheses, but sets up tests of their validity. (See Chapter 9 for a more extended treatment of scientific method.) This method is supposed to carry us as close to truth as we can hope to get, but it must be tempered by Pascal's deep insight that "The heart has its reasons which reason knows not of." Science is of less value—or none at all—when a quality cannot accurately be measured. It must stand mute if asked to decide questions of fairness, beauty, taste, or compassion.

Everyone of Peirce's categories are useful and acceptable in presentation of an idea. Most presentors use all of them at one time or other, and some use all four in every presentation they make. Arranging thought and inferences rooted in the different methods gives a three-dimensional, well-rounded impression of an idea. Reliance on one of them alone produces shrillness or monotony.

With this kit one still faces the task of choosing them with judgment and arranging the various parts with taste. The method of opposites gives the basic framework for development, but there is another one related to it which was used extensively by medieval students. One of the final tests for a degree called for them to stand before their examiners and conduct an impromptu discourse on a question given to them only a few minutes before. Over the years a handy device developed to cope with this test. It is still useful for both improvised presentations prepared on short notice and full-blown efforts. When used well, it embodies all the virtues of a good style: brevity, elegance, clearness, variety, and passion.

On being given the question, the candidate was trained to deal with it in the following sequence: *Assertion:* State the *question,* then your answer and some evidence for it. *Refutation:* State the *opposite* answer and some evidence for it. *Doubt:* Cast doubt on the refutation and show why it is correct to do so. *Affirmation:* Restate the *original* answer in a different way.

This format is actually the method of opposites in its simplest form. Hamlet follows it precisely in his soliloquy: "To be, or not to be; that is the question." Notice how it suggests mature consideration of two sides of the question, weighing the evidence for each, and ending in a sober, clear judgment. Even if the presentor deals from a stacked deck, the audience has seen the presentation done with decent ceremony, and they return the respect shown them. An acknowledgment that possible negatives to the idea exist at least politely offers a hook for dissenters to hang their own views on during the discussion.

Let's try an example in skeleton form. You have an idea that people in an organization (factory, office, store) will be more effective if they are allowed increased freedom in carrying out their work. Here's one way to unfold it using this method:

"We are faced with this question: Can we get a better job from our people if we remove some of the rigid rules and procedures that now restrain them? I believe the answer is *Yes.* I base my belief on recent industrial experiments and academic research in motivational psychology [Here mention some].

"But there is a chance that the right answer should be *No.* Our activity is different from others who have tried it. We have had great difficulty in maintaining the quality of individual work, errors are high, absence is excessive, and productivity keeps falling [Cite figures]. The kind of people we are getting now are not like those we have been accustomed to, and turnover is terrible. If they do badly now with carefully spelled-out instructions and close supervision, can we turn them loose on their own? The whole operation may collapse in chaos. I am aware of the great risks involved.

"Yet, these bad effects may be *caused* by the rigidity itself. The absence of healthy psychological incentives may be responsible for apathy and poor performance. Some of the reports of the successful experiments claim that quite forcefully [Here show some excerpts from the reports].

"After looking at all sides of this question, I conclude that we should go ahead with a trial of this idea. We certainly have not succeeded in solving these problems with our old approaches. They are just not working the way they once did. We are in a new environment, and I believe this is the time to adjust to it with new ideas. If others can do it, why can't we? Here's what I propose."

Notice that the same sequence can be used when you are asked to reply as a member of an approving body, or as a member of an audience whose opinion is requested. You can also build a larger presentation out of various pieces that have this same structure internally, like prefabricated sections of a ship. For example, the above skeleton case could have been one section of an over-all presentation for the forward planning of an entire organization. I keep the sequence in mind by the initials of the four labels: A R D A (assertion, refutation, doubt, affirmation).

MULTIPLE PRESENTATIONS

Presentation of a complex idea can often benefit by having different people present various aspects of it. This is especially true where one man would be required to occupy more than forty-five minutes. If each man selected is expert in the phase he is assigned, and a spectrum of personality types is available, variety comes automatically. Audiences become bored with the same voice or the same type of mind in an all-day session. Multiple presentors keep up the dramatic pace and contribute to a sense of something new always happening. However, this style requires that one man be the over-all leader. He should open the session, use clarifying remarks to show how one piece fits with the others, handle the assignment of discussion questions to the various presentors, and summarize at the end. When this function is not filled, the presentation becomes more and more diffuse, and the over-all idea becomes lost. The leader acts as a lens to focus all the diverse points in the presentations and discussion on the problem itself.

RECAPITULATION

Complicated subjects or presentations always require a recapitulation to sum up the points bearing on the idea. This should be as brisk as possible and emphasize, at its end, the action desired of the audience or the change in attitude suggested. The opening secures attention; development analyzes and informs; the ending seeks conviction and commitment.

Every presentor has more than enough resources to meet the needs of any idea for a proper style. To be a human being is to possess a wide range of intellectual and emotional expression. Even a little courage and awareness releases a great deal of this latent power of expression to inform and persuade in the service of an idea. When that happens, the matching of style and content will be made surely and, with practice, almost unconsciously.

In the next chapter we examine the subtle and overt psychological relationships between presentors and their audiences.

5

Some Psychological Hints

or

What Every Police Lieutenant, Bartender, Reporter, Dog Walker, and Shopkeeper Knows

One approach to the presentation of an idea is to see it as psychological sculpture. The presentor takes a conception that exists in his own mind, and by using the material in front of him—the minds of the members of the audience—transfers his conceptions to their consciousness to produce copies of his own. He faces a challenge similar to that of the sculptor, for each material, like different minds, requires techniques appropriate to its own nature. Clay, marble, plaster, bronze, glass, and wood have some qualities in common, but also differ widely from one another. So do human minds and the characters and personalities they produce. A presentor who looks on all minds before him as homogeneous will convince very few in that audience of the validity of his idea.

In recent years the language and terms of psychiatry have been diffused into our lives, through novels, plays, articles, television, and news stories. A wide range of counselors focus on the human struggle, from infancy to senility. Even undertakers now call their services "grief therapy." Every problem or aberration that exists—from bad marks in school, loafing on the job, drug addiction, on to the malaise of a nation or civilization—immediately triggers explanations rich in the vocabulary of mental illness. These are generally well intentioned, often excuses, sometimes helpful, and rarely productive of real solutions. Charwomen discuss their "frustrations" as they sip their midnight coffee in executive suites; bus riders comment on the "hostility" of a driver; painters "sublimate" their primitive urges; employees call an unpopular boss a "neurotic" or "paranoic"; and gossips sprinkle the nomenclature of Freud on their observations like confectioners use powdered sugar. This is more amusing than harmful in most areas of life, but it can produce two forms of mischief for someone who wishes to acquire skill in presentations. Habitual and careless employment of these terms to label people leads to a viewing of human minds as if they were wrapped in packages; and if you can read the label, you can then presume to know what's inside. Also, excessive emphasis on the aberrations causes one to overlook the much greater mass of normal, noble, and often beautiful aspects of the human psyche. It is as if a gardener developed a passionate interest in weeds and forgot about flowers. In making a presentation, your interest must focus on the normal aspects of human psychology—the weeds of abnormality are merely to be avoided or brushed aside. It is not *your* business to cure them.

Few people know that Freud (who started all this, and who would probably be horrified to see the vulgarization of his work) had great doubts about the training of physicians as suitable preparation for a psychoanalyst. He said that the cloistered existence of young doctors, removed as it is from the daily life and emotional stresses of most people, might be a handicap in learning his techniques in their later life. He felt that certain magistrates, midwives, and older women of sympathetic character might be better equipped by experience and temperament to do the kind of work required. Faced with this threat to the progress of the medical profession, Freud's fellow physicians and their successors succeeded in consigning his view to the category of crack-brained ideas that even genius seems to produce. I mention this to show that one of the most penetrating investigators of the mind's characteristics had high regard for the ability of intelligent men and women to understand the behavior and aspirations of human beings. He believed such understanding could be developed enough to help those in trouble make constructive adjustments to their environments. That level of psychological competence exceeds enormously the level required to make a good presentation. But some appreciation of the psychology of learning and motivation in *individuals,* and of the mental modifications that take place when people assemble in *groups,* is indispensable, if one aspires to skill beyond the mediocre. If Freud was right about the abilities of the ordinary person, then this appreciation is certainly possible, but it does require something better than vaguely felt "principles" percolated from the average person's experiences. Most everyone shares the mistaken belief that we *instinctively* feel the right way of doing a thing. Actually, instinct is the poorest guide to any technique required beyond the cradle. When we are first shown the correct way to tie a shoe, grip a golf club, play a violin, grasp a scalpel, or do addition on a calculator, the method always appears awkward and unnatural. Only after continual practice is the original hesitancy of the correct way turned into a mastery beyond anything that raw instinct suggests.

Another person's mind is a far more complex entity than any tool, instrument, or article. Just as the correct methods of their use come only from generations of trial and error, so observation and reflection on the responses of different minds to ideas requires more than a shared destiny and experience as a human being.

The remainder of this chapter will set forth some attributes of normal mental behavior important for a presentor. There is no explanation of the underlying mechanism. In fact, no one really knows what it is—or rather what they are. We shall emulate astronomers who cannot explain the cosmos, but who do know that certain phenomena occur so regularly that predictions of a high order of accuracy are commonplace. Also, like astronomers, we must be content to observe behavior from a distance, never allowed to watch the mind itself "up close"—only the fireworks it produces. After all, our own mind is the least under-stood of those we encounter. We will also accept behavior as it *is,* and not as it *should be* according to our own view of perfec-tion. Good astronomers do not get angry because a star is in the "wrong" place for a more beautiful design. We must be just as cool in meeting what we perceive as "wrong-headedness" during a presentation. The sense of personal triumph that follows con-version of hostile attitudes into support for an idea is the highest reward of a good presentation. As Edmund Burke remarked: "He who opposes me, and does not destroy me, strengthens me."

The following hints and observations of the behavior of those involved in both sides of presentations should be checked against your own experience, and lead to closer examination in the fu-ture. No one can use them all at any one time, but they represent tendencies to be either used or avoided, as the specific case requires. They are developed around the concept of *relationships* between the presenter and the individual member of the audi-ence; between the presenter and small or large groups; and among the individual members of the audience themselves. We will then treat those psychological aids that strengthen participa-tion, and those that help amplify the perception power of an audience.

THE PRESENTOR AS VIEWED BY INDIVIDUAL MEMBERS OF THE AUDIENCE

Each individual in the audience brings prejudices that influ-ence his attitude and final impression of the presentation. His knowledge and opinion of you, your reputation with others he knows, and even the wording of the announcement that invited him have produced a positive or negative bias. He will tend to delight in the successes and excuse the shortcomings of someone he likes; but will begrudge the successes and delight in the short-comings of someone he dislikes. No one is completely objective. Your occupation is also subject to stereotyped impressions, and individual members will be sensitive to aspects of your behavior that reinforce their stereotype of that kind of job. Think now of what image pops into your mind on being told a presentation will be made to you by: a general, painter, high school teacher, theoretical physicist, steelmaker, statistician, plumber, bishop, social worker, or a politician. These preconceptions, however, can be turned to advantage if you behave in a way that *disappoints* them, for the audience is first surprised, then charmed, and finally interested in what such an "unrepresentative" type has to say. (They also like to tell others about such an experience.) Stereotypes are common to all *habitual* thought—if that is not a contradiction in terms. Consider attitudes toward dogs. On seeing a collie, poodle, boxer, or setter, many feel they are "friendly and intelligent," and people are inclined to strike up conversations with their owners. German shepherds, Dobermans, chows, and Pekingese are thought of as "intelligent but sometimes vicious," and you may cross the street when you see one coming. Beagles, basset hounds, and bulldogs are "nice, but a little stupid" as stereotypes to others than their owners, and usually produce neutral responses.

Members of an audience quickly form an impression of the three possible relationships they can have to the presenter: He is trying to dominate them, treats them as equals, or is submissive. They rightly sense that the dominating and submissive are both actually motivated by fear, and their desire for participation in a subsequent dialogue (the clinching part of any presentation) is diminished. The dominant fears discussion; the submissive fears for his reputation. When the audience senses that they are treated as equals, all working together in the search for the right course of action, they eagerly join in discussion with good will, even if your idea is repellent. Individuals dislike being dominated. It implies that they are not as free to choose, or as independent, as they need to believe in order to preserve their dignity as human beings. If the domination is based solely on higher status or rank, true persuasion cannot take place, even though everyone may say *aye* at the end. The raw form of this approach was used by a high-ranking presenter who said at the end of his proposal, "All in favor say *aye*; all opposed say *I quit*." Dominant presenters produce mixed reactions of envy and contempt in an audience. They envy the presentor's power, but have contempt for a proposal that can only be forced through by that alone. Audiences, after they leave, often show their contempt for a proposal carried by force by taking one of the two attitudes that can kill any idea when it is turned into action. They can carry on as though ignorant of it; or carry it out by scrupulous adherence to the letter, applying its conclusions to absurd, but logically consistent, extremes. Some European labor unions, denied the right to strike by law, often strangle an industry by having their members strictly follow to the letter *every* rule and procedure laid down by the management, regardless of need. For example, a general rule to inspect railroad tickets for authenticity, and to be watchful for counterfeit money can be applied with a microscopic attention to details which exceeds that of jewelers and engravers—and the trains stop without a strike. The dominant presentor always runs this risk of superficial agreement masking deeply felt resentment. His idea, even if meritorious, will not get a fair chance to succeed.

The submissive presentor provokes different emotions, but the failure of his idea is just as bad, and comes a little sooner. The idea does not even survive the meeting. He violates the two rules for successful men of action: "Never take counsel of your fears," and "Never look back." The presentor may not think of himself as a "man of action"—in fact, may detest them—but it will be a rare audience that does not contain them, and they expect an understanding of their point of view. After all, if you don't need them, they would not be there. Since they are going to have to carry out ideas into practice, they know from experience that a mousy, timid attitude can never inspire others. They seldom "buy" an idea without "buying" its author in the process.

The submissive presentor sends all kinds of signals showing his distress. There is a normal tenseness before a presentation which is helpful, for it causes the endocrine system to do its part in supporting you for the effort ahead. Every experienced presentor knows of this and is worried if he does not feel it. He also knows that the tenseness leaves quickly once he starts talking and gets into his subject. The good presentor feels that he knows as much or more about the details of *his* story as anyone in front of him, or else he shouldn't be there. Good presentors also develop the ability to forget the possible effects on their own reputations—for good or evil—during the presentation, for that is of slight concern to the audience. Successful presentors put *all* of their energy at the service of the idea, and do not turn some back on themselves in futile self-criticism. The time for that is *after* the show, not while it's going on.

Most of the symptoms of submissiveness are unconscious. Often, merely being aware of a *tendency* to produce them will subdue them. All of us have lived with our habits and mannerisms so long that we are shocked when we first become aware of them. This can happen when a friend points them out; when we first hear our voice on a tape recorder; or when we are unfortunate enough to see a video tape of ourselves in action for the first time. These habits are of three kinds: muscular movements (gestures), language patterns, emotional reactions, and combinations of the three. It is handy to think of them as linked together in a chain of "brain-hand-voice." A thought or feeling will affect the brain, but the outward sign will be seen in body movement or in a change of speech. All of the natural shading and color in our common conversational speech comes from the emotions we feel while talking, and we will accompany the speech with all sorts of appropriate gestures to emphasize our points. Strangely, when a submissive person talks in a presentation, what came naturally in conversation changes to something odd, jerky, or artificial. His voice tightens, quivers, goes shrill or loud, and all sorts of distracting sounds like "ahs" and "ers" are interspersed with the intelligence he wants to communicate. Here, the brain is overloaded with fright and sends erratic messages to hands and voice. If the fright is bad enough, the person may actually collapse. Others constantly touch their noses with a finger or pull on their ear lobes. Some run hands over their hair, or rub their chins or foreheads. If the energy built up is enough, they may be driven to pace the floor, head down, as though searching for ants, intent on everything but their hearers. All of these things fascinate an audience—like an animal in the zoo— but they can overwhelm all of the content of a talk, very much as excessive static does a radio broadcast. I once became so hypnotized by a nose-toucher that I concentrated on counting the number of touches per minute, and then began to observe variations in the pattern—as a scientist would a gorilla. The maximum touch rate was twelve per minute (in a forty-minute talk), and to this day I don't remember one other thing about the presentation. I'm sure, though, that the presentor felt I was giving absolute concentration to his message.

Tenseness also manifests itself as edginess; every question evokes a sharp, irritating reply. Confronted with this reaction, kindly individuals sense that they are causing pain, and silently disengage from discussion, unwilling to torture the victim.

What can be done to help such people? Two approaches: one physical, the other mental. The excess physical energy can be dissipated before the presentation by a rapid walk, preferably in the open air; or by bowing over at the waist and quickly shaking the loose arms, fingers outstretched, in a rotating, oscillating pattern (athletes often do this before a great effort). If you must be seated in the same room as the audience before your turn comes, use of the previous two methods would cause an eyebrow or two to lift, so something more decorous is needed. Isometric exercise gives second-best solutions, and does not leave any trace. Grasp your elbows in your hands and try to pull them together, then relax, and continue to alternate. Also, if you ordinarily place one leg over the other, link your hands and pull against the upper knee, again alternating. Gripping the arms of the chair as tightly as possible and alternately relaxing is also effective; and the simplest of all, used for centuries by soldiers "at attention," is to clench fists and toes in alternation. There is a secondary benefit from all of these which has a mental aspect. When concentrating on the physical act of gripping at maximum strength, the mind goes blank, producing a healthy break in the vicious cycle of worry (try it now and see). Some people find *exhaling* as deeply as possible for a few breaths before taking the floor a relaxing antidote to the tendency to inhale rapidly which often accompanies nervousness. The best thing about all of these, though, is that as they are used, and presentations benefit, they become unnecessary to think about, for they have become habitual, or truly unnecessary.

One word about alcohol's use—don't. However much you may think it does for your view of things, its effect on audiences is always bad. If there must be a social hour before your presentation, ginger ale and ice will keep your hosts from importuning you and fogging your mind. From a presentation point of view, use alcohol only for celebration, not preparation—including the night before. True professionals carefully prepare themselves for a contest or performance, and to those with submissive tendencies, there is no tougher contest than a presentation of their own ideas to others.

Mental solutions to overcome unfortunate impressions on individual members of an audience apply both to those who suffer from the need to dominate, and to those who feel submissive. All go to one objective: *treat the audience as equals during the presentation.* If you enjoy higher status than the audience, they will be complimented and charmed by your posture as a fellow seeker for correct action. Their egos are not endangered by your potential domination, and participation in discussion becomes safe.

If you are of lower status than your audience, they know it, but also expect to learn something from you. This makes them most willing to suspend the difference if you show them that *you* can do so. Many a promotion had its beginning in a presentation to superiors who saw that the presentor could help persons of greater power. They also admire someone who can do the job of convincing them purely on the merits of his idea, with no need for a push from higher authority. Superiors are always on the lookout for unusual competence, and a presentation to them is an acid test for distinguishing the real from the glittering.

When told to "treat others as equals," the inexperienced may misunderstand what this really means. Here are some things it does *not* mean. Undue familiarity, unusual slang expressions, or off-color stories are offensive to many people—equals and inferiors—and should be avoided. Do not use nicknames for people whom you would not approach that way if you were both in a social or family situation. There is a fine, but rigid, line between taking liberties (which are seen as attempts to put yourself *above* the audience by going too far) and true equality as human beings. The equality to strive for is that every member of the audience is equally interested in arriving at a proper course of action. Everyone at the meeting has a right to be heard, and shares responsibility for the outcome of events if your proposal is accepted. In other words, try always to focus their attention on the *idea* and its consequences, not on yourself. Above all, try to put from your mind your worries about what will happen if you do not succeed in convincing them. One of the ways to do this is by the use of the Method of Opposites (Chapter 3), in which you show that you can understand why someone would say No. Be prepared to cut psychological losses as quickly as a speculator does financial ones. Your sense of personal freedom and respect for the judgment of others will subtly communicate itself to each member listening.

Another quality that strangely reassures a person presented with a proposal is an air of personal disinterestedness. Here you show that you have done a good job, thought through many more aspects of the problem than the audience has been previously exposed to, and produced a judgment for their consideration. But, suggest that your whole world will not become unglued if they reject it. Show that you believe it is only one battle, not the whole war. Hint that you have other approaches that could be tried if they don't like this one. An air of desperation frightens individuals away from you; they don't want to join someone with his back to the wall. Even if you are scared to death, a debonair attitude secures allies; despair causes them to seek escape from its infection. *You* may get pity, but your idea gets no support.

Every audience today contains some amateur psychoanalysts, and they will be alert for all kinds of "symptoms" of insecurity in a presentor. Their diagnoses may be laughable to a professional, but their judgment of the presentation will be influenced by their analysis of a presentor's peculiarities. I recently heard a successful lawyer remark after a brilliant presentation on finance by an eminent young professor that: "Anyone who speaks as loudly as he does must be unsure of his material." The presentation took place in a small room, and this teacher was accustomed to lecturing five times a week to large classes (in the hundreds) without microphones. But the lawyer made no allowance for that, and when this explanation was suggested to him, he felt even stronger antipathy. He replied: "Well, if you are right, then he lacks flexibility, and therefore can't be very intelligent." You can't win over everyone! The amateurs also watch for wringing of hands, excessive smoking (especially those who have given it up), continuous throat clearing, shifty eyes, perspiration, and nail biting. Your only hope is to disappoint them by being aware of their hobby. Artur Rubinstein once was asked the kind of audience he preferred: "Those who have no pretensions to musical knowledge. Those who do, sit like hawks, waiting for me to make a mistake. They don't listen to the music as a whole and never experience its beauty." The amateur analysts offer the same kind of barrier to comprehension. Keep your eye on *them*, for they have theirs on *you*.

INDIVIDUAL MEMBERS OF THE AUDIENCES AS VIEWED BY THE PRESENTOR

Members of an audience are different from one another. They have different backgrounds, education, experience, skills, interests, fears, temperaments, and hopes. The total of their characteristics produces a unique understanding of, and attitude toward, your idea. It is as though each one had a different set of spectacles which distort the image they perceive of an object. The associations they make when hearing an idea are not completely under your control. But by sending the idea forth in different forms and using *different kinds* of illustrations and examples, you can arouse various associations from their experience which will aid them to achieve an understanding that approximates your own. Regretfully, you can also conjure up negative associations which inhibit such understanding. One thing you can depend on absolutely: They will all resist anything that threatens their egos, i.e., their sense of identity and individual worth—other names for self-preservation. If they sniff criticism of their *individual* past performance, they mobilize for counterattack, and their first defense is to clang down the portcullises of their minds against further insult. They rapidly concentrate all their attention to find ways to get back at you, and will actually not hear the rest of your presentation until they dispel their irritation. Never criticize a specific individual in a presentation. If it is necessary, do it very indirectly, and if possible take some of the blame on yourself. In this connection, be especially watchful of those who have no sense of humor, for they lack a sense of proportion of the relative importance of things. What may appear to you as a humorous foible, strikes them as a grievous offense. This is especially important if you use irony when addressing a large group. Everyone cannot see your features well enough to discern that you intend good-natured amusement and not serious comment on their shortcomings.

Another characteristic that can distort your intent is sentimentality. The sentimental person meets an idea with excessive emotional response. If an event is merely unfortunate, to him it is a first-magnitude disaster. If you have a little good news to report, he goes into a state of euphoria, "God's in his heaven, all's right with the world." If a child has a kind word for him, it brings tears to his eyes. If someone politely enters a negative to his viewpoint, the dissenter becomes an enemy who must be destroyed. Cruelty always lives side-by-side with sentimentality as shown by the historical figures of Ivan the Terrible, Hitler, and Stalin. But the uneasy duo permeates the character of many lesser men. They are mercurial—with you one minute, and violently in opposition the next. Often, they live in a world of fantasy, and are quick both to accept those statements that reinforce their fantasy, and to demolish those that threaten it. They have a tendency to polarized attitudes toward others—everyone is either a "first-class man" or a "bum." They abominate subtle gradations of feeling or classification. This makes them very tricky to deal with when presenting an idea that involves complex relationships, because of their need for oversimplification.

A person who enjoys the reputation of being "well-informed" can be very helpful to a presentation if given a chance to display his information in public. He gets great satisfaction from correcting others—even if he has to resort to pedantry. He also likes to furnish the authoritative word on any subject. The more you can let yourself be so "assisted" by the well-informed person, the better his opinion of you and your idea. The one way to lose his support is to contradict his information with yours. If he is wrong and must be corrected, hedge your own correction with all kinds of qualifications to preserve his reputation—at least in his own eyes. If his incorrect contribution is actually irrelevant to your idea, it is best to let it go by without correction.

Every person struggles against his own set of anxieties and problems. The weight of any problem is related to the significance it has for the person who carries it. If an individual intrudes a personal worry, which appears trivial to you, into your presentation, do not let your opinion show. An ironic but true aphorism states: "Other people's problems are far easier to solve than our own." After all, your presentation caused him to make a connection between what you want and his own state of affairs. A sympathetic response based on an attempt to see his personal, if peculiar, association will be rewarded by his attempt to go along with you, if he sees that you understand his difficulties. Quid pro quo is as effective in the give and take of a presentation as it is in diplomacy.

Above all, remember that words are *symbols*, not reality; and symbols are ambiguous. Do not be upset or surprised if a member of an audience has misunderstood your meaning. Look on it as an opportunity to have him learn from you in another way. Use an example or terminology from his own field to illustrate your point, and if he sees your idea in this more familiar dress, he begins to understand. Your grades for flexibility and competence go up in his eyes.

All of the above is merely an attempt to advise the use of tact in dealing with an audience as a collection of individuals. It suggests the benefits of developing a peculiar skill: the avoidance of behavior that unnecessarily offends or disturbs those courteous enough to give you a hearing. I end this section with a stanza by Harry Graham which encapsulates the message:

> Though the noblest disposition you inherit,
> And your character with piety is pack'd,
> All such qualities have very little merit,
> Unaccompanied by tact.

ON THE RELATIONS BETWEEN A PRESENTOR AND SMALL GROUPS

There exists a baffling area of scientific inquiry known as group psychology. It suffers from all sorts of unresolved questions as to what it's up to, and how it goes about its business, but even in its ramshackle state it offers insights useful for our purposes. Common sense alone tells us that people behave differently when in a group from the way they behave in individual conversations. Group psychology begins with this fact.

Presentations are usually made to groups, and we will arbitrarily classify them into large and small, with a fuzzy dividing line at about twelve. Small groups produce a psychological atmosphere different from large ones and require different approaches for maximum idea transfer.

One fundamental observation of group psychology says that two changes occur when individuals are assembled into a group: There is an *intensification* of the emotions; and there is an *inhibition* of the intellect. Wide disagreement exists on the mechanisms that produce these changes, but there is a general agreement that they are explained by the psychological processes that establish emotional connections between members of a group. (The arguments are about the nature of the processes, and need not detain us.) There is also agreement that as the group grows in size, both the inhibition of intellect and the intensification of emotions grow roughly in proportion. Demagogues instinctively know that they can effectively harangue only masses. They are notoriously ineffective in a conference room. Hitler knew what he was doing, giving his speeches in huge, packed stadiums at night, with light from torches placed in military and symbolic formations. It is hard to imagine a better arrangement if your purpose is to drive out all reason and replace it with pure frenzy. This was a cruel and expensive way to test a thesis of academic professors, but one can't blame them for misapplication of a theory. Such an aberration was a modern version of primitive tribal rites, where constant drumming and dancing in large groups produce similar effects—on a small scale—to those at Nuremberg. This also explains why missionaries never defeat witch doctors if they approach their prospective parishioners with intellectual arguments. Their two successful methods have been either to convert the chief intellectually, *as an individual* (away from his drummers), or to use Western medicine (as super-magic) to take on the witch doctor's incurable cases and work their crowbar in from that side. Trade may have followed the flag, but religion follows the hypodermic. The missionary's motives may be humanitarian, but the psychology is important to give them a chance to flourish.

Thus, knowledge of group behavior can be used to enhance an idea's chance for successful adoption. Ignorance of it leads to presentations that are based *solely* on appeal to intellectual appreciation. They neglect the larger role of emotional ties between members of an audience, and usually fail.

In a small group the presentor knows everyone—at least, he is introduced to them one-by-one if he doesn't. The members also know a great deal about each other, and how each of their fellows can generally be expected to react to different kinds of ideas. They have relations of status, areas of competence, special responsibilities, and vested interests, which will give different coloration to remarks they make about the presentation. They will watch each other for their reactions as the presentation unfolds, and what they see will exercise an influence on their own final judgment—perhaps unconscious, but not negligible. Each member of a small audience knows that he will be called on to express his opinion; thus people in small groups tend to be more attentive than in large. Those unsure of their position prefer to hold their expressions of opinion until others have made known how they feel about the idea presented.

If a group contains one or two individuals of higher status or more exalted reputation for competence than the rest, their reactions will be closely observed, and their initial remarks will exercise great influence on the general opinion. For this reason it is wise to determine who these natural leaders are *beforehand*, and direct the most powerful points of your story at them, preferably eyeball-to-eyeball. Also show that you appreciate that certain parts of your presentation impinge on the various areas of competence of each man before you with special force. Make sure you look at the individual involved at the time and allude to his special interest by referring to him by name. When you do this the first time, every other member will be alert for potential reference to his own area of work, interest, or experience. Later, during the discussion period, you will have a good reason to refer certain questions to him—and he will expect it.

The smaller the group, the better it is to emphasize reason and common sense, soft-pedaling the emotional appeal until the discussion starts. You then have better leads as to where the sensitive areas are, especially when a natural leader begins the discussion.

With the small group, avoid the use of outright humor in the direct presentation. If any is used, it should be of the quiet, drawing-room kind. Funny stories or jokes as such have no place with the small group—and seldom draw much more than an embarrassed smile. However, anecdotes drawn directly from the field of work involved in your idea are very powerful. If they contain a wry observation, from a worker in the field, which supports your position, all the better. But don't put your own capping remark on top. Sometimes a tape recording of the conversations of people who have been, or will be, affected by your proposal is very persuasive and authentic. This is especially forceful if they have been participants in experimental situations where your idea has been tried out. The tape recorder is one device that works better with small groups than with large.

In opening the presentation to a small group, get to the problem-statement as quickly as possible and describe the entire presentation format briefly. Indicate the terminal time by the clock (10:45) and announce that full discussion will follow. Also, at the end of the presentation, make a simple, clear, direct request of just what you want them to do, so that the discussion following can go right on to the relevant questions. Do not pussyfoot here! In small groups a brisk opening and a clean finish are very important. Another subtle effect is created if you end the direct presentation just a few minutes ahead of the time you promised. All sorts of overtones of reliability and efficiency surround your idea when this is done—for it is quite rare.

Do not make a direct presentation longer than forty-five minutes, preferably thirty, to a small group, for even a brilliant performer will produce a sense of monotony, which one of the audience will interrupt merely to get relief. If it has to be longer, break the story up into natural pieces, and use different men as presentors. Also, intersperse some discussion—limited in advance by the clock—between direct presentations. You can also use a faster speech rate with small groups than with large. A slow, deliberate delivery, impressive in the auditorium, makes a small group edgy, for they are geared to speed.

In small groups, do not appear too anxious to please by moderating and toning down your original idea to the point of emasculation. The audience dislikes *personal* stubbornness, but admires tenacity for your idea—even if they reject it. Also, as covered in Chapter 7, some questions are raised just to see how strongly you feel about its merits. This is a technique often used by the natural leaders in the audience. It is far better to go out with a bang than a whimper—at least you will be welcome again.

The reason you are before the group is your alleged competence. Two kinds of power are involved in a presentation to a small group. You must demonstrate *power to do* something; the small group has the *power over resources* needed to give your idea a chance. Few groups will ever surrender resources to weak hands. Your job is to convince the small group that your presumed competence is *real*. This is largely an emotional decision on their part. When they begin feeling and thinking: "I believe he's right," you're on the downhill slope to getting what you need.

ON THE RELATIONS BETWEEN A PRESENTOR AND LARGE GROUPS

Presentations to large groups require a different approach from that appropriate to individuals or small groups for two reasons: 1. Large groups are subjected to a presentation primarily so that they *understand* a proposal. Seldom are they used to give final *approval* to a course of action. 2. The principle of greater inhibition of intellect and intensification of emotions as a group grows larger requires more emphasis on the dramatic and emotional elements of a presentation, as compared to its intellectual content.

The physical circumstances of the presentation often prevent the presentor from knowing each individual in the audience. In very large groups he may not know personally anyone except the man who introduces him. The audience, in the absence of personal knowledge of the presentor, is forced to make its judgments of an idea almost entirely from the impressions he creates during the presentation. The individual members bring to a large assembly a higher degree of expectancy and uncertainty, and the general hubbub of their gathering process creates an atmosphere similar to that seen in theater lobbies before the curtain goes up. They meet and greet one another, exchange pleasantries, and speculate among themselves on what they are about to hear. The buzz of many conversations and the noise of people seeking seats add something of a festive air even to the most solemn and serious gatherings. Whether the meeting is a Rotary club luncheon, a commencement, the opening of a Legislature, or a conclave of cardinals, the assembly process of a large group offers convicing evidence of man's nature as a social animal. Such groups require different forms of control; ceremony, ritual, and formality have developed in response to that need, and they augment the emotional element. The wise presentor *uses* these attributes of the large group; he does not fight or ignore them. Of course, he shouldn't go so far as to embellish his presentation with colorful, ancient costumes, band or organ music, and majestic processions, but a presentation to a large group is related in many ways to those human gatherings that do. Oratory is the old-fashioned method of making such presentations, yet many of its lessons and techniques are still quite applicable. (Though a successful presentor today would be embarrassed if told he was considered to be "a fine orator.")

Listen to this description of Daniel Webster, as an example of the old-fashioned style: "Daniel Webster was always the big event. There he was, the greatest orator in the land, and he looked it. People gazed at his massive brow, his deep-set eyes, and they felt his greatness of mind and spirit.

"He'd start cold as a clam, with something everybody agreed was so. Then he'd build his case, calling on their common sense, their better natures, on the names and deeds of heroes past. Finally he'd work up to a crashing climax that, like as not, had folks all choked up and dabbling at their eyes.

"Daniel Webster showed Americans that brilliant logic is at its best when it appeals to men's hearts as well as their heads—when facts are touched with compassion and reason with human understanding."

Few presentors can reach such heights—and if they used the identical style today would probably astonish sophisticated audiences. But the objective of a presentation to large groups is still the same: to move them emotionally in order to achieve intellectual understanding of an idea.

The opening to a large group sets the stage, and should be a clear statement on which most everyone can agree. You can even descend to platitude without harm. Before making the statement, wait until you have absolute silence. Grip the podium, look straight at a specific person in the audience, halfway back, and wait! It may seem like hours to you, but even the noisiest groups come to heel in a very short time—usually within seconds. It is also best to begin with medium-scale loudness—whispers and trumpet blasts went out with bustles. If you have a good story or anecdote *to illustrate your statement,* use it quickly. Nothing attracts a large group's attention at the outset like a story they see themselves retelling later. However, do not use an irrelevant story or joke. They confuse and irritate.

Those presentors with a gift for humor are in their native elements with large groups. If only one person gets a laugh from something you've said, his reaction will infect others, and it will sweep over the audience. Large groups tend to be tense right after you begin, and everyone welcomes the chance to relax that an amusing incident affords. The alternation of humor with deep seriousness gains acceptance for you as a man of well-rounded character and probity. (Presentations to international audiences are exceptions. Unless you are thoroughly at home in the culture and language of your host country, avoid attempts at humor. They usually embarrass, and often offend, persons reared in environments different from your own.) If possible, also weave into your presentation references to specific problems of the persons in the audience, for they need to identify with your message in ways that make it relevant to their lives and concerns.

Large groups, unlike small ones, want to be inspired and are especially grateful for signs that you appreciate their contributions, intelligence, and experience.

The reaction time of large groups is slower than small ones made up of the same people. This counsels a slower-paced delivery, liberally sprinkled with pauses, and a complete absence of fuss and hurry, which puts an audience on edge. It is better to cut than to hurry. Gestures must be large-scale, yet natural and appropriate. Nervous ones of little amplitude or meaning distract if they are too rapid, and have the unhappy tendency to accelerate your delivery.

In anticipating questions, one can safely use rhetorical forms with large groups which are tasteless with small. *Examples*: "One may very well ask why . . ."; "Someone is now thinking: 'Why didn't he . . .' "; "You may feel that you've heard all this before, and ask: 'What's so new about this?' Let me explain."; "The Skeptical probably think: 'Isn't this just another clever gimmick?' Let me tell them why it's not . . ."; and so on.

One method suggested for the small groups is inappropriate for large—the singling out of natural leaders for special emphasis of important points. First, they are difficult to identify in large groups; but more importantly, large audiences actually resent the neglect it implies of the rest of them. They especially dislike it when they themselves do not know the man you notice, for they feel locked out from what seems to be a coterie or "in group." Large groups do welcome recognition of a humble person amongst them, or a "grand old man," well-known and loved by the majority, but who does not have much power over them.

There are two things that lower the respect an audience has for a presentor: a prepared text read word-for-word, and apologies made for appearing before them. Few presentors have the skill to read a script with the nuances, color, and emotion of conversation. If they did, they would be first-class actors, for it takes professional actors many years of concentrated work to do it with even passable skill. Strangely enough, the same men who wouldn't dream of doing it with a small group, turn right around and embrace a written speech as a drowning man clutches a life preserver when they have to face a large group. The results are always inferior to their normal conversation. An audience subconsciously decides that if a speech is read, someone other than the presentor wrote it. Also, they feel that a man who reads a speech does not know as much about the subject as he implies; and, that a man who improvises around a structure of topics in his own words knows far more about the subject than he is presenting. Questions flood the natural improviser, and seldom go to the monotonous reader. The resulting discussion helps one and harms the other.

Apology for making a presentation destroys emotional rapport at the outset. If apology parades as false modesty, the audience justly resents it; if you are incompetent, they will find it out soon enough for themselves. In the development stages of a presentation, you can admit being on thin ice on some technical matters, but this creates a much different effect, for you are then inviting participation on that particular phase from people in the audience with special knowledge, not excusing your bungling of the entire presentation. If you are truly incompetent, it is better not to go on. You will harm both your idea and your reputation. Long-winded recognition of everyone of eminence, and profuse thanks for the invitation have little positive value at the beginning. If you honestly feel them, these sentiments are best woven into your discourse at appropriate places, never at the beginning or the end. Very little is lost by their omission.

In presentations to large groups you are least able to *command* acceptance of your idea. Persuasion must grow of itself in the minds of the audience from the experience you create for them. Any device that enriches the experience is permitted. Some are afraid to show their own self-interest in an idea. Yet this is often useful, if it takes second place to the idea itself. Audiences are not fools; they know that no idea develops without some personal motivation. When that motivation is admitted frankly, and is coupled with a sense of the presentor's own personal ability to carry the idea to realization, together with his willingness to assume a great deal of the risk, a powerful moral authority envelops the idea.

Cautious people are attracted to the courageous. When they see courage in others, they feel a sense of support by just knowing it exists. They may not like the person, but do admire him, and are grateful in a quiet way. We all look for causes to enlist in, and when we see one personified in a presentor with an appealing idea, we experience powerful attraction. If the presentor's character carries a streak of simplicity and sincerity, the effect is almost irresistible. Emotion drags intellect along by the hair.

Suspense and mystery can inject great punch into a presentation to large groups, but you must be careful to wrap up all the loose ends. These approaches require more sensitivity to the audience's feelings than any other, for you must clear up the mystery at just the right time for maximum effect. If done too soon, the effect is childish; if too late, boring. Those not blessed (or cursed) with a keen dramatic sense should avoid them.

The expectation of entertainment which lurks about a large group presentation can also be satisfied by allusions from literature and history, quotations, and poetry. These are almost always deadly in the small groups but, when done well, are viewed as compliments to a large audience's intelligence. I don't know why. Perhaps it is because people are actually more alone in the large group than in the small, and they can reflect on, reject, or warm to such allusions without having to take a position in public or show their ignorance of the allusion's relevence. Master presentors can use openings and closings based on poetry, but it must be selected by a sure hand and taste. When done well, the effect is electric. I once heard a complex account of chemical research (to an audience of six hundred) closed by an Ode from Keats. It seemed to be a signal for the standing ovation that followed.

Skill with the large group presentation comes only from trying out all sorts of things observed as a member of audiences. Continued experimentation and a little analytical reflection on the presentations you like (How did he do it?) are the best prescription for development of your own approaches. Slavish imitation breeds parodies—not skill.

SOME EFFECTS ON INDIVIDUAL BEHAVIOR DUE TO THE PRESENCE
OF OTHER INDIVIDUALS

Desire for respect from one's peers or colleagues motivates most accomplishment. Conversely, the fear of losing such respect inhibits risk-taking with new ideas unless "others are doing it." Persons in hierarchical organizations (every day that proportion grows larger) are especially sensitive to being caught in what are euphemistically called "errors of judgment." To accuse a person as guilty of one makes the worst threat possible to his progress. People who are absolutely insensitive to the feelings of others catch the slightest whiff of such suspicion against themselves.

This conservative inertia of people in groups, large or small, holds back decision until the last possible moment. Should a trend one way or the other emerge, the uncommitted in the group experience great pressure to go along. Political conventions are laboratory models of the phenomenon. The most bitter factional fights, intrigues, and cleavages during the nominating process are finally plastered over by the convention's dying act: unanimous endorsement of the battered but victorious nominee. Everyone involved frantically tries to grab a seat on his bandwagon.

When a group of individuals is exposed to a presentation, they know that they are now in a situation where they can make an "error of judgment," for they must take a position "for" or "against." Police officers see a great deal of human nature under stress, and what they observe of people in groups offers parallels to behavior during presentations. When an incident requiring police intervention occurs in the street, a crowd gathers. As the officers begin asking for witnesses, they receive so many widely different versions of what happened that it is hard to believe that all are talking about the same thing. There's also a fringe of the curious who just want to know, "What's going on?" When it becomes clear that anyone who speaks up may have to appear in court, potential witnesses seem to evaporate; everyone wants to resume bystander status, still in on the action, but from a much safer position. This sort of risk-avoidance is also seen in audiences. It is natural, and has its roots in the fact that the pain of a loss is much greater than the pleasure of an equal gain. What you are asking in presenting an idea is that the members trade an unsatisfactory, but well-known state in the present, for an improved situation, of uncertainty and risk, in the future. Hamlet puts it in two lines:

> And makes us rather bear those ills we have
> Than fly to others that we know not of.

Machiavelli observed in *The Prince* the same human propensity throughout history:

> There is nothing more difficult to carry out, nor more doubtful of success, nor more dangerous to handle, than to initiate a new order of things. For the reformer has enemies in all those who profit by the old order, and only lukewarm defenders in all those who would profit by the new order, this lukewarmness arising partly from fear of their adversaries—and partly from the incredulity of mankind, who do not truly believe in anything new until they have had actual experience of it.

Here we see why reason alone is never enough to predict the future outcome of an idea, and why the emotional force of belief must be used to overcome the natural inertia of "not wanting to become involved." The presentor must show that the *greater* error of judgment awaiting the audience lies in delay or rejection of his proposal. Since this can only be proven in the future, he is of necessity offering faith and hope, not certainty. A good presentor realizes that he is not offering the audience a bargain *from their point of view*. Ideas are always a buyer's market, for they have more places to spend their reputations, resources, and energy than just on your idea. Respect their right to choose, and they will respect your right to their attention. Like all shoppers, members of audiences pride themselves on their sales resistance. They dislike being dominated or rushed while making up their minds, and walk into a shop with the ability to say *No*. Their final choice for purchase is influenced by what others are currently buying, how long they want to live with the product, whether it will enhance the picture they have of themselves, and what others will think of their choice. Ideas, too, are "bought" and "sold," and subject to the same influences.

TECHNIQUES TO INCREASE PARTICIPATION IN DISCUSSION

After a direct presentation to a group, large or small, participation may lag because of the inertial factors above. There are several ways to overcome these.

First, the physical layout of the room exercises a subtle, powerful influence on the resultant pattern of participation. The tendency of a specific individual to participate is related to the distance between him and the presentor. (Some observers state that participation is inversely proportional to the *square* of the distance, but that is a refinement.) Notice how a large group fills the seats in an auditorium before a presentation. The timid seek seats near the back, the great bulk cluster near the middle, and a highly interested few—plus the hostile—take places in the front row. When the hall or room is too large for the group, this is a bad arrangement. If you are really interested in getting participation, your objective is *to minimize the distance between the members and your location.* Secondarily, if you have control over seating of individuals (as in a small group), minimize the distance of the natural leaders and those expected to support your proposal. Any device or deployment which helps this increases participation. For example, if the room is too large and seats are portable, have the excess removed. If fixed, have those near the back roped off with tapes or string. Move the podium as far forward as possible, or if it is too far back even then, use a small table and chair moved in close. At a long rectangular table, take your place in the *center* of one of the *long* sides, never at the foot or head. In setting up seats in a rectangular room, again arrange the seats facing the *long* wall and, if possible, curve them around the presentor's place like half of a theatre-in-the-round. Ignore the stage or platform if it is not helpful to your presentation, for most architects unconsciously place them on a short side of a rectangular room from tradition. At conferences a U-shaped arrangement of portable tables allows everyone to see each other without neck-craning, and stimulates interchange among individual members. These may appear as trivial considerations, but many a presentation has been hobbled, and some ruined, by inattention to the characteristics of the forum used. Rockets are spectacular; launching pads are drab, but nonetheless essential.

Another stimulus to discussion is for the presentor to have ready some questions *he* will ask the audience. Hopefully, he will not have to use them, but they should be prepared just in case. Questions of this kind should be addressed directly to an individual by name, if possible. You can also solicit *contrary* evidence to your position, if all else fails. In a large group you can ask questions that call for a show of hands: "May I see how many (electrical engineers, housewives, statisticians, teamsters, teachers, etc.) are in the audience?" After the hands are up, then say, "I have a question for any one of you which we should have your opinion on." Another approach is to make a statement like: "We have done our best to take account of everything we could think of. But we certainly want to know if anyone more expert than we are in some of these areas feels that we have overlooked something important." If silence meets this, you gain additional points for thoroughness.

The best stimulus for participation is an atmosphere that makes it safe. Courtesy and willingness to treat every question, even stupid ones, seriously, encourage people to risk participation. When they sense that their experience and opinions are really welcome, few will resist the chance to join in.

COPING WITH PERCEPTION OBSTACLES

Perception involves both *receiving* the impressions of our senses and the subsequent *interpretation* of these impressions. Transfer of an idea from your head to another's depends on his first receiving your message with his ears and eyes, and then translating what he receives into its *meaning for him.* Even assuming equal physical capabilities for all members of the audience, their past experience and present mood govern the interpretation they put on what you say or show them. Consider the difference in the effects produced on the same person exposed to a presentation of an idea immediately after he has experienced a dressing down from his boss, and after he has just been given a raise in salary. Or compare the reception of a presentation by the head of a corporation whose stock has been going down, to the same man after it has started to rise again. Everyone, high and low, experiences moods which alter his interpretation of signals from his environment. Generally, the more secure a person feels, the clearer is the perception he brings to new ideas. There is an old definition of an educated man which holds that "He is someone who can entertain himself, entertain others, and entertain a new idea." (Here one should not confuse mere *schooling* with education; that is as bad as confusing plumbing with culture.) Mental security characterizes those who have two qualities: Competence and Motivation. Insecurity attends those who do not. In fact, the inverse of competence and motivation can be tabulated like this:

	Quality	*Inverse*	
Effective Personality (Secure)	Competence	Slogans	Ineffective Personality (Insecure)
	Motivation	Hostility	

(*Suggested by Dr. Frederick Herzberg*)

Audiences composed entirely of incompetent, hostile, and frustrated people can only be dealt with by the techniques of the crowd orator. They hate reality, which has treated them so roughly, and prefer to hear over and over again variations on the slogans that excuse their feeling of inferiority. They insist on perceiving impressions through a telescope, which magnifies the injustice they suffer, and collect slights, which confirm their feelings. Every bartender knows many such people, for they furnish a large proportion of his habitual clientele. These unfortunates are almost pathological cases of insecurity, but every person is incompetent in something, and has hostile feelings against things or persons he fears. The significance of this insight for the presentation of an idea bears on how to cope with the islands of incompetence or hostility that are found in everyone. This is necessary, for if you inadvertently reinforce these feelings, the members of an audience will *not* perceive your idea as you intend. It is as though a large red cloud screens everything you say thereafter. Reporters in need of a story know that they can always produce news by telling a public figure what one of his enemies said about him. Trigger hostility and you get fireworks —but your idea may get burned in the process. You do not have the reporter's neutrality. If your presentation must go into areas beyond the competence of the majority in the audience, then you *must* assume the burden of increasing their competence to a level sufficient to understand your concept. If not prepared to do this, you are on a fool's mission with your idea. Technical, scientific, and other specialists are very negligent in this regard, and Chapter 9 contains suggestions for coping with this grave obstacle to clear perception. "That's the craziest thing I every heard!" may signify a presentation failure, but, "It's over my head," leads to the same destination. This is a more melancholy outcome, because intelligent and careful development can almost always avoid it. Besides, we are grateful to those who help us grow, but deeply resent those who show contempt for what we already know.

Certain words and attitudes ignite hostility faster than you can extinguish it *and are different for every audience.* Unless you consciously select one in order to arouse interest (a hazardous method, but sometimes successful in masterly hands), it is best to avoid them. They can trigger so many bad associations that nothing penetrates the mental uproar set off. Should you deliberately use them to impugn your opposition, you are engaging in propaganda and mob oratory. The intelligent in the audience will feel disgust and turn away. Unfamiliarity with an audience— especially large groups—should be offset by conversation with someone who knows their firmly held beliefs and intellectual affiliations in order to avoid embarrassing lapses. Such reconnaissance will prevent errors that are similar to lectures on the evils of bureaucracy to civil servants; the merits of atheism to religious groups; the virtues of vegetarianism to meat packers; and the pleasures of smoking to the Cancer Society. They may satisfy your own ego (and hostility!) by striking an exhibitionistic blow, but no one seriously interested in getting an idea accepted so indulges himself.

Presentations are social events. People come together for a common purpose and interact with one another. Someone interested in achieving better understanding of normal human behavior can learn a great deal in this arena of ideas. As his knowledge grows, so does his presentation skill; each reinforcing the other in mutual support. When you begin to feel that the small groups are not firing squads, and the large groups not spectators at a hanging, you have passed the worst obstacles on the road to mastery.

6

How to Use—
and Abuse—Visual Aids
"For They Have Eyes and See Not"

Children instinctively draw almost as soon as they speak. They do it as though yearning to supplement faulty oral expression of their feelings about an expanding world. For most of us, as speech skill increases, our drawing skills wither away. Sometimes the process is accelerated by inept instruction, which demands rigid conformity to rules for representation. Strangely, those who cultivate artistic skills often fail to develop their oral skills. The inarticulate painter is a cliché of literature. When others start talking to communicate a thought, the artist seeks his brushes and paints. And yet neither type ever succeeds in completely suppressing the talent of his weak side.

Our entire heritage of art, whether bisons scratched on walls of primitive caves, collossi of Egypt, frescoes of the Renaissance, portraits and landscapes of the easel painters, or the rich variety of our own age, can be looked at as a gigantic warehouse of visual aids. They help us *see* both what we have in common and where we differ with men in other stages of the human drama.

Art communicates the *ideas* of various times and places in ways independent of language. Therein lies its strength and timeless appeal. Most historians feel compelled to include illustrations selected from this warehouse of art to supplement and clarify their narrative. Even the most austere at least need maps, one of the oldest visual aids of all. Thus the instinct of childhood inclines us to use the visual as well as the oral any time we wish to present our ideas with greatest force to others. Few of us would claim such lofty relationships, but the diagrams on a tablecloth developed during an enthusiastic luncheon meeting share a common source with all of man's artistic past. Alexander and Caesar scratched troop dispositions in the sand with a stick to ensure comprehension by their brawny generals. Drawings have been used far more than writing on every construction job since the pyramids. Shipwrights built models of their proposed vessels in order to instruct their workmen. Even Shakespeare had his actors move cardboard trees and canvas columns about the stage to heighten the impact of his dramas. Astronomers, soaring in their intellectual clouds, constructed little merry-go-rounds to keep track of planetary orbits. It is difficult to think of one region in the world of ideas where visual aids have not been either useful or indispensable for understanding.

Language itself employs the visual aids of metaphor, simile, and anecdote when actual ones cannot be used, as in novels and essays. Motion pictures and television programs are nothing but ensembles of visual aids glued together by some coherent idea. (At least the good ones are.) Examples could be multiplied, but they would all make the same point: the eye can help the ear understand.

This little excursion suggests that visual aids *can* enhance the presentation of an idea, but their effective use depends on meeting the criteria of the arts rather than those of pure reason. We will now use some of those criteria as they apply specifically to visual aids suitable for presentation. There are important craft aspects of visual aids (which influence selection of the correct types) as well as elements of over-all and detailed design generally applicable. When these are observed, the visual portion amplifies the presentation; when ignored, visuals produce interference and obstacles to comprehension. Like all powerful tools, visual aids do constructive work only when guided by trained intelligence. Otherwise they are dangerous. Their use does not automatically improve a presentation any more than a power saw automatically improves carpentry.

Some of the following hints and advice may appear pedestrian and obvious. They are included because I have seen many obvious things ignored by all sorts of experienced persons who really had something to say. Their eyes may have been on the stars, but they tripped over cracks in the pavement. Every type of visual aid has its strength and weakness. We shall examine each one's characteristics in detail, but there are some considerations that apply to every type, and we will take these up first.

SIZE

Nothing could be more obvious than the need for a visual aid to be *seen*. Yet this is often ignored by presentors. I once sat through a lecture by a scientist of the highest reputation who scribbled and erased on a small portable blackboard before an audience of three hundred in the Great Hall of the National Academy of Sciences. None of us knew what we missed, except a good hour of our time. One gentleman even gave up after using a pocket telescope.

The only rule for over-all size is that the most detailed text or number should be clearly visible to someone in the last row. You wouldn't use a home movie screen in a theater or the theater's in your living room. If over-all size is limited, then the size of the lettering must be increased to compensate. Sometimes too large a visual is used. (This comes from wrong lenses or distances in projection apparatus.) The effect of this error is just as bad, but instead of the audience becoming bored and frustrated, they begin to make humorous remarks as gigantic images spill over the screen and appear on the ceiling, curtains, furniture, or their colleague's backs. Never take someone else's word that things are the right size. Sit in the furthest place likely to be occupied, and look at your visuals from there. The ten minutes of inspection required is the best insurance you can buy. If things are not satisfactory, make them so. Different lenses, screen, and distances; rearrangement of the chairs; or, if time permits, choice of another type of visual aid, are investments in success. Any amount of compromise with perfect vision is paid for proportionally in lost members of your audience.

Height of the visual is related to size. Audiences will not crane their necks at high angles, or bob and weave to glimpse information near the bottom edge.

Finally, if you cannot solve the problems of size and height, it is preferable not to use any visuals at all. Artists give a great deal of thought to selection of the proper size canvas for a specific subject. Museum directors expend even more effort placing art works in ways that produce maximum effect. You may not have their skill, but your interest should be as great, if you are really interested in the success of your idea. The best reaction to the size criterion is the same for a presentor as for an artist: no one should notice that it has been met.

TYPOGRAPHY

Type founders since Gutenberg have developed hundreds of different typefaces for printing books or newspapers. Almost none are satisfactory when blown up to the large sizes necessary for visual aids. The exception is sans serif ("without serifs"—the little curlicues that help distinguish one typeface from another). This face takes enlargement or reduction extremely well. It looks like this:

ABCDEFGHIJKLMNOPQRSTUVWXYZ
abcdefghijklmnopqrstuvwxyz
12345678910

Notice how closely this type resembles draftsman's lettering, which is made by a pen of constant thickness. The shapes of the letters also hold up well in colors when used in view-graphs and slides. If you do not use type, hand-printed, small letters and capitals are very effective. They are far preferable to enlarged typewriter letters, which are always bad in visuals. When used on flip-charts, or easels with large pads of paper, the hand-printed letters are easily made with felt pens (one type is Magic-Markers). Color is easy to use for special emphasis, and many shades are available.

Script should never be used except in the form produced by second graders—very round and stylized. Unless you wish a special effect, avoid it. On blackboards and blank page easels, improvised script can be deadly. It is far easier to learn to "print" letters than to discipline your normal handwriting to the large size required. Few believe this until they try both. Many "visuals" produced in the heat of a presentation are absolutely indecipherable to everyone involved—including their producers—at the end of a presentation. In fact, too much of this foolishness brings the end sooner than planned for. (We will cover ways to cope with improvised visuals during the treatment of specific types of aids).

The size of type depends on the over-all size of the visual. Again, the *smallest* size letter should be clear from the greatest distance involved. Other larger letters are scaled to the smallest that meets this test of clarity. Too much variety in the size of type in a series of visuals makes an audience jumpy. Keep the size of headings constant throughout a series, and use smaller sizes on the subsidiary content of each visual as an indication of the relative importance of the point made. This is a form of "argument perspective." It is similar to the two kinds of perspective used by artists of the Western world: Linear perspective makes more distant objects *smaller*, and aerial perspective makes them *hazier* and *less detailed*. When we say a picture has "depth," we are acknowledging an artist's skill in these two techniques of conscious distortion. Byzantine artists did not use these methods. Instead, they used a technique much like that necessary for a presentation. The relative size of things in their holy pictures, or ikons, is determined by the *importance* of the person or object shown, and has no relation to whether they are "close" or "far" from the viewer. Most of us find these pictures strange, until we learn the artistic assumptions.

Like considerations of over-all size, the best test of lettering is whether it goes unnoticed. It then causes the least interference with the message carried.

VISUALS USED AS "PROMPTERS"

Many presenters embrace visual aids for their value as "lecture notes." There is nothing wrong with this and often a great deal right about it. But the presentor's needs for prompting must be judged by the impact produced on the audience. Ordinary lecture notes need to make sense only to the lecturer and are usually a mystery to someone else who inspects them. "I don't care how odd they may seem, they make sense to me," is a correct attitude if the notes are not intended to be seen by others. But if these notes are to be made the basis of visual aids (or the aids used as notes) they must *first* meet the test as aids to audience comprehension.

A series of visuals is often reproduced in handout form for members of the audience to take away with them. Some presentations may require that the same story be disseminated to other audiences by the people who first hear the presentation. They will almost always wish to use the same set of visuals that were used for them. Since you cannot control these subsequent versions of your idea, embedding your idea in a coherent set of visual aids ensures that the main points in *your* presentation will be *seen* by future audiences—if not heard. The set of visuals must be able to stand alone and be understood even if unaccompanied by an oral presentor. This is the most stringent test of a series of visuals. The process of meeting this test sharpens them no end, and they then become a superb set of prompters, even in the hands of inept presentors. Coherence demands that each visual's relation to the others in a series be clear. Each one should contribute to the total idea, and still make sense standing alone. These are also the identical tests for objects in a good still-life painting.

Here are some ways to get coherence. Every visual should have a *headline* at the top which states its message. If two or more items are shown to be related (like two graphs that show one item dependent on another), the relationship should be spelled out. The *bottom* of each visual should carry a statement or conclusion of "what it means." This can also hint its relation to the next visual if put in the form of a question. For example, "Car sales appear to depend on disposable income. Can we use this to help our predictions?" Then the next visual shows your answer, and so on. (The method of opposites in Chapter 3 is particularly apt here.)

Another hint from painting, of use to visual design, is this dictum: No picture should contain more than seven major elements. No one knows why. This rule comes entirely from observation of masterpieces. Almost none contain more, perhaps because the complexities of composition and perception of relations go out of control. Statements or items beneath the headline message must actually be relevant to it, or the viewer becomes confused. If he cannot make the connection after thinking about it for a few seconds, the train of persuasion is broken. Subsidiary statements whose relevance to the headline are obvious to the presentor himself must be checked by someone not thoroughly immersed in the subject of the presentation.

There is a way to test a series of visuals for continuity and coherence very quickly. It is well worth the little time required and often suggests the solution to the weakness it discloses. Here it is:

Write down in the same sequence as your proposed visuals the *headline,* and the *bottom conclusion statement,* indented under the headline of each visual. Do not add any other information to the list. This is important. If a crucial point to your development is buried in a *supportive* statement rather than in a headline or conclusion, you can detect it quickly. You will most likely miss it if you merely flip through the visuals themselves. Remember, the audience will retain the top and bottom of a good visual after they see that the supportive material in between has convinced them of a message's correctness. They will usually forget the supportive detail.

After making a listing of the headline and conclusions in sequence, examine it for the flow of development it creates. If there are unnecessary duplications, eliminate them. If there are omissions or jumps too difficult for a viewer's comprehension, add appropriate headlines and conclusions at the right place. These are often available from supportive material on some of the visuals. Only after you have refitted and tailored your list to the idea's requirements can you feel secure that the whole and the parts are in proper balance. You can then safely trust anyone to use them in presenting your idea by proxy; it is very risky otherwise.

Presentors who reproduce their visuals in smaller size as a handout to the audience often commit a great error. This otherwise admirable and considerate act can backfire on the presentor if he distributes the handout to the audience before he makes the presentation. This happens because every individual picks his way through the pages without any guidance. While you are at one spot in your development, his attention is directed to something else in the package. He cannot then pay any attention to what you are *saying*, for the human mind can handle *only one thought at a time*.

The virtues of the packaged visuals become transformed into a vice. A far better way to use the package is to make a statement of this type: "The charts and other visuals which I will use in this presentation have been put together in a small pamphlet which Frank will distribute during the break after the direct presentation. They are quite complete and are intended to eliminate the need to take notes as I go along. We can also use the booklets during the question period if you like." With this approach you *enhance* attention paid you by removing the distractions of note-taking. Few people can take notes without missing something important. Many presentors are flattered when they see flurries of note-writing. They should remember that every time the pencils start, the next part of their story will not be received—at least not as they intend.

DEGREES OF FINISH

A friend of mine who enjoyed a deserved reputation as a superb presentor of complex ideas once made a mistake. He was rescued by the shrewd advice of an older veteran of many high-level battles. The advice struck my friend as completely irrational, but he followed it on faith. It worked as if by magic. He and I have had several discussions over the years as to why. We still do not know for sure, but he does observe the principle scrupulously whenever he uses visual aids. Here is the incident:

My friend was leader of a group of experts who developed an entirely new approach to the training of personnel. In the course of investigations, experiments, and discussions in most areas of his company, his group produced a fine kit of visual aids to present their ideas. Over the months, and after several exposures to many kinds of audiences, they honed and refined their visuals close to perfection by any standards. Starting with blackboards, they went on to the devices we will consider later: flip-charts and view-graphs, and finally two 35 millimeter slide projectors in tandem. Every device to clarify understanding got its chance. Color was used to direct attention to important items; illustrative details on one slide were seen in relation to the over-all picture on another projector; and as each item was presented, the oral narration was perfectly keyed to underline and amplify the visual story.

I saw this presentation later, and it was a model of its kind. The evangelical zeal of the group and their first-class presentation skills soon led to the need for the top people in his company to embrace, reject, or modify the program proposed for companywide use. The executive in charge of personnel was asked to arrange for a presentation to the president and his staff. Before doing so the executive wisely asked my friend's group to run through their latest version for him. They did a superb job. Every detail and lesson they had learned was brought to bear. Timing was exquisite. They had even built an acoustic cabinet for the projectors, so that no one could hear them in operation. When they finished, they expected such enthusiastic compliments as they got when they presented the story to their previous audiences. Instead, the personnel chief sat silently, fingertips together, shaking his head. The presentors were baffled and upset. Everyone of them knew they could not possibly do better. After enduring the silence as long as he could, my friend said to the executive: "What do you think?"

"It's no good. Your presentation is simply too slick."

The group felt a sense of outrage, which they suppressed with difficulty.

To their cascade of questions, the executive answered, "Yes, everything is perfectly clear. Yes, there is convincing evidence on every point. Yes, the alternatives all look bad. No, nothing relevant has been overlooked. Yes, it is a first-class job. Yes, you have carried out your assignment in a thoroughly professional way."

Then what was the matter?

"My colleagues will find the razzle-dazzle offensive and will become uncomfortable. They will feel that they have no place at all to apply their judgment. I'm afraid if you show them what I saw, they will modify your proposal, and *I don't want that to happen*. It's too good."

Then what should they do?

"Make the visuals look cheaper and less finished. Even if it costs a little more, it will be worthwhile. Use only one projector. Make some of the slides in black and white. Put some of the visuals' points on a blackboard or paper easel. Use some hand lettering instead of set type. Miss a few cues when one man turns the story over to another. Right now you come on like professional actors. But don't change the story's *message*. Keep the presentation as it is *except for this session*."

Now it was the group's turn to shake their heads. To their credit, they followed the old pro's advice and succeeded brilliantly. Their proposal became the policy of their company because the executive knew their audience better than they ever would. He detected immediately the clash between what his colleagues liked and what my friend's group had produced. The group had erred in misjudging the "degree of finish" appropriate. They had overshot in an area where undershooting is far more common. Incidentally, when asked to put their story on for high-level groups *in other companies*, the slick, high-finish job worked best.

After I heard of this case, I became sensitive to the influence of the degree of finish on the effectiveness of visuals. Close observation given to scores of presentations leads to these generalizations: 1. As the need to *inform* an audience increases, the greater should be the degree of finish. 2. As an audience's *power to approve* increases, the lower should be the degree of finish. In your *own* organization, the power to approve usually increases with the rank of the audience. Presentations to lower ranks carry a much greater pure information and understanding content. Presentations to audiences outside your organization are almost entirely informational and should employ the highest polish. There is one exception: those outsiders who have governmental authority to approve or disapprove your proposals. With these, the degree of finish should also decline as their power increases. Another generalization applies to the *size* of the audience (see Chapter 5 on the psychological aspects involved). 3. The larger the audience, the greater should be the degree of finish.

With these three guides in mind, the presentor can use his own taste to determine the degree of finish appropriate to a specific audience.

Those with algebraic inclinations (probably a small group) can think of the relationships in this way:

$$\text{Optimum Degree of Finish} = \frac{\text{Size of Audience}}{\left(\dfrac{\text{Approval Power}}{\text{Information Needs}}\right)}$$

(I must anticipate those who will point out that absolutely no approval power makes the degree of finish equal to infinity. My answer can only be: that is a definition of an artistic masterpiece.) This view implies a hard lesson for presentors and those who advise them: the optimum degree of finish changes from one audience to another, as well as from one subject to another.

All of us have seen men of the highest eminence in all areas of life make unbelievably bad presentations to large audiences. They admittedly possess great intelligence and experience. But they carry postures, attitudes, and styles appropriate to intimate groups, where they are highly effective, to the public platform or television studio. They use the *same* techniques regardless of the audience or subject. People who only see them addressing large audiences wonder how such leaders got where they are. Unless they take account of the implications in our little ratio for the optimum finish, such luminaries should have others do the platform and studio work for them. They harm themselves and the institutions they represent if they will not attempt to tailor the degrees of finish to the presentation needs of their ideas and proposals.

Rustic furniture can be charming in a mountain cabin, but furnishings for a state dining room demand the higher arts of the cabinetmaker. The same principles that guide the design of interiors are relevant to the degree of finish for a presentation.

STATISTICS AND CHARTS

One aspect common to most visual aids is the set of techniques used to display numbers or numerical relationships. These methods are often treated in works on statistics, almost as a melancholy resignation to the inability of nonstatisticians to penetrate the deeper recesses of analysis. They project a tone that hints: "Data is best and most fairly shown in columns and tables of numbers. However, many people can only see things from data if put in the form of graphs or diagrams. These must be made with great care to avoid bias, since they can mislead if done by amateurs. Furthermore, they are dangerous weapons when placed in the hands of the unscrupulous." In reading the warnings, one gets the impression that the statistical profession is determined to blot out the canard that there are three kinds of lies: "Lies, Damned Lies, and Statistics." The statisticians do have a case, but audiences today are far more sophisticated in these matters than when the books were written. Someone in most of today's audiences will detect flagrant attempts at distortion of the kind feared by those charged with defending the maiden, "Statistical Truth," from assaults on her virtue.

The main advantage of graphs and diagrams lies in their ability to show a *pattern* in a series of numbers which allows their meaning to be grasped more easily than do dreary columns of digits. If a graph doesn't do this, it should not be used. Hundreds of various ways to bring out the patterns are available, but selection of the "best" is a matter of taste. When not sure, work up the data in several ways. Comparison of the samples will usually show which is best. If you still can't decide, let someone similar to the people in your audience choose the one they like. Bad charts blur the point being developed; good ones spotlight it. Most statistical representations break down into five basic forms: line charts, bar charts, pie charts, distribution diagrams, and correlations. When a point requiring statistical display arises, try out all five in your mind with the data, as though you are trying to fit different styles of clothes to an individual. Settle on the one "that does the most for him" for preliminary drafting.

LINE CHARTS:

These are useful to show what has happened over a period of time and make it easy to grasp trends. Sometimes two or more items are plotted on the same grid to show how different but related measures have behaved over some period. Line charts look like this:

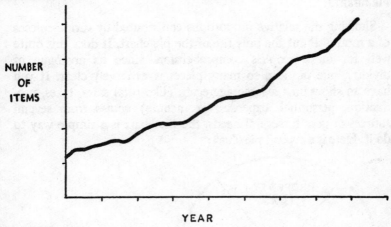

NUMBER
OF
ITEMS

YEAR

BAR CHARTS:

Here the heights of different columns, like different sized rulers, are placed side-by-side to show differences in a *common measure of performance* among a series of different entities. Children, countries, firms, schools, or anything to which a single common standard can be applied are candidates for bar charts. The individual bars can be built up of smaller, identifiable pieces if the internal composition of the entity is important. However, this kind of detail can confuse if carried too far. Typical bar charts look like this:

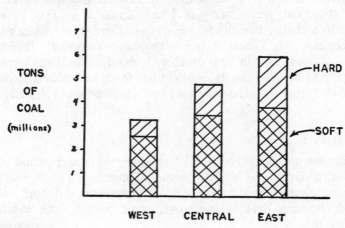

PIE CHARTS:

Showing the relative proportions contributed by various pieces of a total is about the only use of the pie chart. It does this quite well for most people's comprehension, since its analogue of dividing one pie into so many pieces is extremely clear. If you have to show how a large aggregate (like total sales, taxes, production, personnel, expenses, or income) *comes* from several sources or *goes* to several needs, the pie chart is a simple way to do it. Here is a typical pie chart:

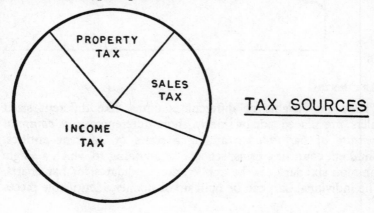

DISTRIBUTION DIAGRAMS

These are used when you need to show how a set of individual items or people can be classified according to different ranges of a single measurable characteristic. For example, to show the grades of all children in a school, you sort them out into piles of those with A's, those with B's, C's, D's, and failures. Imagine a block for each child's name with his grade marked on one side. If you pile one block on another of the same grade as you sort them, you produce a distribution diagram when you push the piles next to one another after all the sorting is completed. Your blocks would look like this:

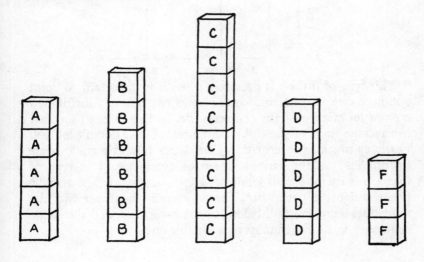

When shown on a Distribution Diagram it looks like this:

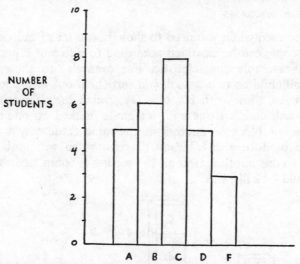

This type of display is necessary when it is important to point out how *one* characteristic of a group of things is distributed *around an average of the characteristic*. In this case, to say that the average grade of the children in a school is C doesn't tell you nearly as much as information that shows how the grades were *distributed* into the various classes of excellence. This type of diagram is useful for all kinds of data—incomes, I.Q.'s, antique prices, weights of cattle, etc. The only requirements are that the individual items must all belong to the *same* class, and the *single* characteristic displayed must be a variable one.

CORRELATIONS

This is a statistical technique which attempts to show how one characteristic of a group of items (or individuals) influences another characteristic. The word itself suggests the idea of joint relationship. When used without competence, correlations can produce ludicrous effects and suggest wrong solutions to a problem. Some howlers of the past have been demonstrations that the decline in tuberculosis correlates closely with increases in cigarette sales, or that the increase in over-all education correlates with the increase in heart disease. The errors in these cases are clear to almost everyone, but less obvious errors often require great skill to detect. One good rule to keep in mind is that *any two items that have experienced growth will always show a good correlation.* But this does not necessarily mean that one was influenced by another. There are many ways of getting around this difficulty (by removing the effects of growth), and anyone who has the need to do so should consult a statistician. If that is too painful to contemplate, a book on statistical methods is a fair substitute. So much for the hazards of correlations, now for its advantages.

We use correlations from common sense every day. It is also at the heart of the scientific method (see Chapter 9). Whenever we say "If I change this, then I can expect a change in that," we are using correlations. These are very useful as visual aids when you need to show the results of experiments or how one characteristic depends on another in a quantitative way. Such descriptions in words alone are extremely difficult and a chart often lets an audience see the relationships in a flash. Words are necessary to show the "why" of correlations, but charts are usually best to show the "what." Let's examine a simple one to get the idea.

Suppose as you looked around you for several years, you suddenly noticed that the older people get, the more they seem to weigh. As you think about it more and want to tell others of your discovery, you finally decide that a good chart would be the best way. What do you do now? You need to get only two pieces of information from many people—their age and their weight. What's the best way? You might set up a booth at a World's Fair (as Sir Francis Galton did at the London Exposition in 1886) and invite passers-by to give you their birthday, and in return you offer to weigh them scientifically, free of charge. Not bad. But after you have several thousand matched items of age and weight, what next? Now you are ready for the preliminary correlation of these two characteristics. You first draw two lines at right angles. Label one "Age" and the other "Weight," and mark off spaces for numerical scales to go as high as your largest numbers.

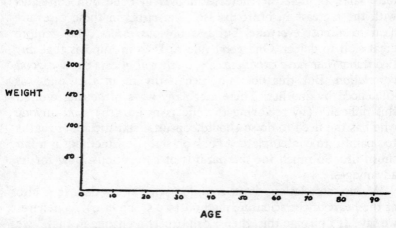

Now plot each individual's two characteristics along these scales as an X.

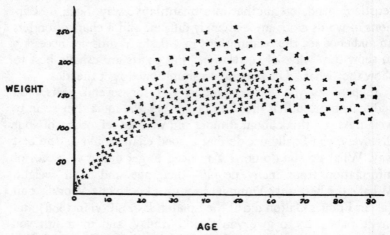

(These are usually known as "scatter charts," for obvious reasons.) If you showed this chart in this state to someone, he would be confused at first. But if he took some trouble, he could see that you are roughly right. Should he ask about the weight differences between men and women, and you luckily noted that originally when you did the weighing, you might wish to draw two *separate* charts, one for each group. After you separate men and women, the X's come a little closer but are probably still confusing. At this point you might draw a line through them to show your idea more clearly, and after that leave out the X's completely. Here is where you need skilled help or extra training. There are many ways to do this badly, and a few ways to do it correctly. Your final visuals may look something like this:

CORRELATION BETWEEN AGE AND WEIGHT

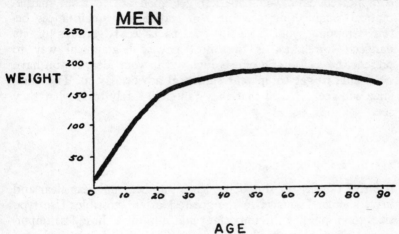

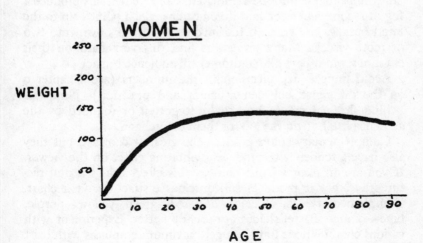

You have taken several liberties with the basic data for the sake of audience comprehension. But if you explain to the audience just what you did, few opponents can argue with your honesty. Notice that even from this little analysis the concepts of "underweight" and "overweight" now make sense in a quantitative way.

This example illustrates the elementary principles of correlation, but the subject is immense. Statisticians have erected a huge structure of variations on its theme, and if you need to deal with complicated data, you had best get good advice from mathematical, engineering, scientific, or statistical acquaintances before wrapping your idea in this package. Regardless of its dangers, correlation is the most powerful graphical way to present the causes and effects involved in your idea. If you have been able to get competent statistical advice, say so. The audience will feel relieved that they can then safely trust what they see.

AESTHETICS OF VISUAL AIDS

Strive for elegant simplicity. Keep numbers and text clear and in vernacular language to the greatest extent possible. Use type sizes to emphasize the important and minimize those less important things that cannot be eliminated. Cluttered visuals produce a fog of incomprehension and if you can't make a point leap to the mind because the visual is too involved, break it down into two or more visuals. Many presentors find this very hard on their emotions, but it pays off handsomely in audience impact.

Avoid unnecessary precision in the numbers (see Chapter 9 on the difference between accuracy and precision). Numerals behind decimal points are usually forgotten or rounded by the audience itself, so do the job for them beforehand.

Complementary colors produce the greatest contrast, but they also have a tendency to produce a vibrating effect on the viewer. If you are an impressionist painter, this effect brings a dull picture alive, but it produces subconscious distraction on a chart. Complementary sets of colors are: red—green, yellow—purple, blue—orange. Pastel shades are usually better. Experiment with various combinations until you get maximum emphasis with least distraction. Children's construction paper and opaque paints (available in dime stores) are inexpensive ways to test color combinations.

The mysteries of artistic "balance" have driven thousands of writers to produce books about it. None are really satisfactory and I certainly don't want to add to this tottering pyramid. There is one trick known to artists since antiquity that is useful to achieve the elusive quality of "balance." Artists avoid dividing a space into equal halves, vertically or horizontally. It produces monotony and deadness. Amateur photographers are advised to "place the horizon in a picture one third down from the top, or one third up from the bottom; never in the middle." This is not a bad rule of thumb, but artists have known of a better division of space. This is known as "The Golden Section." In plain words, it is the cut (section) that produces the most pleasing, dramatic, and balanced effect. This division has been checked by thousands of psychological tests in which subjects were asked to select those space divisions they found most pleasing. The average of all of them falls precisely on the Golden Section known to the Greeks and Romans and constantly used by them. Listen to the fine landscape painter of the Royal Academy, Adrian Stokes, describe it in *Practical Landscape Painting:*

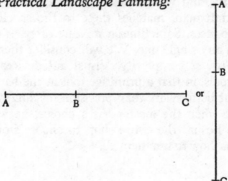

If a line AC is cut at B, so that AB is to BC as BC is to the whole line AC, the proportion thus formed seems, for some mysterious reason, almost to suggest beauty. These proportions occur continually in nature. They may be found in the human figure, in the three bones of a well-formed finger, in the placement of the eye in a head—as between the top of the forehead and the bottom of the chin—the position of the mouth between nostril and bottom of chin, etc., etc. And it is the fact that, in fine works of art, this cut usually coincides with important points in their construction.

This "cut," or division, appears to be the normal one that satisfies, and any departure from it is immediately felt, though we may not be aware of the cause.

The proportions may be kept in mind as 5 to 8 to 13 for they are close enough (i.e., $5/8 \cong 8/13$). Visuals that divide their space this way gain extra power from something that is still mysterious, but actually works. If you can't take this on faith, try it for yourself and see. Also, take a measuring look or two at some fine pictures or reproductions to test Stokes's observation. You will be surprised at how often this device is used—consciously or not.

Now that we have examined those aspects of visual aids common to all of them, we will take a closer look at the characteristics of each particular type. They are tools, and each has its own strengths and weaknesses. The experienced presentor, like any good craftsman, matches these to the specific subject and audience he faces. Sometimes a mixture of types can do the job better than any single one. We will consider them in increasing order of *physical* complexity. Visual aid devices share another quality of tools, in that a primitive tool in the hands of a master can turn out better work than precision machinery operated by a novice. But when the master has a choice, he will do his *best* work when he has the entire shop to choose from. Master presentors know how to use them all.

BLACKBOARDS

This universal device was once found only in the classroom. Not so today. Conference rooms, offices, garages, and kitchens use them because of their best features: They are easy to change, they require no floor space, and many people can see what's on them. Ideas that have a chain of development from initial statements, formulas, or shorthand words can unfold piece-by-piece as the presentor adds to the board like a fresco painter building up his picture stroke-by-stroke. For sheer spontaneity, blackboards are hard to beat. Those who use mathematical symbols prize them for another quality: the ease of erasing as they go from one deduction to another.

One mathematician I know seems to come alive at a blackboard, as an elderly conductor, creaking his palsied way to the podium, suddenly becomes charged with energy when he raises his baton. This mathematician works himself into such a joyful frenzy of writing and erasing that he has one sleeve of his coats cut two inches longer, so that he can use it to erase at high speed without pausing to pick up an eraser, as he simplifies his abstruse expressions. His wife became resigned to the cleaning bills long ago.

Blackboards, however, have serious disadvantages as visual aids. First, they are limited in the space available. This creates the need to erase previous material, perhaps not completely understood, which might be necessary during the question period. Second, when writing, the presentor must turn his back to the audience losing valuable eye contact. While engaged in writing, it is difficult to speak coherently at the same time. The audience hears all sorts of ejaculatory phrases as the man at the board unconsciously shouts out each word or symbol he puts down. The necessary gaps in the oral part of his presentation exert a feedback on him, and he then tries to shorten, condense, or speed up his writing to reduce them. This produces further obstacles to comprehension, for after a time even the presentor cannot decipher what's on the board. This comedy is enriched when partial erasing has been done. Another serious fault is that blackboards almost command the audience to take complete notes. Every time someone must write, he can't give his full attention to whatever is going on in the presentation itself. If he is being paced by a champion eraser, he doesn't listen at all.

For these reasons, blackboards should be used only for those presentations with a high mathematical or symbolic content.

Have one in the room for use by you or members of the audience to illustrate points raised in the question period. They are excellent for such scratch-pad improvising, but don't use them for the connected story of the direct presentation. It is then that their dynamic quality runs amok.

This may be a good place to give some hints for the craft of improvisation for all blank surface visual aids. You should first learn to draw straight lines: horizontal, vertical, and diagonal. Nothing destroys interest faster than a diagram all askew, with shaky, wavy, lightly drawn lines. Here is the "secret" known to artists for centuries: Put your chalk on the board where you wish the line to begin. Then look intently at the spot where you want it to end. Move the chalk firmly and rapidly while you keep your eye on the terminal spot. Ten minutes practice won't make you a Botticelli, but your audiences will notice vast improvement and show it by increased attention. The principle is the same as that involved in ball sports: "Keep your eye on the ball."

Label things clearly, preferably in printed letters. Also try to keep the letters level. Again, a few minutes practice will do wonders. For shaded areas, lay the chalk or crayon on its side and push it to the terminal point, keeping your eye there. Finally, use soft chalk rather than hard; and if you have a choice, green "blackboards" with soft yellow chalk are the easiest on the eyes. I know one professor who carries his own soft chalk. (The janitors stock only the hard because it's easier to clean.) In improvisation, avoid both fussiness and touch-up with the eraser. Broad, strong movements add force and clarity to your point. Besides, everyone can see them.

FLIP-CHARTS

Easels equipped with large pads of paper have become justifiably popular as visual aids. When blank, they are used the same as blackboards and have the additional advantage that each sheet can be saved for later reference or questions. But their great virtue comes in direct presentations, where they are prepared ahead of time. Each page is like a slide, yet can be made very cheaply with hand lettering in any colors needed. As you cover each point and move to the next, you merely flip the sheet over to expose the next visual. Handouts of the charts used can be made by typing up their content on standard-sized letter paper. Sometimes two easels are effective, so that the broader story remains in view as details relating to it are covered on a second flip-chart. When you have a transitional stage in your direct presentation, the last visual showing can be a distraction. Counter this by putting a blank sheet in the series at that point. This is especially needed when two easels are used, since the audience tries to relate what's on the subsidiary charts to the main series. When you use prepared flip-charts, don't use the same easel for improvisation. This requires you to turn all the prepared sheets over until you get to a blank; then you must return them to where you were before the interruption. Unintended comedy can develop when a presentor looks like a housewife trying to hang out her washing on a windy day. Experienced presentors will sometimes remove the blank sheets beneath their prepared ones just to restrain the overly enthusiastic improviser from the audience. Some also place small index tabs made for file folders on the edge of each visual for quick reference during questions. The audience cannot see them, but the instant reference the tabs allow brings a sense of snap and briskness to the session. This contrasts nicely to the impression produced by random rummaging through the sheets, which is far more common.

Finally, flip-charts can be made up and used in the most primitive surroundings. One of the finest visual presentations I ever saw used sheets cut from the wide roll of wrapping paper in a local store. The sheets were taped at the top to the plain wall with masking tape, one above the other, and were peeled away as the story unfolded. The audience was enchanted. They had never before been honored that way in their remote hamlet. At the end they agreed unanimously to the proposal for a dam to be built in their valley. Some said that they had always opposed it before merely because they didn't understand what was really going to happen!

LARGE CARDBOARD PANELS

These were once fashionable, but their use is always a mistake. Flip-charts to small groups are superior, and view-graphs or slides are far better for large groups. Cardboard panels are cumbersome and often warp. They require so much manhandling that they cause distraction and break the continuity of a presentation. Don't use them.

VIEW-GRAPHS

These are transparent sheets, usually 7 by 7 inches, (sometimes 10 by 10 inches), which are placed horizontally on a special projector. Many types of projectors, some quite inexpensive, are available. They are used in almost every training and information facility, by first graders and the highest government officials. The sheets themselves can be produced by service agencies and photographers throughout the country, by certain rapid copying machines, by quick developing cameras, or merely by writing on blank sheets with a grease pencil. View-graphs are extremely flexible and can be effective with groups ranging in size from three or four individuals up to a thousand. The projectors can produce almost any image size required and are simple to operate. Different lenses can be used to meet any situation encountered—but are seldom required. (Any reader unfamiliar with this device can have demonstrations from an army of salesmen.) The view-graph slides are usually mounted on inexpensive cardboard frames and several hundred can fit in a brief case. Projectors are available for rental almost everywhere. There are even lightweight portable projectors, which fold to the size of an attaché case. They are useful if one must make a presentation in remote areas far from his normal work location.

Here are some view-graph hints: 1. Use white lettering on black (opaque) backgrounds (negatives of the original visual as drawn or lettered on white paper). 2. This allows individual lettering on the slide to be easily colored with transparent inks for emphasis. (This ink is inexpensive and comes in small bottles like fingernail polish.) 3. This also allows masking of certain portions of the visual as you develop a series of points one-by-one, with a piece of cardboard laid on the slide. 4. View-graphs of forms (with lines and spaces) can be projected on a paper easel for insertion of variable data when necessary to instruct people in the use of the forms. It saves the tedious drawing of the form for each example. 5. Number and label each view-graph for ready reference during question periods. 6. Use blank walls to project on if screens are awkward.

The view-graph is probably the best general purpose visual aid device. Every presentor will discover or invent many ways to apply it to his personal presentation styles.

SLIDE PROJECTORS

These 35-mm. home-type slides are extremely effective for presentations that require quick pacing, direct control by the presentor, actual photographs of events, people, or apparatus, or very large audiences. The circular cartridge, gravity feed types, are most foolproof. These protect the slides, keep them locked in strict sequence, and consume little space. They also allow random selection of a particular slide during questions. (The presentor should keep a numbered list of his slides near him so he can instruct an assistant to rotate the cartridge to the one wanted with a minimum of fuss). When you want the screen to be vacant, it is best to put a blank slide in the cartridge instead of turning the lamp on and off, as this shortens its life. For very important presentations it is wise to have a spare projector ready in case of failure to avoid delays and burned fingers from changing very hot lamps.

The slides are easily made with any good 35-mm. camera to copy the original visuals (single lens reflex is best). Kodak sells a Visualmaker kit which can be operated by a ten-year-old and produces professional results. Color is no problem at all, and if speed is essential, rapid development is available at a small increase in cost. Otherwise, the regular photographic delivery intervals and charges apply. Most towns have a local photographer who does this kind of work well at reasonable cost. Projectors are rented by most local shops for nominal fees. If you use this technique often, a "zoom" lens is a good investment. This allows changing the over-all size of the projected image without moving the projector itself and gives the flexibility to meet the limits of any size room.

Two projectors can be used to show the broad structure of a presentation on one screen, and supporting details on another. This double technique is tricky without practice, but when done well, it always arrests attention and enhances the grasp of over-all and detailed relationships. Three simultaneous projectors are rarely used, for here you go to the edge of theater techniques and require expert assistants and rehearsals. Without perfect timing and sequence, the effects are comical and do real harm to your idea. It's as though Charlie Chaplin wandered in.

When you have a visual that includes a series of points under one heading, each point can be developed by adding it to the previous slide. Thus the one original visual with six subsidiary points under one heading is developed as a series of *seven* slides. First show the heading above, then with one point, then with two, and so on, until the last slide recreates the original total visual. Color can be used to emphasize the last point *added* to each slide. This technique is also a good one to build up a complex diagram or chart. You add details piece-by-piece, slide-by-slide, from a simple beginning to final complexity, in easily grasped steps.

FLANNEL BOARDS

These enjoyed a short-lived popularity but are generally a nuisance. The background flannel wears thin, and the various pieces of cardboard applied to it are messy to work with. A change of humidity or rough jolt can cause the whole display to collapse into a trash pile at your feet. Don't use them. Whatever the flannel board can do can be done better—and more safely —by the following visual aids.

MAGNETIC BOARDS

These are limited to groups of less than thirty, but have marvelous power to hold attention. The act of building up a complex idea, by slapping pieces of lettered cardboard (with magnetic strips glued on their backs) on to a metal wall or magnetic panel grabs attention almost like a large construction project. The pieces can be moved about, and as arrows and numbers are placed as tags next to important segments you can create a dynamic experience that encourages audience participation. During questions, members of the audience can rearrange and substitute any piece on the whole display. Magnetic boards are especially good when a presentation considers all kinds of alternatives.

The complete fluidity of the built-up visual subconsciously hints that choices, discussion, and decisions are both called for and welcome. Colored pieces can add extra dimensions and values to aid in grasping a complex array of related items.

The "board" can be a metal partition, or a piece of thin sheet steel. Some blackboards are magnetic, and specially treated lightweight panels are commercially available. There is also a magnetic paint sold, which can be brushed on to a plain piece of Masonite, plywood, or a wall. It does a fine job. I once listened to a compelling talk on road safety given to twenty men in a garage. The instructor used magnetic cards placed on the side of a panel truck. The men watched with fascination as he manipulated street signs, intersections, traffic lights, and pictures of cars about. It wasn't long before some of the men talked about their own ideas and experiences and moved the instructor's pieces around to illustrate their stories. Everyone joined in spirited discussion.

When I complimented the instructor later, he told me that until he hit on this idea, all he saw before him were yawns and men looking at watches. Since then, everybody wanted to stand up and talk—if they could use the props. He sheepishly confessed that the story *itself* wasn't changed a bit, but everybody now listened. More importantly, accidents had decreased!

COMBINATIONS

Those of an experimental cast of mind may be interested in some work of a professorial friend who teaches the mysteries of Systems Analysis. He brought his tools and approaches to bear on the design of "the best blackboard." Here is his recommendation: Use a magnetizable writing surface colored off-white (whiteboard), and dark-blue chalk. Project slides or view-graphs for preliminary material; add variations, notes, and emphasis to the projected images on the "whiteboard" with chalk or magnetic cards. His experiments produced gains in speed and comprehension for university lectures on all kinds of subjects, from art history to zymology.

MOTION PICTURES

There are huge libraries of training films and newsreels available which can furnish lively sequences in some presentations. Many firms and government agencies make them available free of charge. Motion pictures offer a welcome change of pace and are especially good to show unfamiliar processes, historical events, and slow-motion operations of mechanical devices. Most librarians can put you in touch with sources.

CLOSED-CIRCUIT TELEVISION AND VIDEO TAPE

Video tape is becoming common, and is especially useful if you need to use a message by eminent persons or scarce experts in a series of presentations. The tapes can also be converted into motion picture film. Local television station technicians can advise you of facilities available in your area. For very important presentations, closed-circuit television cameras can show remote operations as they are going on. The space and missile people use it all the time. It's expensive, but sometimes it is the best way when time is worth more than money.

LIVE DEMONSTRATIONS

Some presentations can benefit from little playlets, or skits, showing how an idea could work out in real life. If you don't need a lot of dialogue, or are merely demonstrating a device, you can safely use people who can learn the jobs or techniques involved. But if crisp dialogue is essential, you had best employ professional actors.

This technique is almost always confined to large groups, and amateurs invariably botch up something important. If you can't go first-class with this method, don't use it at all.

THREE-DIMENSIONAL MODELS

These can be very persuasive and help understanding, but they are useless for presentations to more than five people. Sometimes they are made available for casual inspection during a break or after a presentation. But detailed discussion, while pointing to parts of a model no one can see, is foolish. Visuals of the operations involved are far more effective to achieve understanding. Let those who wish to poke around with the model do so on their own time—not yours. In this connection, it is usually a mistake to pass small models around the audience while you are presenting an idea. It is an absolutely perfect form of distraction.

This catalog represents the basic visual tool kit for presentations. Great presentations occur when the proper tool is matched to the job to be done. As with all tools, one can make them do things for which they were not designed. But such an approach to visuals puts unnecessary obstacles in the presentor's path to success. It's as though he plays the piano wearing mittens. He has to waste a great deal of mental, and sometimes physical, energy fighting his instruments. Inferior presentors stumble into their selection of visual aids from tradition, fashion, fear of innovation, or just plain carelessness. Like all other parts of a presentation, the selection of the best specific aid must be an answer to this question: Which form makes it easiest for the audience to grasp your idea with minimum intellectual effort and maximum physical comfort? Visuals should not be approached as opportunities to display the presentor's mechanical virtuosity. Instead, their use should appear natural and casual, so that only their *message* is noticed—not the apparatus itself.

After you are satisfied that your visuals will do the job you want, submit them to the test of cynicism. This is equivalent to loading sandbags on airplane wings to see where they break. The process is hard on the designer's pride, but it's also the best way to build safer and better airplanes. Here's one way. Gather two or three of your colleagues who are known for their critical or skeptical attitudes. Run each visual past them with a minimum of oral explanation. Ask them to answer two questions at every convenient point: "Does this visual suggest that you ask 'So what?' If 'yes,' then tell me why." "How can this visual be used as evidence *against* my idea?" Don't fight their remarks. Fix things so that the real audience can't make them. In the discussion of cross-examination (Chapter 7) we develop the point that the stronger the attack, the more powerful is its momentum. If the momentum is turned back on the attacker himself, it can help bring about his own downfall.

Strong visuals have great force, and constitute an attack on the existing attitudes and prejudices of an audience. You must prepare for those hostile members of an audience who will try to use the momentum of your own material to trip you.

Since visuals must be simplified variations of your oral presentation, they are always potentially vulnerable to those who insist that you are covering up or omitting important points. The best defense against this kind of guerrilla warfare is to have a copy of each visual in a loose-leaf binder and, opposite it, list the details or examples that support it. A few successful parries or ripostes to such nasty thrusts show that you can easily take care of such hostility. This usually stops it cold, since every success for you is a failure for the opposition.

Finally, remember that visuals do have a high artistic content, and perfection is never attainable in a human life span. Even so, close observation of presentations by others can rapidly sharpen your own. Every time you see a visual used, ask yourself, "What could be added, deleted, or changed to improve it?" When you silently answer, "Nothing," you will have seen perfection—from your point of view.

As Goethe lay dying, his friends used comforting words to ease his ordeal. With his last breaths he whispered: "Open the other shutter," and then, "Light—more light!" Most of us learn by hearing *and* seeing. If we can get our instruction from both together, each amplifies the understanding of the other. When visual aids add their light to your words, the audience will not need to utter Goethe's cry.

7

Making Cross-Examination
Work *For* You

or

Jujitsu Without Tears

Few scenes in literature seize our attention like those which portray the relentless questioning of some alleged culprit by a skillful cross-examiner. Great detectives, champion lawyers, dedicated intelligence officers, or shrewd men of the soil rise to their greatest moments as they smash away at the walls of lies, deceit, and misleading facts that have kept us from seeing the truth. Few novelists or playwrights can resist a chance to use this quintessence of bloodless conflict. It is interesting that in fiction the cross-examiner conquers the cross-examinee almost every time.

This tradition can produce an unfortunate mood in anyone who has to make a presentation, for in our imaginations we usually identify with the heroes of the stories—the cross-examiners. Yet, here you are, committed to expose an idea to an audience who will question you to test both your competence and the validity of your idea. Everything you've read, seen, or heard leads you to believe that the questioners have the best set of weapons. Some are so panicked by this thought that they will never present an idea if there is a possibility of adverse questions. Since this kind of immunity does not exist for any idea of importance, such people must confine themselves to trivial and fruitless commentary on the work of others. But their disabling concern is nearly groundless, and I will try to show why in this chapter.

In the arts of physical combat, whether hand-to-hand or army-against-army, the idea of a flexible response to an attack has been a guiding principle for the successful. The great victors have usually employed their attackers' own momentum to produce his downfall. Thus, jujitsu ("the yielding art") teaches the techniques of meeting an attack *in just the right way*, so that the force of your opponent directed at you is transferred back on to himself. Fencing schools teach another adage: "For every thrust there is a possible riposte." The cross-examiner is your attacker, but, just as in meeting physical assaults, the most important element in successful defense is to realize that the attacker is *more* vulnerable than the defender—if the defender knows how to meet him.

Just as in physical clashes, so also in mental. The worst possible method is to produce an imitation attack in reverse. This is the reply of those in panic, and represents complete loss of initiative. When a cross-examiner gets this kind of reaction, his victory is complete. There are many better ways, but before we get to them in detail, let's examine the attitudes of real lawyers and note the contrast with impressions one picks up from literature.

In observing a working trial lawyer, do we see a cool, haughty knight who yawns through the original testimony of an opposing witness, secure in the knowledge that he can reduce anyone to a quivering mass of nerves, thrashing about like a captured animal in a net of lies or evasions brought out by his cross-examination? Not at all. Most successful lawyers know the great peril to their own case that can come from just one bad question they raise on cross-examination. They also know that they cannot possibly discredit everything in a good direct presentation; that the most they can hope for is to destroy a crucial piece or two. The search for and identification of that piece forces them to concentrate intensely on everything that unfolds, though clever ones do affect a pose of unconcern. Few audiences are up to that kind of effort —and that gives you even better odds.

Some eminent lawyers, in their riper years, have given advice to their younger colleagues on how to conduct cross-examination: things to do and things to avoid. We can make use of their wisdom, not only to become good questioners but, more importantly, to meet those questions that follow the serious presentation of an idea in ways that help your cause. With such knowledge you can at least neutralize the effect of hostile questions. With greater skill the questions can be turned to your advantage and advance your idea with more force than can be safely used in the original presentation.

One may think that a murder trial has little in common with a presentation in business, academic, governmental, or social life. But before positively concluding that, consider that a trial is a conflict between two ideas of who is in the right (or wrong). A presentation is a conflict between your idea and the ideas and opinions that members of your audience hold before they hear you. Consider, also, the *purposes* of questions after one side has been stated. They are identical in both a trial and a presentation: 1. to elicit additional information; 2. to display inconsistencies; 3. to detect falsehoods.

These are double-edged for the questioner, and account for the caution shown by good lawyers. Such caution is often absent in the lawyer's client, who expects his advocate to pound away at hostile parties until they are utterly in ruins. Understandable as this may be on an emotional level, it is usually disastrous if the lawyer gives in to it. An illustration of an actual case from a court in the South may show the hazards of pressing too far.

As an argument developed between two men in a saloon on a hot Saturday night, feelings rose to such a pitch that physical blows soon took over from shouted threats and epithets. During the scuffle the plaintiff lost his ear, which he claimed was bitten off by the defendant. At the trial it soon became clear that no one had actually seen the defendant bite his accuser, and the defendant's mood changed from despondency to relief, and then to elation. Instead of sitting silently, he began to encourage his lawyer with all sorts of suggestions, to the lawyer's immense annoyance. The last witness for the plaintiff was an old derelict who spent all his waking hours at the end of the bar, and who was something of a scandal to the whole town. Here was the perfect chance for the defendant to clear his name and teach the plaintiff a lesson. He insisted that his lawyer go after the witness until the old man begged for mercy. Nothing less would satisfy him. With a look of disgust, the lawyer began. "Were you at the saloon when my client had an argument with Jonas [the plaintiff]?"

"Yep."

"Did you watch the whole time?"

"Yep."

"Did you see the fight?"

"Yep."

"Did you see who hit first?"

"Nope."

"Did you see Bill here [the defendant] bite Jonas on the ear?"

"Nope."

At this point the defendant hissed in a loud whisper: "Don't let him go, get him!"

The lawyer sighed, and with a shrug continued: "Let's make sure the jury heard that last answer. You did not actually see Bill bite Jonas at anytime during the fight, right?"

"Right"

The lawyer bowed to the judge, then turned to the jury and delivered a wrathful speech about the plaintiff's imposition on the time of everyone there with no evidence that anyone had even seen the alleged crime. The defendant was all smiles as the lawyer swung back to the witness for the final blow.

"How dare you, a disgrace to our town, come here to this court, waste everyone's time, to work an injustice on a fine man like Bill? What possible explanation can you give the jury for this degrading, spiteful, and insulting behavior?"

The defendant almost cheered, but the witness shifted his chewing tobacco, looked at the jury, and drawled: "You're right, suh, about me not seeing Bill *bite* Jonas' ear, but I *did* see him spit it out."

This extra information did the defendant no good.

Hundreds of thousands of experiences like this, since the time of Edward the Confessor, have shown the wisdom of some approaches and the folly of others in the conduct of cross-examination. Let's examine the advice of successful practitioners:

Lead the witness to lose his temper, while you hold yours.

Try to pose dilemmas, so that *either* answer harms the witness.

If you can drive the witness to sullenness the jury loses sympathy for him.

Lengthy cross-examination along the lines of an expert's theory are usually disastrous and should rarely be attempted.

Questions should not be so broad as to give the witness a chance to expatiate his views.

Never try to show your own erudition in asking a question.

The *first* question is most important; choose it with great care.

Never give the witness a chance to repeat his original testimony.

Select only the weakest points for questioning.

Stop with a victory. Additional harassment will never be worth the additional risk.

Remember that once cross-examination begins, if you don't break the witness, he breaks you—there are no ties.

The most dangerous advocate is the courteous gentleman who is always fair.

If you have factual information to contradict the witness, first encourage him to make inferences and otherwise magnify his original story.

If you *must* cross-examine an expert, question him on these points: a. his experience and training; b. his opportunity for personal observation of the facts involved; c. the nature of his study of the case in hand; d. any failure to consider relevant conditions affecting the soundness of his decisions.

Intemperate behavior to a witness shows that you are both weak and indecent.

Never ask a question without a good reason.

Never ask a question unless you can live with the answer. Random questions seldom elicit anything helpful and usually harm your cause.

A question puts the witness on guard. He then exploits every chance to introduce qualifications and explanations to set matters right.

Observations and criticism to which no answer can be given are seen by all to be mischievous and unfair.

Never attempt to prove your case by your adversary's witness.

A cross-examiner must be complete master of himself; he must conceal being thunderstruck by the unexpected answer.

Never treat a witness roughly; if he is discredited, it must be done by himself—your questions only allow him to do so.

The maxims above represent a distillation of manuals, treatises, and commentaries published since 1789. It is remarkable how consistently they replay the same themes. Even taking into account the natural and congenital conservatism of lawyers, they all emphasize the *dangers facing the one who asks the questions.* Everyone assumes that the witness is in the stronger position—a complete reversal of the view found in literature. While this may be sad news to the novice lawyer, it is encouraging to anyone who wishes to undertake the presentation of an idea. In addition, the chance that members of an audience will have the years of practice and concentration essential for the development of a competent cross-examiner is very rare indeed. Most questions after a presentation will violate one or more of these traditional maxims. To the extent that they do, such questions offer valuable opportunities to strengthen your presentation—opportunities you can get in no other way. Questions should be much more welcome than feared, for recognition of the positive value of questions is the first and greatest step in converting potential antagonism into support. Once this attitude is adopted by a presentor, he sees his position in a new light and can then comprehend the peculiar strength that flows from merely facing a group of listeners.

THE PRIVILEGE OF THE PODIUM

At any one time in a presentation, someone is in charge of the group involved. Unless he has lost control to someone in the audience, this is always the man making the presentation. It is not uncommon to see members of much higher rank than the presentor defer to his rulings of order or precedence, and his settling of misunderstandings and disputes during question periods. The audience has come to the presentation to be informed and perhaps persuaded about a new course of action or a new attitude. They expect to get something of value. They expect the man undertaking the presentation to do his job, and, in their minds, that includes the *entire* conduct of the meeting. They expect him to have accepted that responsibility when he grasped the chance to present his idea. In return for this silent understanding, they place themselves voluntarily under control of the man at the podium—*as long as they retain confidence in his leadership of the gathering.* The audience will agree to any approach he selects up to the point where they sense that they are wasting their time, or where the leadership they expect becomes capricious, weak, uncertain, or perverse.

This granting of leadership gives the presentor enormous advantage in the handling of questions, if he exercises the power with fairness and regard for the needs of the audience. For example, in some large meetings, questions may be written out on cards or slips, collected, and passed up to the podium for discussion. This is a difficult test of any presentor's skill, for he alone makes the decisions on the order of answer, the arrangement and collation of similar questions and, most importantly, those rejected. The man at the podium must do this without knowing who asked a specific question, and those who find their questions ignored may become quite hostile or suspicious—they seldom forget the slight. (There are ways to anticipate and diminish this reaction, which I will discuss later.)

Remember, the major purpose of questions is to enlarge opportunities for the understanding of the entire audience. Few people wish to destroy a presentation completely, and, even if they think they do, they usually wish only to substitute their own solution for yours. It is extremely rare for them to attack the presentor *personally*, for the hostility that they must display is blatant and will generate sympathy for your own position. You will lose that sympathy only if you defend your position on a personal basis. It is far better to relate such questions back to your *proposal,* not to yourself. Generally, you will know of such people and their views in advance. By stating their views yourself and showing that you are completely aware of the hostile position and parties, you can often neutralize their impact completely. This maneuver is a legitimate exercise of the privilege of the podium and, while frustrating to the opposition, gains you a reputation for objectivity with those who are uncommitted. This makes their later agreement with you much easier, for the open-minded can then feel that they have made up their mind in full knowledge of alternatives.

Probably the greatest advantage that questions furnish is their invitation to expand the ideas involved in your original presentation. This is, of course, the advantage that causes the professional cross-examiner the most worry, but that is the other side's concern, not yours. Every original presentation has to be tailored to a certain amount of time. Design of its composition forces you to eliminate some relevant facts or arguments—often with great regret—in order to meet the time limit. *Do not throw them away!* If they once seemed relevant and important to you, they will seem so to someone in the audience, and he will itch to ask a question about them.

Audiences have a peculiar trait. If you stretch out all the support you have for every point, they become bored or tired, for your entire presentation becomes clogged with so many trees that their view of the forest disappears. If you show that you intend to examine every leaf, they lose any interest they had to start with and begin looking at watches and clocks in desperation.

But after being given an over-all picture, well-paced and supported just enough to suggest the correctness of your view, they will then tolerate a detailed examination of sections of the presentation *when produced in response to a question.* This tolerance is based on the essential fairness of audiences. They sense that your position has been attacked, therefore it is only right that you have a chance to respond. Everyone likes a fair contest, and your questioner brings a new dramatic element to the scene. Many a presentation has been saved by such a shot in the arm.

This point is especially important in presentations that rely on methods of investigation and analysis not completely familiar to the audience. It should be a scandal in the sciences that a large number of their reports break down into: 4 percent ponderous statement of the problem; 89 percent tedious description of methodology; 6 percent references to obscure authorities; and 1 percent hedged conclusions. This kind of structure approaches the ultimate in presentation horrors. It cannot be taken seriously as primarily designed to inform and persuade, and probably results from extending the special approach required for a doctoral thesis (which is a display of personal methodological competence) into mature life. Those who take this course bring to mind the pathetic generals who always plan for the next war on the basis of techniques and weapons successful in the last.

Presentations that must involve such matters should rely heavily on the questions from the audience to develop the methodology. If the audience grasps the problem, acquires assurance in your competence by listening to your development, and finds your conclusions sensible, you have helped them far more than if you try to train them in an esoteric technique, which they may never use again. You will sometimes hear this critique muttered as the audience leaves a bad presentation of this type: "I asked him what time it was, and he told me how to make a watch." Reducing the methods to a paper, made available to those few who are actually interested, and handling a question or two on method in laymen's language with examples, is far more impressive.

Should you attend a play or ballet, you would be astonished to see the author or choreographer pop through the curtain after the overture and harangue you with all the thoughts and problems he faced in bringing you the performance you are about to see. While a tiny fraction of dancers and playwrights in the audience might have an interest, even these would prefer to see the show *first*, before deciding to stay for the lecture on its production. Certainly their questions about technique would be more relevant *after* they've seen what they came for than before. What is true for a performance is also true of a presentation.

Establishment of an atmosphere congenial to the question phase requires explicit attention and planning by the presentor.

Whenever this is taken for granted, control is so loose that it often slips away before anyone knows what happened. Presentations then go rapidly downhill to random destinations, and usually end up damaged beyond repair. Postmortem examiners of these unhappy events keep repeating the mournful question, "Where did we go wrong?" In many cases they went wrong in the way the questions were met. It is here that the inattentive snatch defeat from the jaws of victory. Instead of treating the questions as new opportunities to fortify their presentations, they look forward to them as gantlets to be run, fierce onslaughts to be endured, or irritating distractions from the purity of their message. Some pray that they will get *no* questions, never realizing that this reaction is the polite reversal of applause. Those unlucky enough to get their prayers answered, later wander about in a fog, constantly asking: "I wonder how we did?" Few have the heart to tell them.

Audiences scent quickly a presentor's attitude to questions. In the absence of specific suggestions, they will make up their own minds from your tone and actions, so it is best to state how you propose to deal with questions. They will go along with almost any way you like, *if you make that way clear*, but if you neglect to send your signals, it is then "every man for himself"—just like leaderless soldiers.

One of the most frequent errors in handling the matter of questions springs, oddly enough, from the desire to be a courteous, agreeable gentleman. How often have you heard someone begin with an introduction like this: "We have a great deal to cover in this presentation, and just to make sure everyone understands every aspect of our story, *please feel free to interrupt me at any time so that we don't move on to the next point if anyone has any question at all on what has gone before. In fact, I'll be quite disappointed if you don't.*" Onc cannot compose a better prelude to disaster, and besides, the motivation is suspect. Audiences are intelligent. They know that if everyone did as you asked, no presentation could ever be completed in its allotted time. They also expect that many questions they might have at the beginning are probably going to be cleared up in the course of development. Some presenters piously make this kind of opening statement and then proceed to answer every question with a sharp retort: "We'll cover that later on." Few questioners put up with this kind of treatment for long. Also, a constant stream of interruptions chips away at the over-all structure to such an extent that those who really are interested in following your development find it impossible to see your presentation as a whole, separating out what you said from a series of more-or-less relevant comments from others.

A more subtle flaw in this "nice fellow" opening is that you throw away the most powerful lever for convincing the minds of others: the flash of understanding they experience as they reflect on the problem presented, follow your exposition of its many aspects, and *discover the answer for themselves before you point it out.* Unresolved images or facts that have seized their attention are reinforced in intensity as development progresses and produce a mental pressure which explodes when they see the solution. Even little children resent being told the answer to a puzzle, a riddle, or a trick too soon, for you deprive them of all sense of joy and achievement. Adults feel the same way about problems in a presentation. They want the feeling of learning something new to come from their own insight. Your presentation is merely the guide to let that happen. We rightly call those people "Great Teachers" who produce many more than their share of explosions of individual discovery in minds entrusted to their care. A great presentation produces exactly the same effect.

The haphazard approach, consequently, violates the basic method for holding attention: creation of a sense that something is going on. If you cannot move on without everybody in the room satisfied that he has mastered every previous detail, then the pace of the entire presentation is hobbled to the least intelligent in the room. Nothing will lose the bright people faster than their discovery that you really mean to abide with your opening invitation for interruption. These people are often crucial for the continued life of your idea. Lose them, and your idea dies without a true hearing—or even a good cry.

A final fault with a plea for instant, random questioning is the chance it gives your opposition to tie you in knots before you even get started. They can question the premises, raise all kinds of obscure issues, and otherwise suffocate your child in the cradle. The normal sympathy you can expect under this sort of harassment does not exist, for your opponents are doing only what you asked them to—and everyone knows it. Some in the audience probably regret this happening, but they can't help much as you have tied their hands as well with your opening. Besides, any interruptions they make to extricate you plays into the hands of the opposition. You lose either way if this kind of uproar develops. Such a development does not even have the redeeming merit of tragedy, since it is not inevitable. It comes of simple foolishness; cosmic forces or the anger of the gods cannot be blamed.

Why not inevitable? Simply because a more adroit opening gains all the advantages of courtesy, fairness, and gentility without abandoning control. The audience expects two things: to hear your presentation and to raise questions about it. These *can* be kept separate with no hurt feelings on either side. Consider this kind of statement: "I am grateful for the chance to make this presentation to you today. I realize that you are all very busy, so I'll try to keep this short. In doing so, I may hit a few points somewhat lightly, but I will try to clear them up as we go along. We have tried our best to anticipate any questions you might have, but with a subject as complex as this, we know we must have missed some. We certainly want to get them all out for discussion to make sure that we haven't overlooked something vital. However, I ask your indulgence to let us proceed with the direct presentation so that you can all get an over-all view of how we approached the problem, the various angles we studied, and the recommendations we are making. Some of these may surprise you if you don't see how they were arrived at. This should take about a half-hour; then we can take as long for questions as your time allows. We've also prepared a booklet of the detailed statistical background for anyone interested and you can get one from George, there at the door, as you leave."

Notice the information packed into these seemingly offhand remarks: format, time required, a hint that you are not going into obscure details, a request for questions in an orderly way, and advance notice that one can get the meat of your story—but not its justification—in a summary of recommendations. There's even a little bit of mystery for spice. Few questions can be answered in as short a time as this takes—especially if they come before you're well into the subject. Another bonus is that anyone who has to leave early at least hears *your* side as a connected story.

This arrangement also allows you to capitalize on another fear of professional cross-examiners. Remember, one of their rules is to avoid letting a witness repeat his original testimony. With your direct presentation finished, it is usually quite easy to answer a question by showing that it goes to a point you previously covered inadequately—and then repeat and expand that part of your story in the light of the question. Think how much more forceful this is than having to bring the point forward in isolation, out of sequence, and without the context of the material that both led up to it and followed it.

People in the audience appreciate some recognition that you value their time. They will welcome any sensible discipline suggested, for they then think of others as the time-wasters you're rightly on guard against. Most value this kind of straightforward politeness more highly than the hollow camaraderie of a free-for-all from the start. The art of sculpture suggests a useful image to grasp the relation of the presentation and questions derived from it. Visualize the presentation as an almost-finished statue, which you trundle in for suggestions to complete or improve. Each member of the audience sees things he might not have done as you did, but he *respects and understands the work as a whole.* He is then inclined to put his own tools to work in relation to the whole work. Only the rare nihilist goes for the sledge hammer, and others will usually restrain him. Contrast this to what happens if you drag in a big, rough hunk of stone, and invite everyone to go at it any way he likes. It may be a happening, but it will not be art—or a good presentation.

Even after you have made the more desirable opening, some compulsive soul in the audience may still be unable to contain himself and will intrude a question. You certainly can't ignore it, but the audience is now alert to how you handle it: Will you abandon your high intentions or give up? Don't give up! If the question *is* on the subject, gently point out where it will be covered, either in the problem-statement, development, or conclusion. Point out that if it is not taken care of to his satisfaction, you will handle his question *first* right after your direct story. If the question is a rhetorical one, intended to lay the basis for a long speech by the questioner as he answers his own question, wait for him to catch his breath, and firmly assert the resumption of the original intention of the meeting. There are several devices that can be used to save the questioner's feelings as you interrupt him. For example: "You raise an important and fascinating idea, but it is not quite the same one we studied. I am sure we will all be interested to go into it more thoroughly during the question period," or, "That is such a general and over-all view that we really don't have the competence to contribute much to it. We addressed ourselves to a more narrow segment of the entire field, but after we discuss what we did, perhaps we *should* expand our vision to the extent you indicate."

If you know your man has a reputation as a windbag, or is known to be against everything new or different, or is disliked by a majority of the audience, you can safely use a very rough psychological club: Let him run completely free. As he goes on and on, the audience will begin to see that he is cheating them by using everybody's question time as well as taking unfair advantage of you. Do not interrupt this type; indicate, instead, serious attention to even his most banal remarks, and appear thoughtful as he rambles. If others try to shut him off, restrain them with a silent gesture of the hand, but do not allow them to ask him questions. After a few minutes, these types almost *wish* someone would stop them, for they begin to feel foolish as they sense the irritation building. When he finally stops, make no response to his oratory except "Thank you," and then briskly take up where you left off, as though the interruption did not take place.

The need for a "feel" of the audience brings us to an important but elusive aspect of any presentation: the "atmosphere" surrounding it. Everything seems to have a bearing on it, but nothing accounts for it entirely. The style and material affect it, the room itself plays a part, the visual aids, and so on—all influence it. But how you handle the questions is probably the most important determinant of the final impression carried away by the audience. Think of the restaurants you've visited—the food may have been equally good, but some had a pleasant atmosphere and some had none, yet you are hard pressed to describe just exactly what accounted for the differences. Most people, when asked, mention the "little things," which must be experienced rather than described. So also with presentations. The "little things" are extremely important during questions and influence the way you receive them, your attitude to the questions, and the phrases and tone you use in your answers. Some presentors (bad ones) assume a posture of skeet shooting— every question must be blasted as it leaves the mouth. (You can almost see them swivel after they break one clay pigeon and call for the next.) Others express delight that the question came up and welcome the man who asks it as they would a long lost friend. Thus, the same question and the same answer can create entirely different atmospheres. One of the maxims for cross-examiners is: "The *first* question is most important; choose it with great care." They worry about this for the same reason that the presentor should about his first *answer:* it sets the tone and atmosphere for succeeding questions. Just as your first glance around a restaurant takes in decor, napery, lighting, and the demeanor of the waiters, so does your first response send a flood of silent information to the audience about your attitude toward their questions.

How can you send the right signals? The best way is actually to *have* a positive attitude to all questions, for that will unconsciously influence every move you make and every word you speak.

To begin with, realize that it takes mental effort for someone just to articulate a question. Also, remember that if one in the audience asks a question, that same question was also in the minds of others. When you answer him, you answer everyone. Assume, too, that even if the question sounds odd to you, the man asking it has a good reason for wanting to know your view. Since the motivation underneath a question is almost impossible to unravel (the questioner probably doesn't even know it), it is best to take it at face value in the beginning. If you suspect evil intent behind every question, you will err far more than if you treat them all as true requests for additional information. Many questions are raised because you have created anxiety in the audience. After all, they have heard your idea, and now they must form an attitude toward it. Their question may merely be a plea for reassurance—their way of saying, "I think you've convinced me, but I'd like to be more sure." Since few people will say that publicly, they put their anxiety in question form. If you dispel this anxiety, they are quietly grateful, but will never display it except to support your idea—which is the only result you should want or need.

Other questions may have their origin in the need for many audiences to report or to make a presentation of your idea to others not present at the meeting. They know better than you do the kind of questions they may get when they tell your story, and the alert ones want authoritative answers to help them when they have to explain it later. If you can help these people with *their* problems, you add compound interest to the force of your idea.

Polite and tactful introductions to your answers are the fine lubricant for constructive discussion, and encourage the more diffident in an audience to join in. They consume almost no time, but they are nearly indispensable for the smooth conduct of a question session. Consider these phrases and note that they can precede almost any answer from resounding agreement to absolute denial:

"That is a perceptive question, and shows a complete grasp of our intentions."

"Your question shows an insight into this problem that took us several days to acquire."

"Now, that question penetrates right to the heart of the matter."

"We can always look to Fred to go straight for the jugular."

"You have put your finger on the one thing that has concerned us more than any other in this program."

Everyone can invent variations appropriate to his taste. These should not be automatically tacked on *every* answer, or the effect is ludicrous. You will look like Uriah Heep in *David Copperfield*. Rather you should have them in your mind, alert to apply them sincerely only to deserving questions. However, merely keeping them "at the ready" sensitizes you and makes you eager to get a question to honor in this way. They exert a subtle influence on your attitude. If you receive a batch of written questions from the audience, select for your first answer one that allows you to make a remark complimentary to the questioner. It will keep every one who sent up a question alert for a similar accolade.

All of us relish those events we see that we can tell others about later. We have a high bias toward the unusual or the unexpected. The question period is a rich source of the material that your audience will use in talking about your presentation to other people. Notice how many anecdotes and humorous stories use a question in their telling. They do this for very good reason: The question and its answer are the most elemental form of drama.

Attitudes and character are symbolized in a shorthand form, through question and answer, and register in our memories with great impact. Think back on your own experiences when you were asked: "What happened at the meeting?" How often did you report as a series of questions and answers? Most everyone does—most of the time. In the nineteen-thirties there was a fifteen-minute radio program (a classic soap opera) called *Our Gal Sunday*, which began *every* performance for many years with an unctuous voice intoning, "This is the program which asks the question: 'Can a young girl from a little mining town in the West find love and happiness as the wife of a wealthy, and titled Englishman?'" Year after year the next twelve minutes produced a daily ambiguous answer. Regardless of how many sophisticates spoofed the show, millions of people were compelled to follow the diurnal variations of the drama. A good case could be made that the repeated question, loaded with romantic allusions, was largely responsible for its wide appeal.

When people report your presentation as an answer to questions that may be bothering the secondary audience, your idea is well served. It is not by chance that the great conflicts and issues of diplomacy are referred to as Questions, e.g., the Balkan Question; the Polish Question, the Congo Question, etc. Such a tag keeps statesmen on their toes, for they know that publics at home and abroad are interested in their *answers*, not their descriptions or anxieties. For these reasons, questions should be looked on and welcomed as the vehicle that will carry your idea on its journey to others.

In this connection, do not handle questions as though you are engaged in a *personal* battle. While satisfying to your ego, the effect is always bad for your idea. The audience will remember —and tell others about—the clash of personalities and forget the real basis of the argument. Besides, if you vanquish the questioner as a person in public, you make an enemy. He will snipe at your proposal thereafter to redress his humiliation. Not only Orientals take loss of face seriously. Others who may have had an interest in your answer will shy away from the fireworks of a personal conflict, and are deterred from asking the question again because of the scene provoked. Lincoln's wisdom should be your guide: "The best way to destroy an enemy is to make him a friend"—but seek friendship for the idea itself, not for you personally.

Every presentor must have the intellectual courage to face a harsh truth: The purpose of questions and answers is to enhance understanding of your idea. If the idea is truly unsound, greater understanding of its implications will kill it—and it should. A bad idea that succeeds in gaining acceptance is a worse outcome for society than a good idea that fails. The genuinely good idea will get another chance, but a bad idea sets into motion irreversible forces and events which can do great harm. A feeling for this accounts for the conservative bias of most people who have to assume responsibility for decisions. That bias is compensated only by the build-up of confidence they experience as you successfully clear up point after point in answer to their questions. Innovations take place when people become convinced that the risks are less than the potential gains. Their greatest risk is the trust they must give you in order to believe what you are telling them. If you disappoint them in the question period, *you* have made it "too risky," and their conservative bias is reinforced. Many presenters do not appreciate or even recognize the existence of this natural bias, and seem baffled at some questions that show it. Expect it, plan for it, and welcome questions that spring from it. Answers to such questions offer the best way to display an appreciation of the heavy responsibility your audience lives with. When they sense that you really understand *their* problems as mirrored in their questions, you enjoy the golden moments of communication. Ideas are bought and sold only with this coin.

One psychological aspect of a question always works for the presentor's benefit. When someone has taken the time, trouble, and risk to formulate and ask a question, you can be absolutely certain that you have gained his attention. While he awaits your answer, you have the greatest attention from him he is capable of. Look at the position from *his* point of view. He may feel that he indicates ignorance for all to see; you may try to make him look ridiculous in the eyes of others; he may be perplexed at being taken beyond his competence and really wants to understand what is expected of him. He may start a dialogue without realizing it—or wanting to—and if so, he needs to watch you like a hawk, alert for whatever twist you put on his question by your answer. Many presenters do not realize the effort it takes for someone in the audience to raise the first question after a good presentation. Once the first one is off, the others seem to come along naturally, especially if you establish a friendly atmosphere for discussion. A seasoned presenter sometimes guards against an embarrassed silence before the first question by prearrangement with someone he can trust to start things going. I don't mean "planted" questions *assigned* to be asked, as few things are more transparent to an audience, but merely an understanding that if the first question does not come naturally, your friend will break the ice with anything handy.

I once attended a presentation to a few hundred people where I noticed several typewritten cards being circulated somewhat surreptitiously among the audience. Evidently, the original "plant" rebelled and let his job be shared democratically as the speaker droned on. Nobody wanted to touch them, as the speaker had a reputation for sarcasm to questioners—even to his "plants"! Finally, one unfortunate was caught with a card as the speaker asked, "Are there any questions?" After an awkward silence, the speaker spied this holder of one of his cards. He pointed to him and shouted, "I believe you have a question, sir!"

Shuffling to his feet the poor man carefully adjusted his glasses, held the card before him, and concentrating on the typescript, blurted out, "Yes. In accordance with the instructions here, I must ask you to elaborate the following points."

The burst of laughter that filled the hall terminated the meeting.

Questions also arise because each person uses a vocabulary unique to himself. Every profession, art, occupation, class, school, club, family, or any other social or political unit uses terms and expressions that are well understood by people of the same unit, but ambiguous or mysterious to outsiders. Every audience has some "outsiders" in it, and if they want to understand your message, they may ask you to explain a word used in a sense unfamiliar to them. This is often done badly, with irritability and ill grace, indicating an implied, "How stupid! Everybody knows what I mean by that." Avoid this attitude as you would disease, for such questions come only from those really interested, and you reject potential allies by treating them this way. This is stupidity of a much higher order than that imputed to the question. If you take the time to explain your meaning carefully when asked, preferably translating your term into the questioner's vocabulary, you convert and elevate him to "inside" status. There is another good reason to look at familiar terms afresh. You may have used one from habit, without thought, and it may really be inappropriate. If so, your admission of debt to the questioner will leave him with a glow of satisfaction, which can do your cause no harm.

Deflection of a question to another member of the audience is an adroit maneuver which sends several favorable messages to everyone listening. By doing this you show that: You know the limits of your own knowledge; you are not a "know-it-all"; you are aware of the skills and experience of the various members of the audience; you may do the same thing to every one of them if a question arises in their fields of expertise (This keeps them attentive.) Do not, however, deflect the question unless you are quite sure that the man designated will give an answer favorable to your cause.

This technique is best confined to questions that call for a *factual* answer, not personal opinion. When you call for *opinion* too early, you put your expert on the spot with no warning, and if intelligent, he may hedge and qualify his answer to the point of neutrality. A variation of this method is to preface your answer by noting that there are experts on that subject among the audience, but that you will give your own answer and expect them to correct it if wrong in any way. Most experts in an audience will let you go pretty far before they intervene, for they wish to see where you go with the information before committing themselves to support or condemn your use of it. But they *do* like their presence to be recognized in some way—especially if your idea makes excursions into their fields.

A presentation that acknowledges its debt to the work of others charms an audience—especially if some of these "others" are before you. This acknowledgment should not descend to sleazy flattery, but embody the recognition that your idea has built on their accomplishments. Sir Isaac Newton's remark, that "If I have seen farther than others it is only because I stood on the shoulders of giants," epitomizes this modest attitude.

Everyone believes that what one man can build, another can improve. But almost everyone resents a presentation that seeks to make itself stand out by ruthless criticism and demolition of other men's earlier work. If they are not there in person, some of their descendants, friends, or disciples may be, and they will take you on out of loyalty—a noble and attractive emotion. The tendency to slip into this error is particularly strong during question time, when a smooth interrogator may ask you why you believe your idea is so superior to what they now have, which has served well, and is the result of efforts by generations of first-class men.

You are posed with something close to a dilemma, but there is an escape. You must confess how difficult and frustrating it was to make improvements on something already so good. Mention approaches that failed, for these enhance your credibility. Finally, describe the new knowledge, events, or just plain luck that allowed you to place another course of bricks on top of the fine structure you inherited. Point out how you believe the great men before you would have welcomed this chance themselves, and, where possible, use some of their own predictions, writings, or statements to show the dissatisfaction they felt for what they had built in their own time. Strive for the conviction that you are merely carrying forward the torch you were handed; avoid the impression that you are discarding it as exhausted, and lighting a new one from scratch. Even if the old *is* exhausted, at least make the concession that your new torch can be lit by the dying sparks of the old. Your idea will lose nothing and will gain a great deal from the sense of orderly progress most people find comfortable.

Another way to use questions in generating emotional support for your idea comes from the method of opposites. In answering a question, mention those authorities whose views are *adverse* to your proposal—especially if these are persons whom the audience dislikes. A complex logical chain connecting them to your idea can be developed, but it is not helpful to do so. The audience "reasons" that "If *he* is against this, there must be some good in it."

Today, many audiences suspect that some anonymous group or person actually produced the presentation, and that the presentor is merely its mouthpiece. This attitude (while often unfair) exists especially when the presentation is made by someone of exalted rank. In this situation one can detect a mischievous tone in the questions, as suspicious members of the audience probe for evidence of unfamiliarity with the concepts presented. Such suspicions are confirmed or denied in the question session. If a great deal of the work of a presentation has been done by others, the presentor should prepare himself for questions derived from the maxims for cross-examination. Take note, especially, of the rules for going after an expert, i.e., attack his background and experience, personal observation, nature of his study, omissions of relevant factors.

Presentors whose rank is relatively higher than those in their audience must be careful to avoid excessive reliance on their status if their true goal is to achieve acceptance and conviction on the merits of their case. Cavalier treatment of questions by someone who cannot be rigorously questioned tells the audience that they are really not being presented an idea for consideration, but instead are listening to orders masquerading as a presentation. After a few test questions the audience settles back in a sullen mood, because they have been fooled. At the end of a session like this, you will often hear the alleged presentor plead for questions, but his earlier responses have made it too dangerous. Some phrases used in his irritation are: "Fellows, I want you to feel free to speak up now," or, "If you don't understand, now is the time to clear everything up. It will be too late after we adjourn," or (one of the worst), "Everybody's had their chance to question me about this. If you don't understand, it's your own fault." The resentment this causes in an audience comes from frustration. They probably have many questions about the idea, but dare not cross the great man. Many also secretly feel that without the unfair advantage his rank gives him, they could give the presentor a hard time in a real discussion. These aspects of deference to powerful persons make it difficult for even the best-intentioned of them to judge their true impact on an audience. They have a problem similar to that of an heiress: Are the suitors interested in her or her fortune?

The best way for a presentor to show that he is truly interested in the opinions and views of the audience is to handle their questions as though everyone in the room were his equal—and take this attitude with the very first question.

A related problem faces someone making a presentation to an audience composed of several different levels of rank—above and below his own. He must avoid discrimination in his treatment of questions. If he pays obsequious attention to the questions of superiors and shows annoyance at those from inferiors, both groups quickly see that he is more interested in his personal ambition than he is in the proposal itself. Audiences apply very colorful, but unflattering, labels to such presentors, but more importantly, distrust them. These considerations suggest that the best all-purpose behavior, regardless of your own place in a pecking order, is to treat *every* questioner as an equal. When this happens, discussion shakes off artificial restraints, and everyone involved feels that they have contributed something to the success of a meeting. They have learned from one another, not just from you.

We saw in the maxims for cross-examination that questions should concentrate on the weak points in the testimony of a witness. A good way to disarm someone who follows this line is to present the weak sections of your story with special emphasis, pointing out their deficiencies. Show that you realize more knowledge is desirable, or that you are asking the audience to take risks on your inferences where you do not have hard facts. It is often wise to recapitulate at the end of a presentation all of the risk areas involved in a decision to support your idea. When you do this, the audience automatically thinks of the risks in *not* supporting you, and often tries to articulate support in your favor. Hostile parties may hammer away at the deficiencies, but they will lack the punch of bringing them into the open for the first time. If they go too far, members of the audience feel (and may even say) "He's told us about that! Now, what can we *do* about it?" Every presentation has *some* weak places, and here lies the danger of excessive exaggeration—of either benefits or difficulties. True understanding requires seeing things in proper proportion and relation to each other. When you exaggerate, you place a sharp weapon in the hands of a questioner who can then restore the audience's perspective by forcing you to diminish your original statements. The method of opposites furnishes a strong check on a tendency to exaggerate in developing the original presentation, but it should also be kept under control during the questions afterward. Conversely, if the questioner exaggerates, you have a choice, either to encourage him to go further in distortion, or to restore proportion to the discussion gently, by restating the question before answering it. The latter is preferable, but if your questioner has a reputation for nastiness among the audience, let him show how well he deserves it by giving him a free rein. Bring him up short by a brisk statement of fact, or by reference back to your original presentation (if it was moderate).

Questions are *usually* indicative of the viewpoint of those asking them, but not always. They may be tests to see how strongly you believe in your idea. Be especially wary of the "innocent" or "ignorant" question, for it may be the beginning of an unexpected and offhand test to discredit you in a field removed from your area of competence. A good rule for discerning hazardous excursions is: *Always look every questioner straight in the eye.* You can get more information from his visage than you can by scanning the floor or ceiling as he talks. Sarcasm, hypocrisy, or irony can be completely absent in the *words* of a question, but they are nearly impossible to keep from the facial expressions that accompany them. Great cross-examiners lock to the face of a witness like radar on a hostile missile—alert to catch every nuance or flicker, twitch or hesitancy, for future use. These reactions are under much less conscious control than is our speech.

One mannerism of many presenters has its roots in courtly politeness, but it can create an unfortunate impression on the audience. This is the habit of nodding the head to signify understanding as you listen to a question. A clever questioner may reel off a set of contradictory points in laying the groundwork for his question. If you nod as he hurls each one, the audience sometimes misunderstands each nod as your *agreement* with his point. Train yourself not to indulge in this otherwise gracious habit. The best antidote again is to look directly at the questioner. Concentrated focus of the eyes suppresses the nod. On the other hand, do not overreact to questions with expressions of anger, horror, or agitation. This is rightly seen as ham acting, and discounts your over-all credibility.

Those blessed with a gift for wit must be especially careful how they answer questions. Baltasar Gracian, a Spanish satirist and philosopher, identified the hazard: "Many get the repute of being witty, but thereby lose the credit of being sensible." A quick mind joined to a sense of fun may seize on a serious question as the vehicle to make a joke, turn a phrase, or produce a pun. This is almost always harmful. Even if you bring down the house, after the glow of the entertainment wears off, the audience will see that you did not really answer the question. And one member of the audience who feels ill-used sits smoldering. There is one exception: If you make *yourself* the butt of the humor, it can be engaging (but few wits are good at that).

Should you possess a humorous cast of mind, use it under the controlled conditions of the direct presentation, where no one must be singled out as a target, and *everyone* can then enjoy it. When you have used humor in this way, there is even more reason to handle the questions in a serious manner. The contrast in styles gains you a reputation for being both witty *and* sensible. Should a wit in the audience score off you, relax, and show that you appreciate the sally. But do not turn the meeting into a volley of quips. If you show that you can gracefully take a humorous thrust, the audience warms to you in a far better way than if you insist on topping it—even if you do it superbly.

Allied to the problem of humorous responses are much lower orders of expression, which should never be used: condescension, ridicule, and flippancy. These are powerful engines for producing intellectual enemies, and yet produce no allies in return. Each generates an odor of insult and disrespect which pollutes the entire atmosphere of a presentation. When this happens, questions quickly dry up, for no one in his right mind taunts a polecat.

One gentle form of condescension comes from the use of the word "obvious." This word should be purged from your vocabulary as the question session begins, for if it is used in an answer, the questioner gets the feeling that you think he has defective vision. He slams the door to his mind to shut out any further consideration of your idea, for you have made it too painful to seek understanding. Besides, wily old Prince Metternich remarked that: "The obvious is always least understood." If an answer appears obvious to you, don't say so. Instead, try to deduce why it does not seem so to your questioner. You can often trace the trouble to deficient presentation of your idea originally.

Quibbling and evasion produce disgust. If you don't know the answer, say so directly. (It sometimes pays to ask if anyone in the audience does, especially if you have good reason to believe that no answer exists.) Microscopic dissection of a question, arguments over word meanings, obscure diversions, and long answers to a different question not raised try everyone's patience. You take on the appearance of the loser in a fencing duel from an old swashbuckling movie. There's plenty of action—running up and down stairs, jumping on tables, knocking over candlesticks, throwing furniture, getting caught in the draperies—but the audience soon senses that you will end up being cast from the balcony.

If you find yourself in a jam, you must extricate yourself by your own efforts. It is sometimes pitiful to see a presenter at his wits' end with a question he can't handle. Of course, he can end things neatly merely by saying "I don't know." But no, his eyes dart about for the least sign of help. Rather than utter the hateful words, he lets everyone see that he doesn't know by whining for support from his sponsor, or assistants. There is no more repellent way to throw in the towel.

Persons who carry a large burden of bitterness should not make presentations, for they often feel compelled to vent their frustrations at every opportunity. Their answers to questions are preceded by long introductions of their life and hard times, essays on past injustice, diatribes at those who stole their ideas in the past, stupidities of leaders who don't understand them—on and on down a nauseous trail. They are sometimes people of high talent, but they mangle a presentation beyond recognition during questioning. Such people are well advised to have their ideas turned over to others if they are really serious about getting them accepted. They are simply too crippled to engage in cross-examination, and it is cruel to see them try.

In concluding this chapter, let's establish two tests that a response to a question should pass: Does it inform? Does it persuade? Answers that do neither have no place in a presentation, for the audience attends primarily for these two reasons. The happiest outcome of a question period takes place when the dialogue produces a *new* solution to the problem you presented. But these are unusual. Be content if through their questions—and your answers—the audience achieves greater knowledge and understanding of your idea and its implications for them.

Prepare for cross-examination by listing every view, fact, or opinion that you or your colleagues can think of contrary to your idea. Treat each one seriously and think about your response beforehand. (You may even want to write them out as questions and answers to be distributed later.) In the light of your answers, you may see ways to alter the material or sequences included in the direct presentation so that you can refer back to it during the question time. This is a tough catharsis for half-baked ideas; but one thing more painful than discovering a deficiency in a presentation is *not* discovering it in time to fix it. Be merciless toward your presentation in anticipating cross-examination, and you will need no mercy when it arrives.

Finally, there is one courtesy often neglected at the close of a question period, which can do a great deal for the atmosphere the audience remembers. No matter how rough your reception —or how pleasant—you should sincerely thank the audience for the time and effort they gave to the examination of your idea. Tell them that you are grateful both for the opportunity to clarify your original presentation and for the additional viewpoints they contributed by their questions. Also, in cases where the time limit has been reached, express regret that you could not handle every question (especially important for written ones), but volunteer to be available for anyone who wants to discuss the subject further. Don't say these things unless you mean them. But if you *don't* mean them, the chance that your presentation was worthwhile is quite slim.

8

Building to a Strong Finish

or

A Cathedral Is More Than a Pile of Bricks

One Saturday afternoon before Christmas several years ago, I strolled down an old side street in Greenwich Village. In those days, a number of shops devoted to fine, hand-crafted products were concentrated along two quiet blocks. Visiting the neighborhood was a way of stepping back into a more leisured time— especially on a lightly snowing day. This time, though, there was a great deal of crowding about one of the bowed windows, and curiosity compelled me to see the cause of disturbance. I threaded my way through the good-humored swarm until I could see the front of the shop. Sitting in the window, cross-legged, totally oblivious to the fascinated throng outside, were two eight-year-old boys. They were dressed in well-worn Tyrolean clothes. Embroidered shirts, leather shorts, thick wool stockings, heavy mountaineers' shoes, and yellow hair were all covered by wood chips. These flew from the razor-sharp carving tools in their hands almost as fast as the snowflakes outside. At the front of the window were rows of carved bears, elves, and dogs. The quality of these was remarkable, but the speed of the little sculptors was miraculous. They never seemed to make an error, never hesitated, and always put their full strength into every cut. I watched them closely, for my grandfather was a fine wood-carver, and I had never seen him go at that pace. I noticed that, while the lads chattered constantly, they never took their eyes off the wood blocks in front of them until each small statue was finished.

I entered the shop to purchase one of the bears, and overheard the proprietor explain to an elderly customer what this was all about. "They are Austrian twins, and have been carving as long as they can remember. Their uncle taught them and they work with him in his shop in the mountains."

The old man asked how they worked at such speed, for they did not use templates, outlines, or any mechanical aid to guide the work.

"That's what so impressed me," said the shopkeeper. "I asked them to explain their methods. They tell me that their uncle showed them how every block of wood has an animal or person inside it waiting to be set free by the tools. To let them out, they say that you must keep seeing the animal or person right there in the wood all the time. Then all you do is cut the other wood away from around them. When you've cut away every chip holding them in, then the statue is free! I know it sounds like some kind of fairy tale, but that's what they say, and you can see for yourself that it works."

The old man nodded, but was shaking his head as he waved good-bye.

I never saw them again. My wife liked the bear so much that she wanted another one, as well as an elf and dog. A few days later I returned, but the street was quiet and the window empty. I gathered that there had been some difficulties about child labor statutes. I bought my figures from a clerk, and am looking at one now as I write this.

What do I see? The same vision that guided the tiny hands on their hazardous mission of liberation. As I observed presentations over the intervening years, it occurred to me that the good ones had something in common with the carvers, and the poor ones did not. The sure, deft touch of the superior presentor is under the same kind of control as were the sharp tools. What is the basis of the similarity? I believe it is found in the simplest reason of all: Both the good presentors and the little craftsmen know exactly *how they want their work to end.* They are also able to bring it to that destination. The bumbling presentors, in contrast, are almost as much in the dark about their desired endings as their audiences. It is almost as though they have written a mystery story without a last chapter. The frustration and quiet rage at finding the final chapter missing, after reading for two hours, is quite similar to the reactions observed as an audience breaks up after one of these disasters.

In Chapter 3, we discussed the cardinal rule for securing agreement: *Start where THEY are, not where YOU are.*

The emphasis of this is on the *start,* but it implies movement *toward* something. This "something" can be one of two things: The *actions* you want the audience to take when you are finished; the *attitudes* you want an audience to embrace when you are finished. These are not, of course, mutually exclusive. Actions always signify certain attitudes, and attitudes set up potential action. But from a presentation point of view, it is best to decide on one or the other. Let the momentum built up by such concentration drag along the subtle overtones of the one not selected.

Before agreeing to make a presentation, answer two questions to *your* own satisfaction. No one else need know your answers, but it is absolutely essential for success that *you* produce them.
1. Why am I best qualified to do the job in these circumstances?
2. When I sit down: a. What do I want the audience to do? or b. What do I want them to believe?

It is in all seriousness that I advise you to abandon, reject, or flee from the presentation if you cannot answer these satisfactorily. Presentors who neglect them experience broken reputations and abraded emotions.

They produce effects similar to those pitiful clerics who continue to go through the motions and rituals of a religion after they have lost their faith or belief in God. They are truly lost souls, and have their counterparts in inferior presentors. These men suddenly seem to ask themselves in the middle of their story, as they see their audience fidget or doze, "What am I doing up here?" If that question is answered *before* you grasp the podium, it will not intrude from out of the blue.

One motivation that often prevents a good person from making the decisions necessary is the desire to be known as a "prudent" or "sound" man. Such people undertake a presentation with only a vague hope that they will convince the audience of a proposal they are not too sure about. They begin with a firm resolve to "turn up the volume" on their radar sets to maximum sensitivity, so that they can adjust their ending as natural leaders in the audience begin showing their attitude. Such presentors wish to end up with a majority on their side at any price, even if they themselves have to switch their original position over to the majority. These men do not put on real presentations of ideas. They conduct, instead, long-winded rituals of conformity. In effect, they answer the questions this way: "I am the best qualified to present this idea because my superior asked me to," and "When I finish, I want the audience to do (or believe) what they want to do (or believe)." These answers do not produce outstanding presentations, even though they win gold medals for dullness and ambiguity.

For those who wish to acquire the reputation of a "prudent" or "sound" man, I include this little kit of maxims which are thoroughly tested:

1. Always take a seat at the center of gravity of an audience.
2. Do not get involved in serious discussion of a controversial issue.
3. Take enormous quantities of notes.
4. Smile graciously and nod in assent at all remarks that flatter the audience's past accomplishments.
5. Look grave and concerned if the presentor comes within ten thousand yards of showing discontent with the existing order of things.
6. If finally trapped into expressing your own opinion, look thoughtful and send a cliché reverberating around the conference room. Some useful ones to keep ready are: "Of course

we must crawl before we can walk"; "Great minds have struggled for years with this problem"; "I certainly don't have the answer, but what Mr. S says makes a great deal of sense to me." (Mr. S should be the highest ranking man in the room.)

7. Don't make serious presentations yourself.

Alas, it is with false regret that I must tell anyone who uses these rules that the authentically solid men of our time do not follow them. If they did, they could not make the kinds of contributions to families, businesses, government, education, or religion that fuel any real progress in these institutions. Fortunately, the truly sound and prudent men do not pursue the label itself, for they know it to be phony.

I mention this problem to stress the necessity for a serious presentor to prepare himself for controversy. If his idea is a genuinely fresh approach, or an original insight, it is bound to jar many in the audience. Harry Truman summed it up: "If you can't stand the heat, get out of the kitchen." The best way to stand the heat is to *know exactly what you want to happen*.

Now this does *not* mean that you narrow every remark or handle every question with a single-minded fanaticism aimed at the ending you want. This is repellent to an audience and violates the advice in Chapter 5 on Psychological Hints. You must create an atmosphere of complete flexibility, but *in your own mind* you must have the ultimate goal. Sometimes you can state your objective explicitly (near the ending of the presentation), but you can also suggest it indirectly, or let the discussion and questions produce the articulation of your desired outcome. When this happens, you can then wrap it up as a consensus. Diplomats have an aphorism that encapsulates the indirect approach: "The shortest distance between two points of view is a detour." But wise diplomats who set out on the detour never lose sight of the fact that the detour is only another—and better —way to get where they really want to go. Only inferior practitioners think that the detour is the destination. Some of them, excusing their incompetence, try later to convince their critics that the detour they were trapped in by the superior finesse of their opposition is actually a better destination than the original.

This fools only those who did not know of their original intentions.

These two extremes of narrow-minded, fanatical concentration and random wanderings, coupled with willingness to accept any kind of compromise, are the shoals through which you must steer your idea. If you go too far in either direction, your idea will run aground. An early example of the first comes from Cato the Elder (234–149 B.C.), a nasty sort of Roman puritan, who hated everything he did not enjoy or understand—especially other people's happiness. On a trip to Carthage he saw how prosperous Rome's neighbors were and became a slave to one idea. After every Senate speech, or at the end of every statement, he would say, "Carthage must be destroyed." If he were asked, "How did you like the meal?" he would answer, "It was a noble feast; but, you know, Carthage must be destroyed." After a while this kind of thing got on his colleagues' nerves, and they finally went off and destroyed Carthage—probably just to shut him up! If you select this method of presenting your idea, you should be aware that you can use it only once in a lifetime. People just won't put up with it more than that.

Low forms of politicans—even if in high places—illustrate the second style. Here their sole objective is to get elected, no matter what ideas they must embrace to do so. They acquire and abandon ideas generated by others the way some women abandon dress styles—constantly scrambling to stay with the mob. They never have ideas of their own in which they believe. This quality distinguishes them from the statesman who develops a vision of what a better world should be like, and then presents his ideas to educate and persuade his people to understand and adopt his vision. Even though it may take years, and perhaps result in his personal defeat or resignation, he keeps his eye on the vision. Few of us will ever make presentations on such lofty levels, and with such high stakes, but the same principles are applicable to even the most humble idea.

Before we leave these pathological extremes, it may be well to generalize on the use of roundabout methods: The more indirect the approach to an objective, the greater the skill required. One of the best incidents I know which exemplifies this comes from the life of Talleyrand, Foreign Minister and master presentor, who survived every change in government during turbulent times. Monarchy, Terror, Directory, Consulate, Empire, Restoration, and a new Monarchy, all found him landing on his feet, yet always prosecuting his ideas for peace, constitutionality, and the good of France and Europe. Even his persuasive power was unable to deter Napoleon from leading a campaign against Spain. However, as soon as Napoleon left Paris, Talleyrand for the first time appeared at a large party with Fouché, his political enemy and head of the secret police. Napoleon had shrewdly used the animosity between Talleyrand and Fouché to keep them both in line.

Talleyrand knew that as soon as he and Fouché were seen walking arm-in-arm and quietly conversing, someone would inform their leader. Sure enough, shortly thereafter, Napoleon jumped from a foaming horse, crashed into Talleyrand's presence, and loudly upbraided him in the rudest barracks language, going so far as to pinch his ear lobe between thumbnail and index finger. The entire company stood stupefied, but Talleyrand did not flinch, for he had completely succeeded in his objective. He only remarked, after his fuming master had departed in a rage, as to what a pity it was that such a great man had been so badly brought up! This use of indirection required nerve and clearness of vision far beyond the normal; but if you use any indirection at all, you must have at least some measure of both. The greater of these is clearness of vision, for it generates the nerve.

One way to approach the design of a presentation is to see it as the construction of a cantilever bridge over a river. Halfway finished, the bridge might look like this:

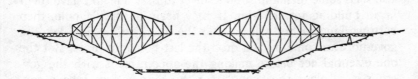

Such bridges are built by starting at both *ends* and building toward the center, using the completed parts as work platforms for the next parts.

One bank of the river is *where the audience is now* in reference to your idea; the other bank is *where you want them to be* when you are finished. No civil engineer can begin his bridge design until his client tells him where these two points are. He would think his client an utter fool if the client told him to "start building where we are now, and as we go along, I'll decide where we will hit the other side." With this advice, the engineer does not even know where to place the ends of the first girder delivered. As absurd as this example may seem, many presentations proceed in just this way. It is no wonder that their audiences feel "left up in the air," for that is exactly the kind of bridge the presentor has built. It goes nowhere.

The remedy for such presentations is the same as for the bridge: Begin the design by specifying the *closing* statements of the presentation. All other parts of development, as well as the opening remarks, will be oriented to that terminal point—the finish of the presentation. In the preliminary design it is not wise to include any indirection at all, for the inevitable diffuseness produced may cause the whole structure to go awry. If you have a clear simple structure, you can always appliqué the indirect parts onto it. You will also know exactly how to have them rejoin the main structure of the presentation—and where.

Notice how our analogy holds. If the engineer on the bank, supplied with rivets, girders, and men, can just get his client to place a flagpole in the ground on the other side where he wants the bridge to go, his design and organizational efforts fall into place. All the men placing girders know that everything they do must be in line with the flagpole on the far side. The engineer can also send some men and supplies over to that side and have them begin building toward him. If they begin at the flagpole, then both working parties will meet in the middle. One fine day, the governor can come by and drop the last bolt into place. But the one essential act before making the appointment with the governor is to plant the flagpole for the termination. I have continually emphasized this point ad nauseam, because its neglect ruins more presentations than any other single factor. Even bad presentations usually have a wealth of good material or content, but collapse due to poor structure. Poor structure is almost always caused by failure to state the closing clearly *before* the design begins. Every presentor should keep an image of the Leaning Tower of Pisa somewhere in his head as a warning.

A good disciplinary method comes from writing out the closing remarks first. State what you want the audience to do, or what you want them to believe, in stark sentences. You may moderate their expression later, but not now. Keep these sentences near you throughout the composition of the entire presentation. Every subsidiary idea, piece of evidence, example, contrary view, or diversion should be examined in the light of these closing statements. Like the steelworkers lining up beams by sighting across to the flagpole, or the little wood-carvers looking for bears hidden in their blocks of wood, every part of the presentation's development must be initiated, included, or abandoned by judging its contribution to the finish.

Sometimes a minor tragedy develops. When the end point selected, as shown in the closing statements, cannot be supported by emotion, common sense, or reason in the development, the conclusion must be altered. It is as though the river is too wide for your bridge design, and there will be a permanent gap in the middle. Some presentors ignore this and think that they can get across by a running jump. Remember, one alert member of the audience may trip you on the run, and it's a long way down to the splash. Polite ones do it by casually charging you with "non sequitur"; others use more vulgar barnyard expressions. Both can be fatal. Honesty, as well as safety, requires you to scale down the conclusion to what your development can support. Strategists call this process "readjusting your ends to your means."

In his haunting novel, *The Spire*, William Golding illustrates the advice. This complex story is one of conflict between the visionary and the practical man, and takes place in medieval times. The dean of a cathedral is dissatisfied that his church does not have a proper spire. He has a small wooden model of the church made, and also adds to the model a removable spire. He uses the two-piece model to illustrate the "before" and "after" of his proposal in his requests for funds to various personages. With funds finally secured, the dean employs a master builder to turn the vision into reality. The saintly dean has a very strong finish, for he shows the builder precisely what he wants as he plants the beautifully detailed, one-foot model spire on top of the stubby church tower. The builder is aghast, for he sees that the actual stone spire will be four hundred feet in the air! He mutters and makes calculations, measurements, and soundings, which convince him that the whole project is insane. But the dean insists and will not cut back his objective in the face of any pragmatic evidence. The builder is kept on the job by all sorts of inducements, but becomes more and more worried as more and more stones are placed. The pillars of the church start to bulge and crack, services must be discontinued inside, and strange noises and groans come from the church walls, as though complaining of the weight added to them every day. Still, the dean keeps on. He enjoys standing in the wind at the topmost level of construction, and neglects all other responsibilities. The story's ending is ambiguous, but we know that everyone's life has been altered, and some ruined, by the beautiful vision of a saintly man who would not "adjust his ends to his means."

I mention this because my plea for a *strong* finish should not be misunderstood as suggesting that its forcefulness be greater than its underpinning. Attempts to make a conclusion stronger than its development can support actually indicates weakness. Friedrich Nietzsche pointed out that one will rarely make an error if he assumes that extreme actions are rooted in vanity. Audiences always assume it, and usually dislike the motivation they unconsciously deduce—unless their own vanity is fortified. This latter technique, however, belongs in the demagogue's tool kit as a standard item. It should only be used in rare cases by serious presentors of ideas, and then only to counter unfair attacks from unscrupulous opponents.

Perhaps this is a good point at which to demonstrate the method of using the needs for a strong finish to discipline the total design. Which type of example should we use?

There is one kind of presentation that nearly all of us are called on to make. Superiors, friends, children, inspectors, parents, and colleagues—anyone we know—often invite us to tell them something about what we are doing in our daily work. The simplest form is posed by the conventional question, "What's new?" or "How goes it?" Few expect a literal response any more than when they ask, "How are you?" Even the kindliest of persons would be startled if you whipped out a copy of your latest medical report and presented it to them. Yet, related to these social conventions, which don't mean what they say, are some presentation opportunities which *do* expect more than a polite reply such as "Not much, what's new with you?" or "I'm fine. How are you?" (There is also prevalent a variation of these replies: "So what's *got* to be new?" This can create a tense situation from a casual encounter—much like border incidents that turn into wars.)

Let's assume that you are engaged in some activity in which others have an interest, and that from time to time they visit you. On these visits you are expected to give them some idea of what is going on in your line of work at your specific location. Whether you are a principal, an army colonel, a sales manager, the dean of a college, a plant superintendent, a ward boss, Secretary of Defense, or head of a hospital, you must give an account of some kind. In fact, anyone who is responsible *for* something is also responsible *to* somebody, or a group of somebodies. They may be hostile or friendly, experts or ignoramuses, high or low, but they have rights to your time. When absolutely no accountability exists, we call this state of affairs corruption. It is the underlying assumption of Lord Acton's famous line in his letter to a bishop: "Power tends to corrupt; absolute power corrupts absolutely." When this condition of unaccountable power exists, serious presentations of ideas are neither expected, welcomed, nor tolerated. The later periods of tyrants exemplify the pure form of such absolutism, and can be found in all institutions ranging from families to nations. Until you ram into this kind of wall, your potential presentations have a place. They should be looked on as opportunities, not as inquisitions. Such meetings are social glue and can hold individuals and groups together through mutual understanding of their respective responsibilities and rights. When the people concerned eliminate this kind of communication, or do it ineptly, discord gets its chance to grow.

I emphasize this need for good presentations because many persons who are incompetent to make them disparage their usefulness. Such people feel that "if everybody did what they were supposed to, we wouldn't need to waste all this time talking." Seldom do they see that the frustration and weariness of crisis meetings usually arise because no one really made clear to "everybody" in the first place just what they *were* supposed to do. In this regard, tailors have wisdom beyond some of the highest officials, for they see every day confirming evidence that "A stitch in time saves nine." But the man who makes that first stitch—or the first presentation—should know his business. *Mis*understanding can be propagated by a bad initial presentation of an idea. When this happens, it would be better if it had not occurred, for now a great deal of salvage work, like a train wreck, is needed just to restore the status quo. The weight of many salvage-type conferences oppresses the spirit and makes experienced persons weary of *all* presentations. Yet the corrective is not elimination of proposals for ideas but, instead, improvement of their quality—especially where poor quality leads to increased misunderstanding. Neglect of the *closing* of the presentation accounts for more misunderstanding of an idea than all other aspects combined. This observation suggests a rule: *Begin at the end.*

How can this work in real life? Here is one fictional dialogue that may illustrate the rule in action:

Scene: The leader of urban renewal efforts for a large city has called a meeting of his five chief subordinates. They must sketch out the forty-five-minute presentation asked for by the Federal Commission that furnishes a great deal of the funds required. The visit will take place in four weeks.

Dramatis Personae:
    Leader
    Construction Head

Planning Head
Health Officer
Social Work and Relocation Chief
Financial Officer

Leader: Well, here we are again, faced with the annual report to our Washington visitors. What do we have to tell them that won't take longer than forty-five minutes? Last year we didn't do too well, and kept getting sidetracked with all kinds of details. I'd like to do a lot better this year if we can. Any suggestions?

Planning: This whole thing is ridiculous! How can we possibly wrap up in less than an hour the tremendous efforts and problems of thousands of people?

Leader: I understand your attitude, but remember, the commissioners have many other groups just like us. If we don't accept this chance on their terms, and help them do their job, we can't expect much sympathy or help. Anybody else?

Health: We've made fine progress in the sewage and sanitation areas, but the disease rates are still high. Do you think they'd be interested in that?

Leader: I'm not sure that it helps us unless we have an intelligent interpretation ready. Let's hold that as a possibility.

Construction: We have some projects ahead of schedule and some behind. The strikes have hurt us and we haven't completed our new schedule to rebalance their effects yet. But if Planning would push it, maybe we can have the new schedule ready in time.

Leader: That sounds good. What about it?

Planning: We can't make the new schedule because we haven't got the Relocation Office's new estimates. Without them, the schedule is nothing but fantasy dressed up in arithmetic. Also, that antique computer I have to use for scheduling calculations is a real drag on everybody.

Leader: Social, can't you get him the estimates?

Social: Sure, but we have never achieved the estimates we worked up in the past, and we want to do a better job. We are now getting demonstrations against us because of our increased pressure to help Construction. Also, closing down the old clinic before we had alternate facilities didn't do us any good, as I predicted. That was just plain dumb; we really led with our chin on that one.

Health: I agree, and it's only because of the College Hospital's cooperation that we didn't have a real crisis. But we can't expect them to always bail us out. We really should have scraped up the money and not just hoped for the best.

Finance: I know, and am sympathetic; but we don't have the power to reallocate these funds after we submit the program. In fact, I've gone past the limit of my discretion several times to do all I can to help, but some of these restrictions really limit our flexibility. I simply can't hide the construction of a new clinic which wasn't anticipated—and I shouldn't be able to. The procedures are designed to prevent such things.

Planning: Okay. We are the culprits because we forced you all to take a chance that didn't work out. But remember, the contractors just couldn't wait, and if we had to pay them penalties with no work going on, the press would rough us up. We can't expect the public to understand all the intricacies of this whole operation, and we had to make the choice with this in mind.

Social: Yes, but the reporters are now giving a great deal of space and attention to our whole relocation effort. We really must improve it. They have played up some pretty awful cases, and I can't say that I blame them too much. We are entrusted with public funds and should expect people whose taxes pay for our work to be interested in how their taxes are used. Goof-ups make news.

Leader: No argument about that.

Planning: What gets my goat is that we are trying to benefit this community, and everything good we do gets no appreciation. But let one little thing go wrong, and the roof falls in.

Health: People's medical problems aren't a "little thing" to them —or me.

Planning: You know what I mean!

Leader: Sure we do. But a catalogue of gripes isn't doing anybody any good. Planning is right in that we have accomplished a great deal in the face of tough problems, but we do have a lot left on our plate. If I reported what we've just heard, I could understand the commissioners recommending our dismissal, and we truly don't deserve that yet. We *have* learned how to run this kind of thing better every day. I believe that if we can use this opportunity in the right way, we will get better understanding of our situation. The commissioners are fine, experienced men. They generally know what the difficulties are, but how do we help *them* with a litany of misfortune?

Planning: Well, I guess it really doesn't.

Construction: You know, when I have my own men in for a meeting, I usually become impatient with them if they just recite their troubles.

Planning: That's right. I do too. In fact I had to let one man go because that's all he did! I want to know what they are *doing* about them.

Finance: We have a rule in our shop: No problem accepted unless you have two proposed solutions to go along with it.

Leader: Now we're getting somewhere. Social, do you have any proposed solutions to this relocation problem?

Social: Yes, we've been kicking around lots of ideas, but most of the good ones call for some reallocation of funds.

Health: We've worked on some, too, and have banged our heads against the same wall.

Finance: They're right, Leader. I've done all I can, but my hands are tied with the present rules. We've exhausted all of the quick fixes. We need some kind of genuine overhaul.

Planning: I agree, and if we had the flexibility, and a better computer, my folks could produce some really dynamic, up-to-the-minute rescheduling that would do a far better optimizing job. This could relieve all of the supervision of a lot of phony crisis work. I know I could do without a whole platoon of expediters who always seem to be getting in each other's way.

Construction: Me too.

Social: We'd do anything to get out of the present straitjacket.

Leader: All right. We now seem to have some ideas which might interest the commission. If they buy them, then they can use their real talents and power for constructive improvement instead of holding our hands in sympathy. They must dislike that even more than we do.

Health: It's also better psychologically. This way we don't look like a bunch of neurotics.

Leader: Thank you, doctor. Now, let's get down to bedrock. Last year we built our whole case on inexperience. That was a mistake. The honeymoon is over, and the commission shares any success or failure we produce. They know it, and we know it. *Just what do we want them to do when I've finished the presentation?* If we can agree on that, then we can build the whole talk around it. Who's first?

Planning: What we really want them to do is to increase our discretionary power over funds and timing.

Finance: Not quite. They have their own masters and you can't expect them to give you a blank checkbook. I wouldn't even trust myself to get any efficiency at all if I didn't have some limits. I certainly wouldn't trust others.

Social: I don't think we really need *more* funds, just more flexibility to use the total we have now.

Chorus of Construction, Health, Planning and Finance: Right!

Leader: Okay. We want the commission to modify its procedures so that we can do a better job in adjusting our efforts to unforeseen circumstances. But we will not request any over-all increase in funds. How will they be sure we're doing a good job?

Planning: We will send their staff a copy of every new schedule we run on the new computer, with all changes indicated and explained.

Leader: Wait a minute! You know that all data processing equipment is reviewed by the central staff.

Planning: Right. But the new procedures should allow us to make substitutions which do not increase over-all outlays. I can do it with present money. Also, with better, more rapid scheduling methods, the waste of effort should be less, and we could actually take a cut in funds.

Health: Hold on. If we get that, it is far better to put those savings on the disease problem, which we've badly underestimated.

Social: I agree.

Planning: It's all right with me.

Leader: Construction, do you think he's right?

Construction: Well, we've been burned once or twice by Planning, but he's right about the waste. I know how much "hurry-up and wait" we've got now. If we could just make a small improvement, we could help Doc out, I'm sure.

Finance: Even if the commission is worried about the idea, perhaps our proposal could be tried out on an experimental basis for a year. It may work well, and they could then make it available to other places in the country. I've talked to many of the other financial people and we are all having the same kind of problem.

Social: Maybe the commission is just waiting for somebody to suggest it!

Leader: Maybe, but we don't want to get carried away. I've written down a list of what we want the commission to do: 1. Order us to develop for their approval more flexible procedures for adjustment to changed circumstances. 2. Use a fast computer for rescheduling to keep everyone informed of changes made. 3. Keep funds at the same level. 4. If desired, try the new ideas out on an experimental basis.

We also want them to feel that: 1. We have produced a good job in the face of unexpected problems. 2. We have our fingers on the pulse of the whole effort and know what we're doing. 3. They can expect improvements from us which may benefit urban renewal management throughout the country.

Planning: If someone told me that, I'd give him a chance to show what he could do.

Social: Do you think you can do all that in forty-five minutes?

Leader: I can if each of you will take these statements and do two things. First, give me some examples of how what we had to do before was hindered by lack of the improvements we proposed. Second, list some current major difficulties which might be overcome if we get what we ask for. Also, give me some of the counterarguments against our ideas.

Planning: There aren't any!

Finance: There always are!

Leader: Hold it! You all know what we want. Also, put down your ideas for visuals—photographs, charts, cases, etc.—if they help make your points in less time, for we must make every minute count. Planning will work out the actual presentation visuals for our meeting next week from the rough ideas you give him. They should all be related and in the same format. We will decide the sequence later. Above all, keep out unnecessary material which does not go to our conclusion. If you are doubtful about something, bring it along next time, and we'll decide on it as a group. Now that I know where we're going, I can start to work on the opening statement. Any questions?

Finance: What if we fail to convince them?

Leader: They will at least know more than they know now, they will see that we mean business, and that we can be trusted to do our best, even if they don't buy our solutions. I personally think, though, that our chances for success are far greater than we now realize. We have focused today on helping *them,* rather than drearily listing our own troubles. That alone represents an infinite improvement over last year's fiasco.

Construction: I feel better now than I have for months.

Social: I want to get with my people right away.

Planning: It'll be great!

Health: I'd almost given up, but now we've got a chance.

Finance: I'll be grateful if I just don't have to say *No!* so often.

(Curtain)

Fiction? Certainly! It differs from many situations in real life in its brevity and the happy ending. Think of the meetings you've attended. Didn't you always prefer a difficult goal, if clearly stated, to a vague suggestion at the end of the gathering that everyone should just go away and "think about" a problem? What did you actually *do* when that happened? If you are like most, you put the notes in a drawer and grabbed them five minutes before you attended the next session of the "problem-solving" group. But if the job to be done was clear, you probably couldn't wait to get started on your piece.

Clear statement of the *ending* of a presentation has another advantage where specialists are part of a group. It mobilizes their imagination and knowledge by showing them where to direct their attention. When several specialists or people of diverse experience address their skills to a common, desired result, creativity has a chance to surface. Atomic bombs go off when different amounts of potentially active material are rapidly brought together at one point. Kept separate, the pieces are almost as safe as bricks. Creative solutions from specialists focusing on a common clear goal produce the quiet explosions of progress in almost the same way. The trick is to show them what is desired with appropriate specificity. Individual experience or knowledge not harnessed in this way is as unlikely to produce a "great leap forward" as atomic bomb pieces are to go off by themselves. In fact, specialists isolated from a need to focus on real problems or goals usually go in for the "great leap sideways." There are now one hundred thousand learned journals published. Those interested in curiosities, which qualify as "great leaps sideways," will find some of these journals a rich source. Every one they find represents a tragedy of misdirected intellect, and has its roots in lack of relation to the real problems in its field.

One writer calls this situation the disease of science. If it is a disease, refocusing on real problems is not a bad place to start for the cure. Great men in every area of intellect can be measured by the greatness of the problems they set themselves. Few of them were unsure of what they were up to. The accidental discovery was a genuine discovery, and not a distraction, only because the discoverer had his mind on a real problem, which the "accident" solved. As Pasteur put it: "Chance favors only the prepared minds." The best preparation for any mind is selection of a goal. (We will discuss this aspect of idea generation more fully in Chapter 11.) As lightning seeks the pointed rods placed on buildings, so talent is attracted to the clearly stated ending of an idea's presentation.

One of the most influential and dramatic presentations of an idea took place in Wittenberg in 1517. When Martin Luther hammered his ninety-five theses to the door of the castle church, he made it absolutely clear where he stood, and welcomed debate on his position. Many people before him had raised similar points, but Luther's presentation could be grasped by peasant and professor alike. Widely distributed by the relatively new invention of printing, the clearness of what he wanted his audience to do could not be ignored or misunderstood. Theologians and nobles, craftsmen and intellectuals, all had to measure their positions in relation to Luther's. Some joined him, others fought him; but none could remain indifferent to his proposals.

Should we do less when presenting our own ideas and programs for improvements? Of course, few of us are Luthers, but everyone can at least give his ideas the best start possible. One way is to couple two pieces of advice for structural punch: *Start where your audience IS, but show, with the greatest clarity, Where You Stand, and What You Would Like Them To Do.*

Your finish can only be as strong as the end of a presentation is clear. To torture an old proverb: "He travels furthest who knows his destination."

9

Coping with Special
Knowledge and Its Jargon

or

Undermining the Tower of Babel

The passage in Genesis that describes the aborted construction of the Tower of Babel carries great significance for our own era. After their adventures of the flood, the survivors found a pleasant place to put down roots, and began building a city with a tower in the center to reach up to Heaven. Things were going along fine, everybody knew what to do as they all used one language, and success looked like a sure thing. However, the Lord had other plans. An entire earth had to be populated, and with everyone looking forward to a relaxed and affluent life in a brand-new town, there was no incentive to leave, especially after all they had been through. Inspection of the project showed that they had made remarkable progress, so the Lord selected the most subtle and powerful method for breaking up a human community: "Let us go down, and there confound their language, that they may not understand one another's speech."

This maneuver was perfectly correct in that it did "scatter them abroad upon the face of all the earth." As an exercise in

241

management it is hard to criticize, for all three criteria for first-class management practice were satisfied: See where you are, know where you want to go, and choose the best way to get there.

Unfortunately, now that the earth is full, we face exactly the reverse problem today, and should logically diminish the variety of tongues if we want to get on with improvement of our world. Yet the commands of a different god, specialized knowledge, continue to "confound our language." This hampers common efforts by persons of different disciplines and backgrounds. The present momentum is too great to turn back, and schemes that try will share the same fate as Esperanto and other universal languages—passionate commitment from a handful of ineffective advocates; amused indifference from all others. We must accept the fact that a lively field generates new terms—or new meanings for old ones—almost as fast as it generates new knowledge.

And yet our more complex human affairs require that many specialties be brought to bear on the large problems of today. Seldom do the people responsible for the resources of men and money necessary to utilize expert skills on programs and projects have deep knowledge or competence in even one field. Never do they have it when several different kinds of expertise are involved. The more intricate interdependence of all parts of society has also created a need for many other people—not only those who say *yes* or *no* to a proposal—to acquire clear understanding of ideas which may have severe impact on their own interests, development, and livelihoods. As a consequence, if your idea requires the use of special knowledge, you must be prepared to undertake its translation for dissemination to a great number of nonprofessional, intelligent laymen who constitute an approving body, your colleagues, or fellow citizens. They can not be expected to cooperate unless they understand the relevance of your idea to their lives. They can only achieve understanding of specialized matters with your help. Anyone truly interested in bringing his idea to the arena of ordinary life welcomes every chance he gets.

This chapter is designed to help the specialist make the most of his chances. Those who do not care whether anyone understands them or not are rare, and must satisfy harsh conditions for the attitude to be authentic—and not an elegant cover-up. They must be: 1. independent of the control of others for all necessary resources used in their work or, 2. truly contemptuous of the intellect of others not fellow professionals in their sector of work, or 3. such men of genius, so far in advance of their contemporaries, that no one can possibly share their insights until long after their death. Unless you are certain that you can meet one of these tests, it is worthwhile to learn something of the techniques useful for unfolding esoteric ideas to intelligent persons interested in your work. They may not be equipped by previous training or practice to absorb such ideas in the technical form natural to you, but many great men have mastered the art and continually renewed enthusiasm for their subject by making it meaningful to others. First-class teachers all do and, as a result, are the unsung trustees of our culture. In our world each of us flip-flops between the roles of teacher and student every day of our life. Besides, the exercise of translating is usually challenging fun, and the different perspective it produces can offer entirely new insights into your professional practice. Enrico Fermi, Nobel Laureate and father of atomic fission, taught first-year physics to minds new to a subject in which he was pre-eminent. His example should chasten many of lesser attainments, who consider such activity beneath them.

This chapter divides into six parts: the nature of translation; how perception comes about with complex ideas; aspects of pedantry (the poison of understanding); deleterious motivations of specialists which inhibit successful presentations; methods of approach to transform the insights of special knowledge into ideas of relevance to laymen; and ways to deal with numbers and statistics which enhance comprehension.

Before beginning our excursion, let's take note of that wisest of physicians, Sir William Osler, who said "In science the credit goes to the man who convinces the world, not to the man to whom the idea first occurs." (Not only in science, Sir William.)

An idea not passed on might just as well have left its original mind unstained, for it adds nothing to the common culture. He who does set out to bring new knowledge to others gets—and deserves—their gratitude, and sometimes even fame. These are the people who have produced our entire intellectual heritage. In fact, one could make a good case that the specialist who does not do his best to communicate has not fulfilled his side of the implicit social contract (which allows him to acquire and develop his knowledge) with his family, employer, university, community, or nation.

So much for the "why"; let's move now to "what" and "how."

THE NATURE OF TRANSLATION

Specialists have a morbid fear of "popularization." They often purge from their ranks those elder members of a profession who pass the years beyond original, creative work by writing accounts of ongoing progress designed for the vulgar masses. Yet these same specialists are extremely flattered when asked for permission to translate some piece of their work into another language. Let's take advantage of this tendency. One way to look at a presentation to nonexperts in a field is to see it as a translation into another language: the vernacular. Fowler (of Oxford English Dictionary fame) calls the vernacular, "words familiar to us as long as we can remember—the homely part of the language in contrast to terms consciously acquired." No translation is more difficult—or more rewarding in the long run. The hazards of translation to any other language deter many otherwise brave souls, for a good translation must traverse a narrow ridge between unintelligibility and unintentional low comedy. Consider these examples. In English we use an expression, "once in a blue moon," for an infrequent event. As you translate a story into Spanish and encounter this phrase, could you guess its equivalent? It is, "Every now and then a bishop dies." Logical? Hardly.

An acquaintance, eminent in engineering, was once a delegate to a scientific congress in Budapest. Every modern facility for simultaneous translation into twelve languages (including Swahili) was provided, and yet my friend said he never spent a more baffling session than one devoted to methods of metal forming. The lecture was given in Turkish. It detailed a fascinating story of progress in a developing country, but my friend kept going off the track with continual references to "water goats." He could not figure how these animals were of any possible use in the mills. Later, at dinner, he confessed his difficulty to an Englishman fluent in Turkish, who smiled and said, "So that's the best these literary types doing the translations could do with *Hydraulic Rams*." Everyone has his own favorites which make the same point. The absurdities are even worse when the "translation" is made into the *same* language. Consider mathematics. This "queen of the sciences" has a certain feminine wiliness, for, unlike most other disciplines, it uses very common words to represent the most complex concepts.

Few people would admit that they do not know the meaning of the following words: set, domain, rational, real, imaginary, integrate, definite, infinite, variable, series, function, probability, argument, constant, factor, group, complex, operator, proof, rigorous. Yet, if a mathematician overheard someone express his opinion of their meaning, he would hold his sides with laughter. (Try it on a mathematical friend.) An intelligent layman could listen to an advanced discourse on mathematics, "understand" every word, and actually be less informed than when he entered the room, since he would have acquired a great deal of misinformation.

Every discipline that uses mathematics can fall into the same trap. Biological subjects, on the other hand, use words from ancient languages to describe commonly known items: *patella* (kneecap), *carpus* (wrist), *gluteus maximus* (buttock), *Ilex opaca* (holly), *Betula papyrifera* (birch tree), *Castalia odorata* (water lily), *Taraxacum officinale* (dandelion), *Dolichonyx oryzivorus* (bobolink), *Marmota monax* (woodchuck), *Ondatra zibethica* (muskrat). (Mathematical biologists must have a terrible time.) These two extremes of simple words for complex ideas and jawbreaking labels for everyday things are found, in various mixtures, in the working languages of every craft, profession, or specialty, from ditchdigging to brain surgery. If you must convey something of their meaning to others not privy to the science or art involved, then you must either decode them into terms your audience already knows, or teach them the meaning, if they really want to learn the jargon itself. If you don't, you might just as well deliver the talk in Phoenician.

"But," the expert objects, "each of these terms has a special meaning of great precision. They have been developed over generations primarily to prevent misunderstanding. How can we possibly throw them aside just to please a bunch of people, worse than amateurs, who won't take the little trouble required to grasp our terminology?" One reply is if you do not *need* understanding from the people in front of you, don't make the presentation. As in the days of Caesar Augustus, you may detest Rome, but if you need something only Rome can give, or *have* to go there, it is wise to speak as the Romans do. Another answer comes indirectly from the art of map-making, or, as called by its practitioners, cartography.

Map-makers begin with an honest appraisal of their limitations. They know that no matter how careful and skillful they become, they can never represent the entire truth and reality of the actual earth itself. Besides, nobody needs it. For several hundred years cartographers have developed techniques to represent *certain aspects* of the earth's surface designed to fill *specific needs* for particular users. The spectrum of details and features runs from a mere grid of latitude and longitude with a few dots to represent points of interest, to breathtaking works of art, which show the detailed physical features of a continent with clarity.

I once navigated an airplane from San Francisco to Honolulu at night, using a "chart" made up by drawing lines of latitude and longitude on a sheet of brown wrapping paper with two X's on it—one for San Francisco, and one for Honolulu. (We had short notice for the flight and no available maps.) To my surprise, the uncluttered sheet, empty of irrelevant matter, like depth markings in fathoms, was far easier to use than the official charts, and I adopted the method for subsequent work. This incident illustrates the secondary benefits that flow from orienting a piece of technical work directly to the need of the user. People listening to your presentation are trying to make use of your knowledge *for their purpose*. Most are there to learn something that will have a bearing on the future decisions facing them. If you can achieve the state where you look at your information or techniques from their point of view, the proper emphasis will come almost automatically. But this is more difficult than it sounds, especially when there are several different individual needs.

Map-makers approach this problem in a direct way: They have different maps of the same place for different purposes. For example, they have maps that 1. preserve *equality* of different *areas*; 2. preserve *angles* from one point to another; 3. preserve relations between actual *distances*; 4. are good for polar areas only (since they must eliminate the equator); 5. are excellent for areas around the equator, but get worse and worse as you approach the poles (which they can not even show). No matter which selection is made for the user's primary purpose, distortion, or elimination, of other relationships is inevitable. But this is the important point: The user does not care about aspects that are irrelevant for his purposes, however interesting to the surveyors or explorers who gathered the data. The user is grateful for the hardships, skill, and science that were necessary in order to give him what he wants, but he needs to get on with his own job, and not spend time on what are, to him, unnecessary distractions from his objective. A cartographer who refuses to hand over his newly drawn maps to frantic sea captains unless they agree to sit still for a lecture on how they were made would find future prospects grim. Yet many specialists seem to hoard their nuggets of hard-won knowledge, and actually sulk if a client in need of them shows the least sign of impatience with a boring, long-winded chronicle of prospecting. A good antidote to this attitude is for the specialist to imagine how interested he would be if his client insisted on explaining every nuance and difficulty of the client's discipline or occupation.

Maps are imperfect translations of reality into a handy, useful size, in symbols and language suited to their users. This is the same objective for a good translation from the technical to the vernacular. Specialists are often irritated by the need to translate. But even the law courts will not allow a defendant unfamiliar with the normal language of the court to be convicted unless all evidence is made clear to him in his native tongue. He also has the right to present his own testimony to the court, and it must be translated for the jury. Lord Reading of the King's Bench set aside a conviction for the murder of Mrs. Thompson by Kun Loo, a Chinese who spoke no English, and who was denied these rights.

If translation is so important in such earthy affairs, think how much more essential it is when a specialist presents "evidence" to those who carry responsibility for the lives and destinies of others. Proper understanding of the messages of experts becomes increasingly important as leaders encounter difficulties that demand special knowledge. Contrast the difference in persuasive impact of Einstein's actual letter to President Roosevelt suggesting that he prosecute atomic research, with a scientifically impeccable sheaf of papers, covered with arcane formulae carrying the same message buried in hieroglyphics. This may seem an absurd example, but every day some expert makes a grab for the batch of formulae and declines to write the letter. Preference for his technical language makes an expert unnecessarily vulnerable to opponents of his idea who are willing to use tactics of the crowd orator against him. The expert (by definition) is superior in some way to his audience. A streak of resentment attends any relationship involving inferiority, and the wise expert strives to minimize it. By using terminology beyond the knowledge of the audience (without making its meaning clear), an expert reinforces their feeling of inferiority. He becomes a sitting duck for opponents who enjoy casting slurs on those educated beyond the average. If the feeling of inferiority gets out of control, even an intelligent audience will welcome an unfair attack on the offender who has made them so uneasy.

By contrast, should the expert's language bristle with words drawn from Greek and Latin sources, and he takes the trouble to show that their original meaning—to Greeks and Romans—was understandable to those ancient laymen, the audience feels relaxed. (They have also acquired something to spring on others later.) Here are a few samples: *exothermic*—Greek for "external" and "heat," thus a chemical reaction which gives out heat; *polytheism*—Greek for "many" and "god," thus belief and worship of more gods than one; *electron*—Greek for "amber," which, when rubbed, produces "electricity"; *hematogenesis*—Greek for "blood" and "birth," thus "formation of the blood"; *paleolithic*—Greek for "old" and "stone," thus the Old Stone Age; *sericulture*—Latin for "silk" and "raising," thus, care of silkworms; *hyetography*—Greek for "rain" and "writing," thus charting of rainfall distribution; *entropy*—translation backwards *into* Greek of the English word "evolution."

The list for any single discipline may be quite long. Specialists can exercise the forgotten intellectual muscles of their apprenticeship days by making up a list of "translations" like the above. Some technical presentors distribute their decoding table to an audience as a kind of glossary. If the presentation is the beginning of a continued program of informing an audience, this is a good way to give those members of the group who want to understand a helping hand they can accept without diminishing their ego. As the series goes on, it then becomes safe to inject technical terms into the discourse—in homeopathic doses.

Another variation of the "translation-through-etymology" approach is useful when a specialist from one discipline is presenting an idea to specialist members of another field. (This is becoming more frequent today when *teams* of specialists are assembled for an attack on a complex problem. The new field of "Operations Research" begins with the assumption that a mixture of disciplines is *essential*.) The presenting specialist "translates down" to the ancient vernacular meaning and then asks for a "translation up" to the other specialist's technical language. This is an effective way to get started on the road to meaningful, interdisciplinary communication.

CREATIVE PERCEPTION

Arthur Koestler finds that art, science, and humor each produce their "breakthroughs" by confronting one view of a problem with another view of it *from a different angle*. Elting Morrison, the historian, also notes that innovations in technology seem to occur when someone competent in one field becomes extremely interested in the problems of another. These "marginal

men" then bring "ways of looking at things" used in their original area to their new interest. Often, specialist workers in the
new area cannot do this (just as the "marginal man" did not do
it in his original field), since they have mastered the standard
professional approaches so well that their habits of thought
automatically reject the new approach. The wise specialist is
always on the lookout for such "new angles of vision" when he
makes a presentation to an audience of intelligent persons who
are not experts in his own area, but who show intense interest in
it. Alertness for such potential mental excitement can put a fine
sheen on a specialist's presentation, and makes the specialist
sincerely eager to communicate. That's the only way he can bait
the hook for the "marginal man."

People test the authenticity of an idea by matching it against
their own experiences. If unfamiliar terms or concepts prevent
them from making the match, they will never be able to accept
its authenticity emotionally. They may agree that you are a brilliant man, learned in your field, and a credit to your profession,
but they will not apply your proposal if they cannot see its
relevance to their affairs. Some specialists are happy just to receive such meaningless compliments. (Since his hearers did not
understand, how much are their appraisals worth?) These people
are best left to write for abstruse technical journals, since their
bungled presentations actually harm the chances for a good idea
to become a force in human affairs.

When someone asks a specialist for an answer, he expects a
direct answer, pinpointed to his question. He hates to go the long
way around and prefers a simple "I don't know" to a long-
winded equivalent. He also becomes bored with a series of hypo-
thetical "ifs" as a foundation for an answer, and detests having
his question "answered" by another question. What he seeks is
the feeling that, once you tell him what he wants to know, he can
see the outcome of applying your knowledge to his own concerns. These desires put intense pressure on the specialist who
dreads being responsible for influencing a decision unless the
questioner knows as much about the matter involved as the expert himself. The beginning of the expert's wisdom is to recognize that such a level can never be achieved by decision makers
—or he would not be the expert he claims to be. Decision in-

volves mutual risk. The layman risks his reputation by following the expert's advice; the expert risks his reputation by influencing the layman to do so.

One international incident illustrates this point. A State Department official was informed that an uprising had just occurred in Angola, and he was expected to propose an appropriate response. He called in the experts on the area, told them that a Naval squadron was in the South Atlantic, and that he wished their advice. Several hours later the experts presented him a thick binder on Angola. It contained the history of the area since Vasco da Gama, the tribal structure, geology of the region, population statistics, trade and economic data, recent reports of agriculture, and so on. The official grabbed it eagerly, but after a quick examination, wearily put it down, turned to the experts, and said: "Gentlemen, you misapprehend my problem. Do I ask the Navy to tell their admiral to sail north, or south?"

SOME PITFALLS

Two dangerous traps must be skirted by the specialist presentor. These are pedantry and cant. Both have swallowed many well-intentioned presentations.

Pedantry is an undue display of learning, often accompanied by slavish attention to rules, obscure details, or unnecessary precision. Cant is an insincere appeal to principles—scientific, political, moral, or religious—which are not truly believed, acted on, or understood by the presenter. Cant is worse than pedantry, but both are deadly to persuasion. Pedantry has its origin in fear; cant, in corruption. The pedant often believes he is motivated by an integrity to his discipline, which demands absolute adherence to special meanings and procedures; he would rather be meticulous than helpful (The word "meticulous" itself comes from the Latin for "fear" and "timid".) Cant is usually resorted to in dealing with embarrassing questions. There is always a hint of the bludgeon about it. Those in an audience who detect its use consign the entire presentation to the wastebasket of their minds. Those who don't are misled.

Here I must risk going to the edge of pedantry by discussing the difference between accuracy and precision. Most people use the two words interchangeably in normal conversation, but failure to understand the difference between them leads many a presentor astray. Unnecessary precision overburdens subsequent discussion with so much irrelevant detail that it cannot get off the ground.

Let's begin with two propositions: A statement can be accurate but not precise. A statement can be precise but not accurate. Thomas Jefferson giving instructions to the explorers, Lewis and Clark, might have said: "If you go westward, you will see the Pacific Ocean." This is an accurate statement, but not very precise. If Clark had said "Do you mean that we should head 276° away from north, Mr. President?" he would be trying to increase the precision of his accurate instruction. We see the same thing in everyday life, and sense that there is a different degree of precision appropriate for different purposes. If a friend casually asks you the length of your living room as he sits comfortably on your sofa, he would think you a bit batty if you answer "34.6742 feet." But if you are purchasing wall-to-wall carpet, the salesman taking your order by telephone would not know how to quote a price with the answer: "between 20 and 40 feet."

The same principle should guide the specialist presentor both in selecting the level of detail and in treating intricate sequences of causes and effects involved in his idea. Surveyors use automobile speedometers to get a rough idea of the acreage of a wasteland, but they use optical apparatus of the highest precision in laying out an aircraft assembly line or a skyscraper foundation. Precise statements, even though inaccurate, are attempts at intellectual magic. For example, "There are 162,317 Pygmies in Central Africa." The actual number may be closer to a million or a thousand—no one really knows for sure. Gambits like this are quite frequent in technical presentations and try to take advantage of the normal tendency to confuse precision and accuracy.

The best rule for technical presentation is: Make accurate statements, but support them with the least precision and detail necessary to make the point. Any level greater than this becomes pedantic and boring. Only the Almighty knows the wasted labor of hard-working multitudes spent securing excess precision of facts necessary for decision or approval of an idea. Don't add to this already scandalous pyramid of nonsense. Your audiences will be grateful. (We will discuss how to handle statistical and mathematical information near the end of this chapter.) Vernacular languages embody the folk-wisdom of a people's needs, and develop shades and nuances appropriate to their everyday life. In English we have *one* word for reindeer; the language used in Lapland has *fourteen* words for reindeer—animals central to their existence. The same principle of economy should be observed in translations to the vernacular from jargon as apply to translations from Lapp to English.

William Cowper summarized our guiding rule:

> "Knowledge is proud that he has learned so much,
> Wisdom is humble that he knows no more."

FOIBLES AND TAINTS

Before moving on to specific methods and tests of translations, let's examine those motivations of specialists that hold back the descent (or ascent) to the vocabularies congenial to an audience.

First comes fear of criticism by professional colleagues. This has its roots in a polite form of jealousy. There is so little "room at the top" of any specialty, whether abalone fishing, opera singing, poetry, or zoology, that the scramble for eminence allows few slips. Motion picture directors are "as good as their last picture," and their compensation shows it. Other worlds are not as harsh, but all specialists experience similar effects on a smaller scale. Thus a specialist has loyalties to two separate groups: his colleagues and his clients. They have widely different criteria of successful practice. Colleagues judge on the basis of contribution to the common body of knowledge or art; clients judge by how much help they personally receive. Each specialist must face this dilemma in his own way, but those who elect to sever every loyalty except that to their professional colleagues will never influence the larger world of affairs. They become mental hermits, even though they may live in superficial contact with nonspecialists. Any good work they do must be conveyed to the world by others equipped with more courage. The proper conduct of a life oscillates between involvement and withdrawal, between action and contemplation. In the words of the New Testament: "Render unto Caesar the things which are Caesar's; and unto God, the things which are God's." Both are entitled to some attention.

The only antidotes to fear are knowledge and courage. I have observed that most specialists who take the plunge to make their work understandable to intelligent laymen become exhilarated by the challenge, and then delighted at their reception. With experience, their fear leaves, and courage enters. Most audiences *do* want to learn and are willing to go further than halfway to meet an expert who tries to help them. A goodly portion of experts who try, find—often to their surprise—that their increased influence is not unnoticed by professional colleagues who have been watching them out of the corners of their eyes.

While one can sympathize with the fear of professional criticism, there is one behavioral trait that is never excused. This vice is snobbery. Snobbery marks those who make birth, wealth, schooling, or intelligence the sole criterion of individual worth. Snobbish specialists make competence in their specialty the sole criterion. They give themselves away—like other snobs—by cringing to those superior and by being overbearing to those inferior. Inferiority or superiority is determined only by their single specific criterion of excellence. In extreme cases they show oriental servility to eminent colleagues, but insolence and ridicule to everyone else. They are also prone to name-dropping. Such experts never persuade others. These are the men who believe that "trivial is what the other fellow does"—and act on that belief. They also believe themselves to be high priests of orthodox professional opinion. "Heterodoxy is what you believe; orthodoxy is my doxy" describes their attitude. This tendency to snobbery, like pneumococcus germs in the lungs of each of us, lurks in the character of every specialist, waiting for a moment of weakness to sprout. Hygienic recognition and resistance helps to suppress both.

Another characteristic of many specialists is their need for appreciation. One can also sympathize with this, for their expertise requires years of study and hard work to acquire. But appreciation is like love; when most aggressively demanded, it is most likely to elude. Help the audience with *their* problems, and the appreciation will come naturally. If they have to endure a story of your life and hard times to get your help, they will feel you have already collected the appreciation you demanded. Morris Kline describes a happy variation of motivation in his treatment of what impels mathematicians to sacrifice and drive for mastery. He mentions the excitement of a quest for new results, the thrill of discovery, the satisfaction of mastering great difficulties, and pride of achievement. He adds others like the delights and aesthetic values that come from surveying orderly chains of reasoning, from the sheer contemplation of the results themselves, and from grasping the ideas that make demonstrations work. Notice that every one of these is a *human* attribute, not cold science. Someone who has experienced these rare and lovely moments may wish to share them in detail with others. He deplores those who want only practical application of his results. It is with a melancholy sigh that our advice must be: Help them first, and be content to share your delights only with those who have a taste for them. Don't call them; they'll call you.

Finally, avoid intellectual blackmail. Special knowledge gives the technical presentor an advantage he can exploit for a short-run gain. He can do this by responding to a difficult question with involved and complicated analysis, exotic terminology, blackboards full of formulae, or obscure historical and legal niceties. If he does this, he puts the victimized questioner in the position of having to admit either that he understands what may in fact be completely meaningless, or that he is beyond his depth and thus an ignoramus in the eyes of the presentor. You may handle the problem of the moment, but you have created a greater one, which could last your entire career. If someone competent in your work is in the audience and sees what you really did, the harm to your professional standing may be irreparable. Extortion of any kind merits retribution—and often gets it.

APPROACHES AND FORMATS

We now turn to approaches that can aid a specialist who has decided to cross his personal Rubicon and make his idea known to laymen.

First, work your idea out completely in any terms and techniques congenial to you. Use advanced mathematics, foreign expressions, historical examples, computer programs, literary and scholarly references, trade names, shop talk, or slang—the whole arsenal of intellectual, artistic, and industrial discourse. Modern, medieval, or ancient it matters not. When you are satisfied that the resulting presentation would meet the approval of your specialist colleagues, you are now ready to begin its transformation for laymen. Do not bother to write out the original in connected prose. It is better to put it down in topical form, with the structure showing clearly. In fact, placing each point on a card or small sheet of paper will facilitate the rearrangement required, and also allows you to make deletions, clarifying insertions, and notes for visual aid ideas with little trouble. (Before spreading these out, it is wise to number the originals serially, so that after initial frustrations you can restore the original order for a fresh start.) This is an irritating process until you do it a few times, and attention to mechanical details removes a great deal of potential nuisance. Spread all of the numbered sheets (or cards) out on a large table. Use the floor if you like it and there's no one about to make snide remarks.

We will discuss later several *forms* that can be used for the final presentation, but before doing that, you must do something which appears easy and unnecessary, but which is actually quite difficult. It constitutes the make-or-break stage of the transformation. This is to determine and list two things: the assumptions implicit in your original technical presentation; the assumptions you can safely make about the knowledge of your audience. If these are identical you are making a presentation to your specialist friends, and you need go no further. If they are not identical, your job is now cut out for you in this way: You must make *explicit* the assumptions and knowledge required in your original story, and these must be brought into line with the assumptions about the knowledge of the audience. You can do this two ways: Translate into their vernacular *all* the assumptions involved that are beyond the knowledge of the audience; or school them on some points so that their existing level of knowledge is raised to that necessary to accept the implicit assumptions you wish to leave implicit, for whatever reasons you have. (This latter course is equivalent to that used by a literary translator who gives up on certain foreign words as "untranslatable" and plugs the original language right into the text of the new language. He usually concedes that he has to clear up the meaning somewhere, even though he may take a hundred other words to do so.)

Now go back to the original and mark every word or symbol that carries a technical or obscure meaning from the viewpoint of the audience. You can deal with these either by finding rough vernacular equivalents, or you must take the time to *define* them in the vernacular if you wish to use them in the presentation itself. Often these terms or symbols can be easily translated by picture, chart, model, or other visual aid. If these are not appropriate, a story or anecdote can illuminate such difficult points as occur in many legal, psychological, or artistic distinctions. Use the characters in the story to personify the principle at work. (Audiences identify with a fictitious person far more easily than with an unfamiliar principle.)

Once you have earmarked every place your audience can go off the rails, insert the additional clarifying sheets or cards among the originals. You are now ready to rearrange your material into a form more congenial to your audience than to fellow specialists. Write down in a few sentences what you believe to be the most significant message in your presentation *for the audience*—not for you (if they are the same, so much the better). This statement will furnish the heart of your opening and the foundation for your closing. What you want them to *do* provides the closing itself. Write this closing down, too.

With this core message and closing in hand, go back to your original sheets, which now have the additions produced in the terms-and-symbols-clarifying stage. Earmark those absolutely essential for both understanding of the core message and persuasion to the action you want. Be harsh with yourself in this part of the process, for it is always easier to add to this select list than to delete an item once marked (I don't know why, but it always works out that way). Move the items not selected to another part of the table, but save them. You may need them later to fill holes, or as ingredients for visual aids. They will certainly be useful in cross-examination.

Before you now are all the bricks needed to build your presentation, but what sort of building should it be? A palace, fortress, shack, or a wall? At this point the process allows your individuality free play. The job ahead is very similar to that of the film editor. He has before him all of the scenes for his picture, which have been photographed in bits and pieces. What the audience is allowed to see is entirely in his hands. How well he selects and places the pieces in sequence will determine how the final picture affects its audiences. Many actors lament that "My best scenes are on the cutting room floor!" This is often true. They are rejected not because they are bad scenes, but because they did not contribute as much as others *to the central theme and intent of the story.* You must be as ruthless as the editor, not only in selection and sequence, but above all in the rejection of great—but irrelevant—material. Specialist presentors invariably find this painful. Some can't bring themselves to abandon these children of their minds, and their presentations suffer.

Several "building plans" are particularly useful for specialist presentations. Here is a sample catalog, with a brief description of each type.

THE CHILDREN'S HOUR

Children have an immense capacity for understanding the elements of a technical subject. In fact, it takes more than a decade of inept instruction to stamp out their interest in any subject. They prefer the exotic and mysterious, the dark past and the far future, to the everyday, for their powerful imaginations have less restraint. Whether the subject be dinosaurs or space travel, Egyptian archeology or Indian art, African mammals or

Australian aborigines, courtroom procedure or the Age of Chivalry, children bring fresh minds and an eagerness to know, if you can grab their imaginations. They actually see themselves in the situations described and later play out what they have learned. They are unafraid to display ignorance and are quick to ask questions—often of the most profound type. To answer: "Why is the sky blue?" scientifically will tax the resources of most adults—and few adults ever *ask* the question. The physicist who quickly answers that "it is due to scattering of the upper air" does not satisfy them until he explains scattering and how you get it. If he does explain it dramatically, he may get vocalization of wonderment ("oohs" and "aahs") and even applause. (Parents of this kind of audience are in for a lesson in one-upmanship from their offspring that evening.)

Children are intelligent and resent being "talked down to" or given soothing replies which avoid answering their questions. In this respect they are like all audiences. An audience of adults exposed to a specialized subject for the first time is quite similar to a group of children—only more cautious. A specialist asked to present information about his field to a school assembly of children will usually do a fine job. Strangely, if asked to do the same thing to a group of adults, he will often do badly. The reason for the difference springs from his unconscious acceptance of the knowledge level of the children, the fact that they have no power to affect his reputation, and his eagerness to find examples, stories, and visual aids to illustrate difficult points for them. If such specialists gave the same presentation to the adults as to the children, they would do far better in communication of their ideas to mature audiences. Fables and parables have been used by the greatest teachers of the human race. They can infiltrate the most intricate and mysterious insights of philosophy, religion, and science into ordinary minds with a marvelous economy of words. Their power lies in the ability of an audience to "fill in for themselves" all the attributes of the "speaking" animals or persons in the fable or parable. When used in stories, words like *tiger, mouse, fox,* or *woodsman, thief, old man, soldier,* conjure up instantaneous associations which take scores of pages to describe by other methods. I once heard an outstanding presentation of data-processing techniques to a worldwide congress of experts which developed around a fable of the burdens and behavior of clerks throughout history. Punched cards were treated as Sumerian cuneiform clay tablets, magnetic tapes as rolls of Egyptian papyrus, and high-speed printers as cousins to Gutenberg's experiments in Germany. This presentation is still considered to be the best in the annals of that sophisticated organization. The fable itself took twelve minutes and would have fascinated a class of sixth-graders.

Specialists can often find in this approach a helpful format for their presentation: Develop the idea as though it were designed for a school assembly. The child in us is always present and never more so than when we face the unfamiliar.

FIRST NIGHTS AND TRAVELOGUES

Attendance at a new play or return from a journey to places unfamiliar to your friends furnishes an analogue to the problems of a specialist presentation. When we meet friends afterward, we will often be greeted with a request like: "Tell me all about it!" The play may have occupied three hours and the journey a year, so this request cannot be taken literally—nor is it meant to be. What do you do? We have all met theater bores and travel bores. They get that way *through inattention to the interests* of the person making this open-ended request. The specialist's career has been a journey to intellectual, scientific, political, social, industrial, or artistic regions unfamiliar to most of us. Yet we are eager to hear what he has to tell us, if we can relate it to our own experiences.

At an afternoon gathering to welcome a distinguished European scientist I overheard a female undergraduate gush, "Oh, professor, I've been dying to meet you. Please sit down right now and tell me all about your cryogenics. By the way, what *are* they?" Had he really undertaken the task of explaining his lifetime of investigations into the behavior of materials at very low temperatures, he would have been foolish, and she embarrassed. He obliged her instead with a story of what happened to a matchstick—like one in her hand—which accidentally dropped into a flask of liquid helium in his laboratory. It took five minutes, she acquired an exotic piece of knowledge, and then bounced away to rejoin her friends. She still clutched the match, and was eager to display her new mastery of cryogenics to them. The scientist, amused, slowly shook his head and smiled, hands upturned as if to say, "What could I do?" He did just fine, for he had neatly calculated just how much of his expertise was needed to meet the needs of his audience in a way related to something she could understand.

Travelers who delight us usually capture our imagination in two ways. First, they contrast customs, scenery, and people of the foreign land to those we are familiar with. Second, they usually recount in detail only an incident or two on the whole journey which brings to life for us the nature of the daily life, attitudes, and spirit of the people they met. Notice that both approaches are audience-oriented; the first by contrast, the second by personifications with which the audience can identify.

The "review" of a play, for a friend who asks about it, can be done by sketching in the plot, the message of the play, the performance of the actors, contrasts and similarities to other plays you know your friend has seen, and an opinion on whether you think he should go. He will appreciate this personal view of *someone who has been there* far more than if you hand him a copy of the script, even though that is much more responsive to the *letter* of his request. The script, like a technical or learned paper, takes no account of *his* individual needs.

Here we see the entire purpose of a specialist presentation to laymen: to have someone competent make clear the *meaning to them, in their terms,* of work in some field. Even if they could conceivably extract this meaning for themselves by exhaustive study of the scholarly literature, they still prefer the more personal link to special knowledge which the specialist before them promises to furnish. After all, they cannot engage in question and answer sessions with a learned journal. Even the most bookish of Presidents, Woodrow Wilson, said: "I would never read a book if it were possible for me to talk half an hour with the man who wrote it." The specialist presenter stands as proxy for *all* the men who wrote the books in his field. He should do such experts credit as their representative, to whom the audience can talk.

To use the travelogue and first-night approach, the presentor must answer these questions for his audience: What do they *want* to know? How much do they *have* to know? Which aspects will *interest* them?

OVER THE COFFEE CUPS

No man can ever be a complete hero to his wife or family. They know too much of his weaknesses and failures to swallow pontifical statements, even if he is the world's most eminent expert in a particular subject. Should the morning paper carry an item in his field, his wife may ask his opinion of it as she sips her breakfast coffee. How he answers her specific questions and discusses the implications in the limited time before he leaves for work suggests another format for specialist presentations. She knows her expert too well to put up with long-winded introductory or background material. The event described is usually tersely written, and she expects a quick appraisal of its significance. If that strikes a responsive chord, her toleration for additional background material goes up. If not, she turns the page. What usually infuriates her is to use the tired riposte "What do you think it means, dear?" She rightly senses that this is a gambit to escalate your expert status by correcting her misconception, and that you will be out the door before she gets an answer to her original question. Both domestic relations and specialist presentations benefit from the same treatment: Answer the question at hand *first;* if the answer provokes further interest, elaborate.

In the presentation, you create the "event," but this statement should be as terse as the newsman's whose skill caught the morning readers' interest. Techniques used in most news stories are based on this little drama of the breakfast table. Headlines use few words to blast out the message. The first lines cover who? where? what? when? Successive paragraphs produce greater and greater detail as they answer the how? and why? Laboratories follow a similar route. In using a microscope, one first positions the slide with the naked eye, then uses the low-power lens, finally going on to higher and higher powers of magnification for increasing detail. Only bunglers start with the high power, wasting a great deal of time (and scratching lenses) just trying to find the spot they want. They seldom find it, and finally use the correct procedure.

Coffee is also served in living rooms to small social groups at the end of the day. Here again the normal rules of social behavior guide an expert when asked his professional opinion during polite conversation. His approach to questions on these occasions also suggests appropriate conduct during specialist presentations. One of the best guides to this form of discourse is found in the *Dialogues of Alfred North Whitehead* by Lucien Price (Mentor, 1964). Few presentors could match Whitehead's scholarship, but fewer still possess his genius for clarity and sensitivity to his audience when engaged in conversations dealing with that scholarship. Specialist presentations are also social events, and there is no double standard for etiquette.

TRIALS AND OTHER TRIBULATIONS

Specialists are called on more and more for advice and testimony to aid courts and Congressional committees. In courts, experts, like all witnesses, are expected to present facts. But unlike other witnesses, experts are also allowed to present their opinion as to what those facts mean for the purposes of the court. The age-old tests of evidence apply to both facts and opinion: Are they relevant, competent, and material? In plain words, how does the expert's testimony: 1. relate to the issues in the specific case; 2. qualify as being authoritative enough for the court to be guided by it; 3. justify itself as important enough to affect the outcome of the case in hand. Law courts use another rule known as *de minimis*, which is a shorthand expression for: *De minimis non curat lex*, or, "The law is not concerned with trifles." Application of this rule to many specialist presentations would strip them of much of their fat—and it would do them no end of good. Congressional committees are more relaxed in their procedure. They are interested in broad policy considerations for future legislation, not with specific decisions measured against precedent and existing statutes. Yet the most effective appearances before them are made by those who observe the stricter rules of the courts without being required to.

This ancient form for presenting evidence to official bodies offers another approach for the specialist presentation. Determine what the issue is; develop facts that bear on it measured against the rules of evidence; and then sum up the meaning of those facts both by stating your opinion and by showing how your expert interpretation of the facts leads to that side of the issue you favor.

The most difficult part of this form lies in the absolute necessity of clearly stating the issue before the audience. Without this, nothing that follows can be tested for relevance, competence, or materiality.

SCENARIOS, OR FACTUAL FICTION

One of the most rapid and dramatic methods of presenting a complex idea and its consequences comes from the "story in the future," or scenario. Here, the presentor sketches out a series of incidents and their background, based on a set of initial assumptions which presumably could become factual. Each incident (or "scene") calls for a decision. As a specific decision is made, it creates a new set of incidents, calling for new decisions, and so on. The process goes as far as imagination can carry you. The richness of this method is also its weakness. You can readily see the huge number of final outcomes as one makes different decisions for each incident involved (thus setting up a completely different chain). The scenario fosters identification of the audience with the decision makers at every point. At these points the expert presents the technical or other special knowledge that bears on each particular incident and decision required. If the audience disagrees with a specific decision (a fork in the road), their inducement to participate in discussion grows rapidly.

Here's a quick example, greatly oversimplified: The Suez Canal is completely blocked in winter. The price of oil rises immediately in Western Europe. The charters of all tankers are rapidly bought up. African ports experience a boom. Refineries in the Mediterranean decline in output. Refineries on the Atlantic rise in output. Orders for construction of supertankers are received in Japan. The feasibility of a pipeline in Israel is enhanced. New production and import quotas are needed to restore equilibrium. Political repercussions are felt in every oil-producing country. . . . and so on, and on, and on, to the limits of the audience's patience or willingness to speculate.

Notice that every point brought up shouts for specialist knowledge to test its validity. It can also use such a wide range of knowledge that everyone in the audience can have something valuable to contribute to at least one point. Note also how the chain of subsequent events is altered if one of the consequences is not likely or valid.

Expert knowledge is hung on the various branches of the decisions like Christmas decorations on a tree, starting downward from the top. Several different scenarios starting from the same set of initial conditions can bring out more of the complex factors involved than any other method, given the same time.

In using scenarios, however, one must be on guard for their tendency to luxuriate. Comprehension can be lost in a jungle of confused and contingent conditions without an experienced guide.

The impact of a good scenario comes from the fact that human responses, made by men of affairs in complex circumstances, can be best described in plain language and ordinary dialogue. This disciplines the *expression* of the special knowledge, for it must be made clear to *those who have to decide* after "hearing" it, as each incident occurs.

BLIND MAN'S BUFF—SCIENTIFIC STYLE

There are many phenomena in scientific fields that cannot be figured out with the kind of elegance we usually associate with grave men in white coats. Such things as the behavior of actual airplane wings, the flooding of a river, the spread of infectious diseases, acoustics of an auditorium, or patterns of road traffic, cannot be cooked up in a test tube. The classic scientific approach, where you hold everything constant and let only one factor change to see what happens, cannot be used. Everything is going on at once, as in most situations involving human beings.

There is an approach to such problems which is dignified by the term "dimensional analysis." It actually boils down to a thoughtful man, chin in hand, looking at a panorama in uproar, asking himself, "What can have something to do with it?" He then looks at the various parts, gets some hunches, and watches for the action going on to see if events seem to be influenced by the part he observes closely. It is all sort of disorderly, like a sightseeing tour, but the elements of unexpected guess and quick insight produce a high element of interest. It is the way of the naturalist rather than that of the biologist.

The specialist who has an idea, which may appear quite radical unless there is an appreciation of the complexities of a real situation, can use this framework to build that appreciation. He sketches in the rich mixture of phenomena that need explanation, examines several obvious factors, goes on to not-so-obvious ones, and finally shows the destination: his idea of the underlying factors that can be altered to change the events or things to bring them closer to the desires of his audience. The solution of a thicker wing, a new type of dam, different methods of controlling epidemics, novel ways of recording price changes, or strange kinds of upholstery for auditorium seats will not seem so odd or absurd *after the audience has seen that the more obvious things, which they all thought of, won't work as well.* This method is similar to unwrapping a package enclosed by many layers of cardboard and paper. Excitement builds up as each layer is removed, and when you get to the last, their expectations are at the highest pitch. At this point, present your solution. It had better be a good one, for this style constantly hints that it will be. If you end by saying that you don't know what the answer is, the accumulated emotional tension can have a vicious backlash. If you do have a good solution, this method allows—and often demands—a great deal of special knowledge to illuminate the shortcomings of each obvious, rejected solution as you develop the story. This approach is especially good for reporting the results of a task force or committee who were assigned the job of finding a solution to a specific problem enmeshed in a web of complicated circumstances. In effect, you take your audience over the paths you followed, including the dead ends, until, after successive failures, you break out into the light.

IN THE LATER STEPS OF SIR FRANCIS

After his mixed success as a lawyer—rising to Lord Chancellor, and then convicted of bribery—Sir Francis Bacon turned aside from the casuistry of the Law and laid the foundations for what we call the scientific method. In his words, he developed —about 350 years ago—the way to form "a closer and purer league between the two faculties of the experimental and the rational." This is the approach that comes most naturally to scientists in any discipline, for they have been shaped and molded by it in order to survive as card-carrying professionals. Besides, by its use the men in white coats succeeded in overthrowing the tyranny of the men in black. (It worked so well that some scientists aspire to tyranny themselves from time to time, but that is another story.) The scientific method is a procedure for conducting scientific *work*, but in the raw form of detailed chronicles of experiments, it is not well suited to presenting the results of that work. However, the *structure* of scientific method described below furnishes the specialist a potentially superb framework for presentation of his ideas, conclusions, and recommendations. When done well, an audience experiences that thrill of discovery that attends educational experiences of the highest order.

Most of us think that we use it all the time, but scientific method is an extremely subtle blend of dogged, routine drudgery and the greatest flashes of inspiration. Disputes still rage about the underlying philosophy, but its continued ability to deliver the goods we want has neutralized humanist critics. So much so that ours is the first era where "unscientific" is used only in a disparaging sense.

When one uses the framework of scientific method, he creates a halo effect around his presentation, but pays for it in the care he must take to avoid boredom or disappointment.

There are several labels given to the phases of scientific method, but I will use those generally accepted. These are: Observation, Hypothesis, Experiment, Verification.

First, one must recognize that a phenomenon exists. This means that something is happening that is not satisfactorily accounted for by current theory or the general opinion of experts in the field. Once that is done, some way is set up to make observations of the phenomenon and gather data about it—preferably quantitative measurements (you'll see why in the next stage).

After assembling "enough" data (a tough judgment in itself), the scientist peers at it, thinks about it, searches for relations among the data and, in mysterious ways peculiar to each scientist, called *inductive* reasoning, finally formulates a preliminary generalization to "explain" the data. This shaky generalization is known as the hypothesis.

With the hypothesis in hand, the scientist (or other colleagues good at this phase) then uses *deductive* reasoning to draw out logical inferences from his hypothesis. Since mathematics is a high-powered engine of deduction, if the hypothesis can be put in mathematical form, every manipulation, stratagem, and technique from the entire weaponry of mathematics can be used to extract the greatest number of inferences with the least effort (but verbal logic can be used instead). After the hypothesis has been put through this torture, some of the deductions (i.e., inferences) look better than others as candidates for the next phase. Deductions often come in very long chains, but the final one selected has a direct relationship to the beginning hypothesis. It boils down to a statement like this: "If the hypothesis is true, then logic says that this last deduction is also true." The "If-then" form of reasoning is common to all deductive methods. Now the fun begins. The last deduction shouts to be tested, and an experiment is designed to oblige its demands. The deduction now turns into a *prediction*. It says to the experimenter: "If you look for such-and-such a relationship, you should find it—if I am right."

Now the experiment phase begins, and the instruments and schemes for detecting the *predicted* phenomena are deployed. The mathematical type of deduction allows these predictions to be made in quantitative terms, and thus lets the experimenter match his actual data against the predicted with the ease of merely comparing *numbers*. If the prediction and the experimental data agree, this is considered a proof of the hypothesis. Verification is now required. The experiments are made again, by different scientists and perhaps by using additional deductions, to verify the hypothesis. If everything still stands up to this battering, then the hypothesis is granted the title of a theory (if grand enough), a law (of less nobility), or a rule (just barely in the scientific peerage).

If the experimental data do not agree with the predicted data, then the scientist first checks the chain of deduction. If that is correct, he must then scrap his original hypothesis, find a new one, and start the whole process over again. Laymen usually hear only of the successful hypothesis, but the great bulk of scientific workers encounter far more of the bad ones. In fact, in the noblest institutions, disproof of a faulty hypothesis is considered a very respectable outcome and quite worthwhile. But the greatest fame does not lie along that road.

So much for one of the finest keys ever fashioned to unlock the secrets of nature. What are its lessons for specialist presentations?

First, if you use this framework, an audience of laymen expects only the *happy* outcome: hypothesis proved! This approach is deadly if it results in *negative* proof, for the audience does not know what to do. (There is one exception: That is the case where you are asking for approval to make a fresh start. However, even in this unhappy situation it is best not to use the scientific method framework, for it prolongs the agony and harms your future cause as the dreary chronicle unfolds. Straight confession of failure has the merit of quick surgery, and allows more time for your *positive* case.)

Second, there is a strong tendency for the presentor to go into excessive detail as he lovingly lingers in the deduction phase. Skip as many steps as possible. Many good specialists give only the hypothesis and the final deduction in their talk, consigning the mathematics and logic to a document available to those few interested.

Third, do not overelaborate on the tedious aspects of data collection and observation. While important to the over-all process of the *work*, they tend to clutter and confuse the presentation. Place emphasis on any *novel* apparatus or technique, for that is what most laymen recognize as scientific advance. But be careful to show how it was *essential* to the results, otherwise they will class it as gimmickry and accuse you of cracking peanuts with a punch press.

Fourth, be aware that you are compressing into a brief presentation the work of many people over a period of years. You cannot possibly give them all individual credit. The advice for Travelogues and First-Nights above applies with greatest force to the use of the scientific method framework. Finally, never treat the presentation as merely the oral form of an article for a learned journal. Keep footnote items for supplementary *documents*, and save your time for those parts of the work of greatest significance and interest to the audience.

PUTTING NUMBERS IN THEIR PLACE

Specialist presenters often rely heavily on statistics and other kinds of numbers to support their points. They are right to do so. But a single-minded concentration on a number itself—without regard to the image it produces in its context—often creates ridiculous effects. An item in *Punch* illustrates the possibilities: "The figure of 2.2 children per adult female was felt to be in some respects absurd, and a Royal Commission suggested that the middle classes be paid money to increase the average to a rounder and more convenient number." The lesson here is that averages should *always* be rounded. Solid numbers stick in the mind; decimals don't. Most people reared in countries accustomed to English measures find vulgar fractions like a quarter, half, twelfth, or sixth far more congenial than their decimal equivalents. Give a handyman an instruction to drill a ⅛-inch hole and you'll get a nod of understanding—and the right sized hole. Tell him you want one of .125 inches and you'll be greeted with bafflement. Most audiences are like the handyman. Simple fractions create an image of cutting something up—a pie, a piece of wood, or a potato. Decimals conjure up fearful pictures of sophisticated tools like micrometers and vernier scales. People usually enjoy dividing up something, but find precise measurement with instruments a tedious chore, which they see themselves botching up. Fractions sooth; decimals alarm.

At the other end of the scale, very large numbers are meaningless unless reduced to a human scale. If you say that a corporation has invested in its tools the sum of 100 million dollars, this will be admired or resented, but not really understood or appreciated. If you do nothing more than the third-grade arithmetic of dividing up the 100 million by the five thousand people on the payroll, you show that the firm has had to raise twenty thousand dollars for every person's job. Most people can relate that to their home mortgage or annual income and will keep listening. Also, changes, or differences, in big numbers create a dynamic element and should be made explicit. Many specialist presentations lose their audiences when everyone in the room starts doing subtractions and additions on envelopes or scraps of paper as they struggle for comprehension. All this can be avoided if *you* do the work ahead of time by anticipating their attempts to relate the numbers to *their* concerns and experience.

There is one exception to these hints. If your audience really enjoys playing with numbers to avoid coming to grips with real decisions, you must humor them. However, such presentations are really ceremonies, not honest examinations of ideas. They are often used only to reinforce previous prejudices. If you can, let someone else play the part of high priest at these events. It is a hollow role.

Chapter 6 (on Visual Aids) discusses patterns of numerical representation which enhance the comprehension of an audience. If your material must involve a great deal of numerical information, these are almost indispensable. But if you can't use them, do not try to describe numerical visuals in prose. Such a naïve approach requires a skill beyond that of most novelists and never works out well. This unhappy situation calls for a complete re-thinking of the presentation to make it fit the strictly oral form.

We close this chapter with one of those profound insights that are produced only by poets. Every specialist presentor should have its message embroidered on a sampler and hung in his work area—or better, engraved on his heart. William Wordsworth is the author of this sage advice to every specialist: "Wisdom oft is nearer when we stoop than when we soar."

10

After the Votes Are In

or

Turning Words into Work
(*and Vice Versa*)

Napoleon was not a humorous man. Yet one of his remarks does disclose an inclination toward irony. He was once asked how you went about winning a battle. His reply was: "It's quite simple. One commits oneself, and sees what happens." The answer is interesting not because of what it says, but for what it takes for granted. Napoleon, of course, knew this. Because he felt so few were capable of making the plans and preparations required *before* the battle, his advice is actually dangerous for the unprepared. It might even tempt someone who did not see the irony to take him on, since he made success appear to be solely a matter of nerve. In contrast to this cavalier answer, there have been few commanders throughout all history who could match the early Napoleon in thoroughness of preparation for an engagement. In later years, inattention, distraction, diminution of energy, and self-delusion produced a sloppiness in planning which contributed to his downfall. Even his unparalleled experience could not compensate for the grave deficiencies that resulted.

What significance does this have for a presentation of ideas? When Napoleon said, "One commits oneself," he wrapped up in this phrase several vital assumptions: One has conceived an idea, studied the terrain and the opposition, gathered resources, considered effects on other countries not involved, is informed of attitudes back home, and finally instructs his marshals and men in what *he* intends to do, and explains what he expects *them* to do.

When a proposal becomes a project (or a plan becomes a battle) the presentor steps over the line that divides dreamy aspiration from concrete reality. He must then lay out his *specific* plans for approval by those above, and for the instruction of those below. He should also keep in his mind the fact that he will be called on from time to time to give presentations to both groups throughout the life of the project. How he conducts the first presentation will influence every subsequent one, because the first presentation details the entire future plan. The audience pays great attention to the ideas and expectations expressed, for their spirit of risk and adventure reaches its highest pitch just before launching. Subsequent oral reports of progress—or lack of it—will always be related back to the plans first described, even though their accomplishment may take many years. Here is a diagram of the process:

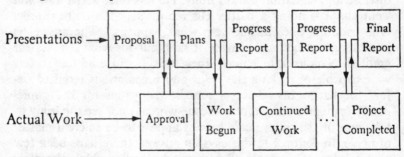

The diagram can give us a useful insight, for it suggests that each presentation requirement is only *part* of a series. They should all have similar basic characteristics to help the audience relate one to the other, and to the *entire* project from conception to completion. Therefore, the *structure* of the "Plans" presentation (how the various parts all fit together) should take account of the need to report subsequent progress with that same structure. If this is ignored, your subsequent presentations will suffer the same fate as the victims of Procrustes. He kept an iron bed available for weary travelers, but stretched the legs of those too short for it, and amputated the feet of those too tall. He simply couldn't stand a bad fit. Your first "Plans" presentation is the iron bed. Make sure that future presentations can be placed on it without undue torture for future audiences. You can be sure that they will be as tough as old Procrustes. They have the right to be, since their acceptance of your plan implies that you will inform them as to how foolish or wise they were in committing their reputations, resources, and energies to its ideas. Thus the *words* of your plan set work afoot; and the results of that work must be translated back into words for you to carry out your end of the bargain. How to do it?

For centuries there has been one set of activities that exists as a continuous stream of proposals, plans, projects, and programs. These are, of course, the management of military and naval establishments. Regardless of whether one deplores or applauds the need for them, they do offer an enormous reservoir of experience useful for structuring *presentations that deal with specific projects*. It was not by chance that many of the great engineering works of the past were led by men trained in the flexible deployment of resources on new endeavors. Whether the project was digging the Panama Canal, building railroads across continents, or exploring and developing new regions, the ways of structuring and organizing to carry out a project came quite naturally to those whose schooling constantly taught them to approach projects in a certain frame of mind. The successful ones were not successful because they were good *soldiers* (in fact, many were quite bad as soldiers), but because they were able to organize and lead diverse resources to a common purpose. Of course, many great managers never come near such establishments, but examination of their methods suggests that they approached their projects with frames of perception very similar to those of the successful officers on civilian projects. I cannot afford to be misunderstood. By discussing *approaches*, I do not mean over-all philosophical attitudes, temperament, or character. Certainly not reliance on military discipline of the theirs-not-to-reason-why school, which is probably the best recipe for failure in today's world. What I *do* mean is the art of selecting a goal (or mission), breaking down the over-all task into workable problem areas, assembling resources in sensible ways to achieve the goal, and adjusting resources committed as unforeseen events occur. This is no more than a description of the art of management.

One reason why a mission-oriented framework fits the project-type presentation springs from its basic nature of conflict. The military is in conflict with an enemy; the presentor is in conflict with the fears of failure in the audience and with alternative suitors for resources. The project itself is in conflict with all of the uncertainties and risks of the future. As we discussed in Chapters 2 and 3, the conflict between two images, one existing and one desired, is fundamental to any kind of drama, including presentation. The method of opposites builds on possibilities inherent in conflict to develop and display to the audience the implications of a problem. Matching different kinds of resources to the project's goal allows this method full play.

To get specific, what happens when a goal is given to someone trained to the mission approach? He immediately begins to think in terms of the five categories of activity that will need consideration. With singular lack of imagination these are known as G-1, G-2, G-3, G-4, G-5. But what concepts lie behind these stark labels? First, they represent the five staff sections of commanders, from the highest to the lowest. Everyone in a leadership position has a similar understanding of the structure of resources. This allows communication about essential factors to take place with a minimum of explanation. Orders are *given* in this structure, and reports are *sent back* in the same structure. The labels are actually the five "paragraphs" of what is known as a Field Order (though for some operations, like the invasion of Europe, one "paragraph" may require a four-foot shelf of documents). These paragraphs follow a statement of the mission to be done.

Here are the paragraphs: G-1 Personnel (Status of Our Own

Forces); G-2 Intelligence (Status of Opposition Forces); G-3 Plans and Training Required to Carry Out the Operation (Project Timing); G-4 Supply Matters (Including Communications, Food, Transportation, etc.); G-5 External Relations. This structure can be applied to *any* human activity that uses organized resources. Whether it be a city, circus, university, festival, school, convention, corporation, garden club, church, or a pacifist demonstration, the *way of thinking about the project or program* embedded in this structure can be useful and efficient. It can also help prevent omission of important factors.

When a project is organized in this way, delegation of responsibility is simplified and separate presentations can be made for each section. In fact, the "briefings" used both for men in charge and for the men who do the work are really nothing more than specialist presentations of each piece of the over-all plan.

Notice, too, how reporting the progress of various efforts as they unfold in the real world is made as simple as possible. Those in charge can easily grasp the essence of reports from the men who are actually engaged in carrying out the work of the original plan. Wise persons know that nothing ever goes absolutely "according to plan," for every plan is a bushel basket of assumptions, deductions, and predictions. The elder von Moltke summed it up this way: "No plan can survive contact with the battle." He also said, before the Austro-Prussian War, "Gentlemen, remember that any instruction which *can* be misunderstood, *will* be misunderstood."

These aspects of projects are often ignored by inexperienced presenters, who discuss a project as though all expectations, hopes, and details are absolutely certain to be realized. These people either learn painful lessons on their first project, or they are not trusted with any future ones.

A good way to look at any project is to see it as a proposed voyage from one port to another—and you are to be in charge. You have selected the destination and secured tentative financial backing for the trip. You must now detail your specific plans in a presentation. We will use this metaphor to illustrate how the Field Order structure can help organize both the trip itself and its presentation to the backers. If successful there, a little rearrangement and change of emphasis can produce the presentation for the crew.

Begin by writing down a statement of the purpose of the voyage. Say why it is a necessary thing to do, and the benefits it will confer. Do not write anything about resources needed or specific plans (means), but confine yourself to the primary purposes (ends). This is what the military call the *mission*. It stands at the head of the order, and everything in the subsequent "paragraphs" will be measured against it. The ultimate report of success or failure will undoubtedly begin with a quotation of this original statement. Take care that it can stand up over a period of time—perhaps years—and not embarrass you later. Let's speculate on such a mission as Columbus might have written for his presentation to Queen Isabella. (I shall use the modern English of officials rather than the lush flourishes of Renaissance Spanish and Italian.)

The purpose of this proposed voyage is to settle once and for all several controversies which now frustrate expansion of the Spanish Empire.
1. Do unknown islands to the west really exist?
2. Is the earth truly round?
3. Is there a better route to India than the risky passage around Africa?
I personally believe the answer to each of these is *yes*, but no one knows for sure. If I am right, and Spain underwrites this trip, your Majesty will have legal title to all the lands between here and China. We will bear our true religion to untold millions of those who now know nothing of Christ and thus carry out His command to spread the Faith. We will also bring to the benefit of these unknown people the advantages of modern science and technology and will help multiply the production of their lands through improved management. The riches they will gladly send to Spain in return for the advantages they receive will allow your Majesty to extend the good works so well begun for the prosperity of your subjects. I am also worried that if Spain does not support

this effort, less civilized nations will do so from motivations far less honorable than your Majesty's.

I believe the entire project to be feasible, and the rest of this presentation will detail how I propose to go about it if I get your support.

So much for the mission. Now we will use our "organizing paragraphs," returning to Columbus from time to time to put flesh on the skeleton of more abstract considerations.

Since most of us are fortunately not under the rigidities of military life, we do not have to worry about maintaining the *sequence* of the paragraphs. Presentations have a much higher need for persuasiveness than do orders from generals. As admirable as firm discipline may be for generals, some rearrangement of the five parts is often more congenial to the audience's background and makes more sense to them. However, as a set of bins to collect different aspects and angles of a project initially, the five categories should be thought of as equally accessible. Only when you get to the moment of presentation must you finally decide on sequence. Let's go along for now with the traditional sequence, and wait until later to see if rearrangement makes any improvement.

PERSONNEL (G-1)

In this bin you place all considerations and factors affecting the *people* you will need. Here are some of the questions you should consider. (They usually demand that you produce answers. Even though the interaction of the other paragraphs may cause some duplication, it is far better to duplicate on paper than to omit it in actuality. When different "paragraphs" are assigned to different people to draft, as often happens in large projects, things will fall in the cracks if the leader insists on no duplication or overlap. Remember that the Child Jesus was lost when both Joseph and Mary thought the other had responsibility for surveillance. Duplication can be taken care of in a split second with a blue pencil while in the planning stage. Omissions in the real world of the project can be fatal or, at the very least, embarrassing.)

Personnel questions: What skills are essential? What backgrounds would be helpful? Where are the sources of people you need? How would they be assembled? What is their compensation to be? How many people do you *need?* Can you *use?* Who will supervise them? Whether you are building a pyramid or making a movie, the process of answering these will disclose gaps in your present information which must be filled. You must expect someone in every audience to ask every one. Ask these of yourself first, but be sure to get answers that at least satisfy *you* before taking the platform. When members of an audience say that "this idea is not well thought out," what they really mean is that there were too many questions of this type unanswered either during the presentation or the subsequent discussion.

Let's return now to our fictional Spanish court, where Columbus is discussing the G-1 side of his proposed voyage.

I have given a great deal of thought to what kind of staff would optimize our chances for success, consistent with the financial constraints of the Crown. The detailed personnel requirements for our task force will be found in Roll 1, but let me quickly summarize the personnel recommendations, and give some of the reasons behind them. We are trying to do something never done before. The potential rewards are incalculable, but even with the best people we may encounter difficulties beyond our powers. Your Majesty should have the best men in their fields assigned to this project if we are to minimize the risk of failure. We will need two captains, in addition to myself, and I am happy to tell you that the two Pinzon brothers, both renowned master pilots, have assured me of their services if the Crown gives its support. We shall need crews for three ships, soldiers, carpenters, linguists, surveyors, physicians, and priests. A few experts to appraise commercial potential, and some men of science to classify the flora and fauna of these unknown regions will be indispensable for your Majesty's future expeditions. Since the voyage will be arduous, I would like the strongest and youngest men available for each occupation, in case we encounter new diseases.

I have assurances from friends in Palos that the crews and
soldiers are almost completely gathered, and a few critical
vacancies can be filled by judicious pardons from the local
prisons there. Three scientists have volunteered from the University of Salamanca, and the merchants of Cadiz have come
through with a physician and the mining and textile experts.
We expect our linguist, Luis de Torres, to arrive any day. We
have enough holy friars volunteering to baptize all Europe, for
their zeal has been fired by the vision of carrying the gospel to
these unknown lands. In short, your Majesty, I can put my hands
on the eighty-seven men I need if you will say the word—but
not for long. I have promised them all, except the friars and scientists, that deposits of gold will be placed with the Palos bankers
in their names before we leave, and that if we do not return in
one year, their families will receive them.

These men will accept my leadership, but I will be advised by
the Pinzons, the chief scientist, our spiritual leader, and the
military commander in the conduct of affairs affecting personnel.

[Examination of the *actual* payrolls suggests that Columbus sub-
stituted able seamen for the soldiers and priests—evidently a
command decision in the interest of prudence.]

INTELLIGENCE (G-2)

The phase of a project described as "Intelligence" may conjure up fantasies of glamorous locales where spies and other
covert operatives furtively pass around secrets from the min-
istries of world powers. There is still an element of this sort of
thing in political and military operations—not quite glamorous,
yet far from dull. But all authorities agree (after they retire) that
it represents a very small part of any nation's intelligent intelligence effort. The greatest amount of labor and time is spent in
just keeping abreast of everything openly available about a subject, nation, or person. The best brains are reserved for the task
of making a meaningful pattern of the truckloads of information
available, and the best-of-the-best brains spend their time search-

ing for and describing the areas of ignorance which need more work done to clear them up. Why all this hustle and bustle? Why this strange mixture of cerebration, humming computers, and frantic travel? In the framework of our organization for projects, someone needs it in order to write paragraph 2!

An audience listening to a presentation of a project's plan or progress wants to know the risks involved before they agree. Some individual members have picked up gossip and random information about the project, or ones like it, and a few have made deductions about what your project really means by using inadequate or incorrect data pulled together from their own sources. The intelligence section marshals the ingredients to describe what is known, and what is unknown. Here you tell about the chances for success, and about ways to diminish the chances for failure. You also lay the groundwork for the methods you will use to keep the audience informed of how things turn out in practice. This section requires a delicate touch. You can drive the audience into fright and panic by overstating the risks, or lull them into disappointment and disaster by understating them. The method of opposites is the choice of master presentors of intelligence information. Its technique creates a sense of balance between optimism and pessimism, between the known and the unknown.

Here are the questions you must consider in preparing for the intelligence part of a project: What has been the experience of others with similar projects? What do you have to say about current rumors concerning your idea? What authorities or experts have you consulted on the various unknown areas and what are their opinions? Where have you obtained the information on which you base your conclusions? What changes in previously successful policies of the audience will be required to embrace your proposed project? Who else is likely to compete with you and cause you to fail? Why are you qualified to undertake this project? Notice that these questions are applicable to proposals to expand a school, conduct a campaign for election, market a new product, begin an archeological expedition, or establish a hospital—in fact, *any* project at all that entails risks.

How might Columbus have handled this?

We turn now, your Majesty, to a review of the existing knowledge and opinions that bear on this expedition.

As you know, I have long studied this matter, and for eight years have pleaded for the chance to try. But your Majesty's holy war with the Moors, finally succcessful this year, has kept us from a serious attempt. These years have not been wasted. I have collected facts and reports from sailors and travelers, studied the rare books of the universities, corresponded with men of science, and traveled myself to the present limits of your Empire. My brother, Bartholomew, accompanied the great Diaz on his voyages to the tip of Africa, and is now one of the most learned map makers in your realm. He has recently returned from England, and reports that interest is stirring in this same project there. King John of Portugal a few years ago tried to steal my plan, but he trusted it to the hands of an irresolute captain. This trip ended—as it deserved to—in mutiny, for the captain did not believe in its purpose. It is true that there are some who say I am mad, but when Marco Polo returned from China, no one believed his reports until he produced the jewels sewn inside his garments. I have had scholars inspect Marco Polo's original writings. By calculations using the most advanced analytical methods on Polo's data we are convinced that China and Japan can be reached by a month's voyage from the Canary Islands. The results of this scholarly work have been independently confirmed by astronomers at La Rabida. These comparisons are on Roll 2. I myself have talked to many fishermen in Madeira. Most have seen remnants of products and plants strange to Europe— but similar to those from Asia—float in from the western seas. Scholars have also told me of Norse legends which describe voyages to the West five hundred years ago, but these may be fictional.

With the infidels blocking Europe's expansion in the Mediterranean, and the Italians dominating what trade remains, our destiny *must* lie to the West. All countries on the Atlantic will soon awake to this last, open opportunity, and then we will have to compete and struggle. Now we need but sail. Everyone who has spent time investigating my plan is either completely enthusiastic, or at the least open-minded. *No one* has said that it is absolutely impossible, and all agree that no further knowledge will be forthcoming until someone actually sets out.

I believe in this to the extent that I gladly put my life in your hands as leader of the expedition. I will be responsible for any failures, and eager to bring your Majesty the fruit of the success I know awaits us.

Notice that intelligence can never eliminate *all* doubt, but that it attempts to minimize the total uncertainty by any and every means. It uses the most reliable data available, but checks it with rumors, observations of others, or anything that can help fill the vacant areas of knowledge. Its final conclusion is always a *judgment,* never the clinical certainty of a formula.

If you have only a limited amount of emotion to spend on a project presentation, place most of it on the intelligence section. Passion, belief, and hope may be the only bridges across some chasms of ignorance. Many a successful project has used them before, and many will do so in the future. Halls of Fame are rightly peopled by those who did things for the first time. This is equivalent to saying that their members went beyond the known. But accurate knowledge produced by the intelligence effort allows the leaps into the unknown to take off from the most solid foundation possible.

One of the traps for timid project presentors comes from their attempts to eliminate *all* risks by increased intelligence work. This can never be done for real projects. After some point, additional improvement in information requires more work and time than it's worth. Intelligence is important, but it is a *foundation* for the leap, not the leap itself. The leap is the province of "paragraph 3."

OPERATIONS AND TRAINING (G-3)

Here is the native habitat of men of action and the breeding ground for leaders of men (the word "operations" itself comes from the Latin *operatio* meaning "work").

The operations "paragraph" assumes the already stated mission as the "what" of the project, and selects, from the innumerable alternatives of "how," one course of action to accomplish the mission. Personnel, Intelligence, and Supply (covered next) furnish the chess pieces Operations deploys and arranges for the effect desired. Responsibility for the over-all design and plan of the project rests here. It also includes development and selection of alternative courses to meet contingencies. A first-class operations job covers the entire life of a project, from baptismal rites to the hymns sung at the burial service. Eeryone involved should be able to see what he is expected to do, when his part is to be finished, and how it fits in with the work of others, by consulting the specifications of the operations section. An analogy of the operations "paragraph" is the orchestra score of a symphony. The concert itself is the mission, the players are produced by Personnel, their instruments are furnished by Supply, the hall is selected and filled by Intelligence, and the conductor is in charge. But the complete score in front of him and the individual parts on the music stands of each player constitute the Operations plan. It tells each man which note to play and when to do so, subject to adjustment of the total effect by the conductor, as they all contribute their specific skills to the project. Managers, mothers, police chiefs, schoolteachers, conductors, top sergeants, theater directors, and mayors share one common bond: They all carry an "operations plan" in their heads (that is, they do if they are at all good at their jobs).

If a project requires that new personnel be trained in existing techniques or that existing personnel learn new techniques, this is best covered in the Operations section of a presentation. Because the training required derives from the actual plan selected, it can only be understood and scheduled in relation to the plan itself. The training may be done in many different places or different groups, but it is the operations section that calls the tune and takes responsibility that the training gets done. Violation of this principle has wrecked projects ranging from church bazaars to economic development programs of emerging nations.

Here are the questions which should be answered in the Operations section of a project-type presentation: When will the project begin? When will it be completed? Where will it take place? How will it be organized? What will be the responsibilities of the various parts of the organization? What is the schedule for the activities of the various parts? What training is required? How will the training be done? What contingent plans are ready in case of miscarriage?

How might Columbus have covered this with Queen Isabella? Let's see.

We now come to the exciting part of the proposed voyage. With the personnel I've selected and the information gathered on expected conditions, I have formulated a plan for the operation.

We shall leave Palos before the middle of August to avoid bad weather and also allow us to return before the winter storms. We shall use three ships for several reasons. Experience has taught us that when three ships travel in convoy, the hazards of mishaps at sea are greatly reduced. Also, with three ships I will command the flagship, and use it as our headquarters at the capital city where we will anchor. I can also dispatch one ship back to Spain to let your Majesty know of our success as rapidly as possible. The third ship will be dispatched on subsidiary voyages to various parts of the lands to survey and chart the best routes, and to aid me in arranging more formal visits with my flagship. During the voyage out, we shall sail within sight of one another at all times.

We shall use an improved system of navigation developed by the Pinzons and myself, which depends on the determination of latitude and dead reckoning beyond any accuracy known today. This secret method allows us to duplicate our voyage with larger expeditions in the future, and will ensure return of our messenger vessel by the most rapid route.

We must train our crews in new methods of sailing to take maximum advantage of these methods. This training will be done by intensive drill on the first ten days of the voyage, which will bring us to the Canary Islands. My knowledge of the ocean currents has been gathered over many years of travel, ranging from the South Atlantic to Iceland. This will allow us to set courses which maximize the contribution of prevailing winds and currents. After reprovisioning at the Canaries, we will then sail southwest for twenty more days.

If our calculations are correct, we should at that time sight the easternmost islands of India, China, or Japan. We intend to carry a royal banner to plant in these domains in order to signify the claims of your Majesty for all time. If all goes well, I shall then sail on to the seat of the Great Khan to effect an alliance between our two empires. (Incidentally, it would be helpful to have high rank conferred on me temporarily by your Majesty to facilitate these negotiations.)

As soon as this is done, I shall dispatch one of our ships to Spain to inform you of the arrangements. We shall also establish a base for future operations, and our commander of soldiery will be placed in charge. We hope to have our technical experts effect agreements to open up mutually profitable trade and secure concessions for Spanish merchants to be named by your Majesty. In this way, you will recover the underwriting expenses. I estimate that we will arrive in thirty days, move to the capital in another twenty, and return before the end of the year.

In case unexpected hazards overwhelm our best efforts, we shall carry a hundred sealed bottles, with messages inside, to be thrown into the sea. The messages will guarantee a reward from your Majesty on delivery to your court. If we have time, we shall also write down the circumstances of our misfortune in sealed bottles for guidance to your future expeditions. (These will promise the highest reward.)

This plan has been developed by the best minds available and contains the experience of practical men who have repeatedly risked their lives on successful pioneering ventures. This is a most ambitious project, but all of us are eager to start and are convinced that the details contained on Roll 3, constitute a plan that can succeed.

Visual aids are very useful in describing the details of operations, for they involve schedules, maps, and all the paraphernalia of action. The temptation to be resisted in the operations section is that of furnishing too much detail in the presentation. The audience may easily become overwhelmed. A good operations presentation is like a fresco rather than an etching. Strive for the big picture, but give assurance that the fine details are available and will withstand critical inspection. If you have alternatives available, mention them and explain why you picked the plan you did. Also, if your audience contains authentic experts in some relevant discipline, incline as far as possible to incorporate their suggestions in your final plan. Most audiences can see themselves involved in the action implied by operations, and their suggestions usually concentrate on this section of a presentation. Operations aspects carry inherent interest for stimulating discussion, but often the vote for approval or rejection will depend on whether the bill is too high. This brings us to the fourth "paragraph" of a project presentation.

SUPPLY (G-4)

Few projects enjoy the situation described in Matthew VII: 7 "Ask, and it shall be given you; seek, and ye shall find; knock, and it shall be opened unto you."

Every leader of a project faces two harsh constraints: time to complete it and supplies to carry it out. To some extent, the two are compensatory, in that a given project may generally be done faster if more resources are available, or will take longer if less are rationed out. There are, of course, exceptions. One can't speed up a scientific or artistic discovery by putting twice as many men on the job, just as ten chickens assigned to produce one egg cannot do it in one-tenth the time. Also, a chasm cannot be crossed by a series of small steps. But for projects involving known techniques and not limited by biological clocks, or thresholds of minimum effort, the trade-offs between time, supplies, and personnel are intuitively appreciated by everyone. This relationship of time and resources is a rich source of variations in discussions of the supply part of a presentation, and experienced presentors expect it and use it.

Financially minded audiences believe that their job is finished when they arrive at a judgment of the total funds to be made available for the project. "Financial expert" types are also inclined to bargain resources in money terms. You ask for 100,000 dollars, they want to compromise at 50,000, etc. Unless your project is strictly a financial one, it is most unwise to confine the supply section of a presentation to money alone—even for financially minded audiences. Here are some reasons: You invite bargaining. There may also be threshold effects; that is, a certain minimum amount may be necessary just to get started, before any results at all come forth. Backers should know how much *additional* risk they are putting into the project by chiseling on what's really needed. Experienced bankers know that if a man of proven judgment and performance says he needs 20,000 dollars to carry out a program, it is far safer to lend him 22,000 than to cut him down to 19,000. But in order to make such determinations, an understanding of what the cash will be used for is essential. If the resources are trimmed too closely, it is far better to postpone or cancel the project than to raise the risks of failure to the point of foolishness. You wouldn't try to fly the Atlantic on half-full tanks, yet inexperienced project presentors often let themselves get caught in exactly analogous situations, because they have not shown the dangers of such "economies" to their audience. Even Winston Churchill let his belief in a project lead him into this trap—once. When asked the lesson of the abortive Gallipoli campaign, he said that never again would he attempt to carry out a bold plan with less resources than necessary: "Men are ill advised to try such ventures."

Strangely, when tight-fisted approval bodies see that the supply side of a desirable project is well matched to its goals and mission, their reassurance restrains any tendency to petty chiseling. In fact, if they really admire the boldness and merits of a plan, they will often add to its chances of success (i.e., diminish *their* risk) by providing some margin of reserves.

This behavior says that when unconvinced of the merits of the proposed operations, they prefer to avoid arguments over its details and find it more decorous and dignified to choke off its sustenance. Withheld supplies signal failure to convince of the project's value. The supply part of a presentation, then, must show how the physical resources requested are absolutely essential to the operations. Lump sum requests for funds can never do that.

Another mistake made by inexperienced presentors is to leave the supply needs unadjusted when the audience escalates the scope or scale of a proposed operation. This is equivalent to bargaining, but is more subtle. Instead of asking that the proposed job be done for less, they insist on a larger job being done for the same amount or in less time. A cardinal rule for project success is that the only time to get resources is *at the same time the operations are agreed on.* Afterward, it's too late. Better to be a hero when the job is finished, than at the budget meeting which authorizes it.

Blackmail is as bad when tolerated as when perpetrated. Many eager innovators have been turned into dark reactionaries because they have let their enthusiasm for an idea blind them to its needs for minimum supply. Their resulting failure had its roots back at the initial presentations, when they sold their idea's chances in return for mere toleration of a half-hearted attempt. There may be rare times when "half-a-loaf is better than none," but if this proverb tempts you to give in, confront it with another: "Well begun is half-done." Inadequate supply causes stumbling even before the start.

Some shrewd men make successful careers by rescuing good projects that founder due to inadequate resources. They do this by resuscitating such projects with the small amounts of additional resources that should have been made available in the first place. If you don't want these scavengers picking your bones, pay sharp attention to resources. Supply affairs do not have the zest of Operations, or the fascination of Intelligence, but they need as much care as the horses that carried their knights to glorious victories.

With these gloomy admonitions out of the way, here are some questions that must be answered in the Supply "paragraph": What buildings, rooms, or land will be needed? Is construction necessary? What amount of payroll is required and for how long? What services and supplies must be purchased from outside suppliers? What service and supplies will be provided by other parts of the organization? What transportation will be needed? What special tools, furniture, or equipment must be rented or purchased? What storage arrangements are necessary? What financing alternatives exist? These questions are applicable to establishing a college, organizing a gambling casino, or planning a camping trip for underprivileged children.

Columbus might have tried it this way:

Roll 4 details the entire list of supplies required for this voyage, but I will cover the more important features to show how they are absolutely essential to our success.

The three ships have already been optioned, and I can have them only if I sign their charters within the month. The flagship, *Santa Maria*, is of 100 tons, 117 feet long and fully decked to protect supplies. The other two are caravels, of 50 tons each, are 50 feet long, and have only partial decking. While an austere fleet, I believe these ships will do well enough for my eighty-seven men. We will arm them with 4-inch bombards to fire granite balls. These will be supplemented by smaller guns which use lead projectiles.

We will carry two types of goods: cheap tools and merchandise for trading with the lower classes, and costly gifts suitable for the leaders. We will use ships' chandlers and provisioners at Palos and the Canaries to assemble supplies for a forty-day passage. We expect to secure supplies for the return trip in the Eastern lands, but must carry some gold as well as goods to insure purchase. It would be an inauspicious start for international relations if we had to commandeer supplies and live off the land.

Hand weapons for everyone aboard must be provided, as well as muskets, powder, and ball for the soldiers. Payrolls will be disbursed on our return, but will be deposited with the bankers before we leave. Navigation instruments are quite expensive. The captains and I will furnish many of them ourselves, but there are a few additional things we should have. The Church has generously offered to equip our friars completely for their missionary work and services to our men.

Everything we need has been kept to an absolute minimum to speed our trip. Larger crews would require more supplies, more supplies would require larger ships, and so on. We have ruthlessly eliminated every item except the essential, and have limited even these to levels near their danger points. These requirements cannot be reduced any further without enormously increasing already great risks.

The supplies for the whole expedition, detailed item-by-item on Roll 4, add up to an outlay of 1,500,000 maravedis. I have secured loans of 500,000 maravedis in my own name from merchants who have faith in my vision. I respectfully request your Majesty to make the additional investment of one million maravedis. By such expression of support you can cause this expedition to set sail in two weeks.

Vagueness in the Supply part of a presentation poisons its persuasiveness. There is something about furnishing a list of items and accounts, even though estimated, that reassures the audience. The reasons are probably twofold. First, such an itemization suggests thoroughness of planning, and neat rows of figures imply that the project is one of concreteness and solid practicality. Second, the audience can carry the list away for additional study and use it in the future as an audit or check against actual performance. This helps reduce anxiety about possible failure, for they can at least feel that postmortems can be performed with decency. Visual aids are often very effective —and sometimes essential—in presenting the Supply aspects convincingly.

An audience may not completely understand in detail the vision of the operations, but everyone can grasp the reality of bolts, nuts, freight cars, typewriters, dishes, convoys, land, buildings, machinery, or payroll checks. When their imaginations are applied to the mundane articles of Supply, they gain better appreciation of the scope and nature of the proposed operation itself.

EXTERNAL RELATIONS (G-5)

Any project of more than trivial importance creates impacts on others not directly involved in the project itself. These may be other businesses, organizations, universities, churches, fraternal groups, learned societies, etc.; or various agencies of local, state, federal, or foreign governments. You need permits to build a porch or to hold a parade, licenses to operate a pushcart or to export medicines, zoning rulings to establish a business, certificates of accreditation for a curriculum, health inspections to serve food, prospectuses to sell securities, foresters to oversee tree-cutting, and tariff approvals to haul commodities for others. Almost any idea today sets the web of existing legal relationships atingle.

All of these are rooted in socially desirable goals, and the mere thought of disturbing them often chills the blood of the man with a good idea. His opposition often plays unfairly on this anxiety, and no one knows how many potential innovators have been turned into arch conservatives by cowardly advisers masquerading as prudent men. Yet, we are fortunate that many of those who do have good ideas intelligently take account of these relationships and accommodate their projects to social and legal demands. A project of real value can always do so, but it must be considered as part of the over-all society in which it takes place. Any new idea of necessity constitutes a disturbance. If designed to solve a problem, the idea tries to transform an existing state of affairs into another state closer to the heart's desire. In this game, one man's transformation is another man's disturbance.

Some of the questions to be answered in "paragraph" 5 of the project-type presentation are: What approvals or documents must be secured from domestic or foreign governmental agencies? What agreements must be signed by others? What contracts are involved? Who may oppose the project on legal or social grounds? What bonds or insurance must be provided? What liabilities are assumed in undertaking the project?

It is easy to see how these questions can dampen the spirits of the most ebullient. They are like a thunderstorm during a garden party, and usually come from the dour, grim-visaged members of an audience if not anticipated and answered by the presentor himself. Even when answered in advance, faint-hearted, anxious members of the audience may not like the answer given. At these points, the presentor needs to draw on the deepest reserves of his character. He has probably spent long hours with melancholy experts to hammer out his answer. When he sees all that effort going up in smoke, his first impulse is to fight a battle to the death against modifications. This impulse *must* be held in check.

Entertain the objections with the greatest courtliness, and indicate an eagerness for alternative solutions. Other members of the audience expect someone expert enough to criticize to show how his expertise can help answer the questions. If such critics don't even attempt to help, their colleagues usually dismiss their criticism as totally destructive. When this happens, their influence diminishes rapidly. By showing a willingness to use alternative answers, constructive suggestions superior to your own answers may come forth. If the audience warms to these alternative solutions, embrace them quickly, providing they do not damage the project's chances. Agreement on questions of external relations is the best signal you can get that your proposal is accepted.

How might Columbus have handled this?

We will need a charter signed by your Majesty to signify that we are an official expedition of the Spanish Crown. This will give us priority for the local resources of docks, warehouses, and inns necessary to assemble our force. We will also need to have military guards furnished for the assembly area since secrecy of our detailed plans is essential.

The chandlers and ship owners will accept contracts from your Majesty instead of cash as surety for our performance. If we are successful, then your Majesty's liability can be discharged by the riches we will bring back. Only if we are lost would the Crown have to indemnify these financiers.

We can expect many kinds of covert opposition from Portugal, and perhaps hostile raids from unmarked ships in their employ. To counter this, your ambassadors to the Portuguese and the Pope should secure agreements that will prevent molestation of our passage through the Western Seas and also ensure the legitimacy of your claims to our discoveries. We should also have documents by which you and King Ferdinand authorize me, as your viceroy, to sign treaties with any rulers I encounter. Finally, a special letter of credit would be desirable. This would be countersigned by your chancellor, and only be used in grave emergencies on the return passage. I have consulted several lawyers here at your Court, and they know of no other liabilities assumed by your Majesty which can be attributed to this proposed voyage. I have had drafts of suitable documents prepared for examination by any experts you care to name, and they will be found on Roll 5.

Notice how the dismal language of the law adds an air of respectability to an apparently insane project. It was probably this kind of halo effect produced by legal phraseology which made otherwise sensible people think that the Volstead Act had a chance to succeed. This quixotic attempt to eliminate the use of alcohol must have looked downright silly unless clothed in the majestic phrases appropriate to constitutional amendents.

Thus the aridity of questions involved in External Relations can be looked on either as obstacles or as stepping stones across a stream of social or legal precedents. Expert presentors, with access to truly competent advice, are seldom stopped by such questions. They often use these questions to show their own nimbleness and ingenuity in the ways they approach and cross this stream.

After all, lawyers since the Code of Justinian have known that every precedent they search for was once a new response to changed conditions. In its youth a precedent enjoyed only upstart status; age brought respectability. Most projects experience a similar life cycle. Don't fight it; use it.

We will now let Columbus rest in his grave after the spins we have given him in the last few pages. Before we do so, let's pay final respect to the one quality necessary for a project proponent that he had in abundance: dogged persistence. He conceived his idea in 1476, and for the next sixteen years made presentations in quest of support to everyone who would listen. As great as his voyage was, maintaining enthusiasm for his idea throughout those disheartening years is an even greater accomplishment. Few men can exceed him in this regard. He stands as a model for the inexperienced presenter who cannot even contemplate disappointment, or learn from it. A harsh maxim for soldiers, which they seldom voice, but most believe, states that: "It takes the lives of ten thousand men to make a good major general." That's probably why most soldiers prefer to serve under a general who has already paid that unspeakable tuition. Mastery in presentation exacts its own price in disappointments and failures of persuasion. Like that of the general's, this education is so costly that wise men extract the last drop of instruction from each mistake. But few pay as high a price as Columbus, whom we now let rest in peace.

This completes our examination of the methods used by successful men of action in organizing the elements of a project for presentation to others. One can use other labels for the five "paragraphs" involved, but their content and questions to be answered remain the same. One can also rearrange the sequence of the various sections. There is nothing sacred about the subscripts of one, two, three, four, or five. But do such shuffling in full knowledge that you expect to live with the sequence throughout the life of the project. Any reshuffling of parts in subsequent presentations is mischievous for two reasons. First, you throw away the powerful, rhythmic effect of the repetitive form. This similarity of pattern subconsciously bridges the time gap to the previous presentation, and lets you safely use phrases like, "As we discussed before on this point," or "You will recall that last time we were unable to be definitive about this particular area, but now we have the missing information," etc. Second, if the audience does *not* perceive the same pattern in a series of presentations, they become confused by trying to relate the two different presentations. This is especially upsetting if they bring their previous notes or material distributed at the last meeting. Others become suspicious that the rearrangement is a cover-up. Neither of these reactions does a presentation any good.

Every meeting, from a parent-teacher association to the most august legislature, uses some form of rules of order to conduct its affairs. Such rules have little merit in *themselves*, but expectation and agreement on sequence embedded in the rules of order allow information to be communicated with less confusion than if at each meeting the chairman rearranges the rules. The "rules of order" for a series of presentations are unconsciously embedded in the *first* one. Choose this first sequence with care. When unable to decide, you will probably do best by falling back on the "paragraphs" arrayed in the classic, numerical sequence of the Field Order. At least all the old soldiers will feel at home.

Many projects today are extremely complicated and thus are in danger of coming unglued at some crucial spot and falling apart. Large urban renewal schemes, aerospace operations, re-organization of government departments or business firms, flood control, or the logistics of disasters of all kinds involve many things going on at one time. Different people or groups carry out essential, individual parts of the total effort, but they must be brought together at various times and places. If this interlocking is not controlled with care, the over-all objective that the whole thing was designed for in the first place cannot be realized.

Many clever men have produced many clever ways to control the meshing of complex subordinate tasks into a grand design. They are known by several barbarous acronyms, such as PERT or CPM. These come from their original labels: Project Evaluation and Review Technique, or Critical Path Method. There are dozens of variations of each, and every day someone adds to the pile. (If anything is out of control, it is probably acronym generation, but that's another story.)

Anyone who comes within hailing distance of any project of importance may be exposed to these techniques, expected to use them, or find his limits of action controlled by them. A few remarks about their nature and how they can be used and abused in presentations may be helpful, since they play such a dominant part in modern project management. Their names may change to accommodate the needs of fashion, but their basic ideas will be around for a long time.

These techniques are ways to develop and display schedules of interrelated activities. There's not much new in that, of course, for Xerxes' chief of staff was probably quite competent at handling this sort of thing. What *is* new, is the built-in ability of these schedules to be quickly adjusted for breakdowns in the various subordinate activities. By their ability to carry out constant rescheduling of all the parts (sometimes daily or hourly) they produce options for the managers to select. For example, some breakdowns may not affect the completion date at all, some may postpone it beyond critical deadlines, some unexpected accomplishment may allow earlier completion, or massive redeployment of resources may be required to prevent collapse of the entire project.

In earlier and simpler days, one brilliant man could do all this in his head, but modern complexities have grown faster than brain cells. If better techniques are not used, the manager must impose a stifling rigidity on all of the parts. This forces him to suffer the breakdowns, but also prevents him from taking advantage of lucky breaks. An example of this occurred in World War II during the invasion of Germany. A great master schedule for all units had been prepared and approved in London. As the Third Army raced across Europe, they found an intact bridge across the Rhine at Remagen. General Patton frantically pushed units of his army across it, and exultantly signaled headquarters of his good fortune. Shortly thereafter he was visited by a staff officer from headquarters who lectured the general on how his rash act was not in accord with "The Plan." One of this plan's assumptions was that no bridge would be left undemolished by the retreating Germans. The general's reply could not be printed without violating every guide to polite language, but one can sympathize a bit with the staff officer. If he wished to take optimum advantage of this unexpected stroke, he faced the impossible problem of adjusting the entire Allied effort sprawled across a continent. Entirely new schedules for every unit would have to be developed overnight and sent to thousands of organizations. Faced with this enormity, the staff officer preferred to tangle with a potent and colorful deviant from "The Plan."

The new approaches of PERT and Critical Path methods were designed to overcome this kind of noisy confrontation. How do they do it? They arrange all the activities necessary to a project in a long list, and estimates are made of the amount of time required to complete each piece of assigned work with an assumed level of resources. Also, each activity listed is tagged as to: 1. What other activities must be completed before it can begin; and 2. What other activities cannot be started until it is finished? For example, in construction of a building one cannot install plumbing before the foundation is dug, or put in ceilings before the concrete floors have been cast. Obviously there are certain delays that hold up everything and others that hold up nothing. If the steelwork falls behind schedule, the starting date for final painting scheduled eight months hence is affected; but if electric light chandeliers are lost or stair railings are not delivered, the rest of the building's subprojects can continue without adjustment. Unless you can link all of these subprojects together in a long series of dependencies, it will be difficult to know which projects are really essential to keep on schedule by any means (as they affect the completion date) and which have a great deal of leeway. The essential ones are said to be on the "critical path" of the network linking all activities in the project.

This means that any project on this critical path affects the completion date, and should get the leader's full attention. But —and this is the important point of these systems—as events occur unexpectedly, and reports of actual accomplishment are received, *the projects on the critical path change*—and the leader's attention should shift to the new path. Just *finding* the new critical path after initial reports from the real world is a slow and tedious task. For this reason the tracing and retracing required to find it is usually handled by computers.

And now I come to the real reason for this extended discussion. Some presentors who must report progress or discuss the control method of a project at an initial presentation blithely announce that no one need concern himself about schedules because "all of the scheduling will be done by computer." *This is invariably a mistake.* It makes as much sense as saying that you are going to let all of the scheduling be done by a Chinese abacus operator who will be located in Hong Kong and who does not speak English. Some managers would prefer his accessibility to that implied by the inane and thoughtless remark that "all scheduling will be done by the computer." I mention this because threats to the audience's sense of "being in charge" lead to their rejection of the benefits of these new methods—and that is a shame. Experienced and talented men are unwilling to buy better control in return for a state of benign slavery to a blinking, buzzing, and bloodless box of electronic hardware. This tragedy occurs because of misunderstanding caused by the presentor himself, who really did not mean what he said. If he *did* mean it, then he is totally incompetent to lead any project.

These control and management methods constitute a revolution in tools, but tools are still designed for men to *use*. A sensible man will only handle a powerful new tool if he gets instruction in its safe and proper use. My own experience has been that the first time an audience is exposed to these methods, it is best to explain in some detail how they work without reference to any computer. Show them how the various parts of the project are tied together by building up the linkages through a series of visual aids. Magnetic boards (described in Chapter 6) are best for smaller groups, but a series of slides, slowly increasing in complexity, step-by-step, are better for larger audiences. (There are also some good animated motion pictures available.) You then mark out the "critical path" through the forest of subprojects and then show how it is altered by unforeseen changes in the circumstances originally assumed. After they grasp the over-all idea of the method, someone in the audience almost always proposes a computer to do the tedious work of charting the suggested alterations of the original schedule. When this happens, you are home free. If no one does, you can safely introduce it yourself. They now see the place of the computer *in relation to themselves* in a proper light. All it really does is to display to them as rapidly as possible the layout of new circumstances on which they can exercise their judgment, *after* the computer has done its work strictly in accordance with their instructions. Now the relationship of slave and master are correctly understood, and the threat to their security suggested by an inept presentor is revealed as completely groundless.

I have never seen adoption of these advanced methods without this kind of instruction, but have also never seen a rejection of them when well presented. Most people in charge of human affairs do want to learn and keep up with improvements when competent experts take the trouble to teach them. However, they rightly resist being steamrollered by insolent high priests who insist that everyone blindly worship at the feet of their particular technological idols. Such resistance is the path of sanity; the high priests teach a false religion.

The message of this chapter is simple: The longest journeys begin with a single step. A project-type presentation is a proposed journey, and its initial step is the presentation to an audience whose support is necessary. Make sure it is a firm step and in the right direction, for the vision disclosed will affect your own life and the lives of many others.

Oscar Wilde's wit once hit on an insight which illuminates the relation of a project to its presentation. When most believed that art imitated nature, Wilde pointed out that nature often imitates art. What he probably meant was that how we *see* nature is affected by how works of art have *taught* us to see it. The presentation of a proposed project attempts to describe its parts in faithful imitation of how the presentor himself "sees" it. But the presentation to an audience will influence the project itself, since the presentor teaches his audience how to "see" his idea as embedded in the project's presentation. Throughout its life, a project will always be perceived by an audience through the spectacles fashioned for them by its initial presentation. Some distortion is always present, but proper structuring of the relationships among the various parts can minimize it.

A presentation of a proposed project is like running a motion picture newsreel of the future past the audience at high speed. They cannot possibly see every detail of every frame, but they are usually eager to grasp the "event" or over-all idea. More than in any other type of presentation, the project-type is influenced by the personal impressions created by the presentor. He is presumed to play an important leadership role if the project is authorized. He must show: that he has a worthwhile objective clearly in mind; that he has considered every relevant matter (as covered by the "paragraphs" of the Field Order); that he is enthusiastic about the chances for success; that he is willing to risk his life, reputation, or time; that people are eager to follow him; that the audience can afford to trust his judgment.

If he passes all these tests, no audience can resist giving quick approval. Should he fail just one of them, the audience is wise to put its money on another horse. Form in the presentation is rightly considered indicative of form in the world of the project itself. Responsible audiences rarely play long shots on the character of a project leader. Their lives are risky enough already. It is not enough to demonstrate talent. As Gracie Allen said: "Everybody's got talent; but can they wrap it up?" The presentor who shows that he can "wrap his talent up" for application to a proposed project is the one to bet on—and most people do.

11

Sources of Ideas

or

Hunting, Fishing, and Trapping in the Country of the Mind

Every human being has creative potential. He has had to handle a flood of sense impressions and ideas from the time he was born (or even before) just to survive and grow. Every one does this in ways unique to himself. Some retain the ability to seek and encounter new knowledge with the wonder and delight of a bright child until they die of old age; others find this ability handcuffed before adolescence. The first are the high-voltage idea generators; the others become time servers and cultural dropouts, careening from one physical stimulus to another merely to avoid boredom. Are these differences due solely to fate, unable to be influenced by the individual himself? If true, then all human effort to improve ourselves or understand our world is absurd. There are some who say they believe this, but they also continue to live. Their mere existence is the best refutation of their alleged belief.

If individuals can influence both development of their own abilities and alteration of their environment, then we leave the dark jungles of alienation and enter the land of affirmation. Our search then narrows for *means* to transform latent capacity into ability. We will concern ourselves with development of one specific ability: the generation of ideas. Here in this last chapter are set out several approaches used by others in the hope that the reader will find some of them helpful. They are presented in full awareness that only the individual can teach himself. The most that teachers can do is make it a little easier to learn by showing how individual potential for idea generation has been tapped by others before him.

Serendipity entered our language as a description of this phenomenon: Significant discoveries are often made by searching for something else, entirely different. Horace Walpole coined the word from the title of an old fairy tale, *The Three Princes of Serendip.* As these royal folks travelled about, they seldom found what they were in quest of, but instead always fell into situations and accidents that proved better than their original goals. Their luck grew out of two qualities. First, they did set out on journeys and thus created an environment far richer in accidental possibilities than staying at home. Second, they were sagacious enough to see chances for improvement of their situation in the unexpected events. Successful "idea men" take almost exactly the same approach. In this they have kept alive the attributes found in children before we train away their original creative and uninhibited curiosity, and before we restrain their playfulness. Since they are not expected to know much, children are not afraid to ask: "How does it work?" "Why is he doing that?" or to show their ignorance. This makes them models of open-mindedness, always on the alert for wonder and delight at the unexpected. It takes years to suppress this, but when finally achieved, we produce an individual who is a model of conformity. His original gifts of wonder and sensitive observation have been reduced to a comatose condition. His work becomes a carbon copy of others, he has no opinions of his own, and he seems always at attention, awaiting the commands of others to be told what to do. Such individuals truly believe the slogan of George Orwell's *1984,* "Freedom Is Slavery." But even such diseased cases of total adjustment can be roused, for like Sleeping Beauty, their gifts are sedated, not dead. We just have to find the right stimulus to bring them to life.

An outstanding manager told me of the most intellectually stimulating incident in his life. It took place twenty years before, but was as fresh as yesterday to him. The executive was sent by his company as a Fellow in a graduate training program, for men of unusual promise, at the Massachusetts Institute of Technology. On the first day, all of the Fellows were addressed by Norbert Wiener, the founding father of Cybernetics. Wiener had been a child prodigy, philosopher, linguist, novelist, mathematician, and expert in several other scientific and artistic fields. His credentials as an idea generator were impeccable and awesome.

Wiener began with an ironic flick: "I have never before stood before such a splendid array of future captains of industry. I'm deeply impressed; but, tell me, do any of you ever do any *thinking?*"

The audience remained silent, reacting prudently to the tone of veiled hostility.

"Come now, don't be afraid to speak up. Tell me some of the great thoughts you've had recently."

Silence.

"None?, well let's see what you can do with these." He looked down at the list of names in front of him, stabbed his pencil into it to select his victim and called out the name of the manager who told the story: "Ferguson. Let's find out what you know about giraffes and whales. What do you think happens to a giraffe's blood pressure when he raises his head? Does it go up or down?"

My informant said he had no idea.

"Think, man! You're an engineer and must know something about hydraulics. Don't you have to pump harder to raise a liquid to a higher level? Isn't blood a liquid, and isn't the heart a pump?"

Yes, my acquaintance admitted, and now that Dr. Wiener had pointed out the analogy, he could see how the blood pressure would have to rise.

"Wrong!" shouted Wiener. "It stays the same, and *nobody knows how the giraffe does it!* Don't you find that interesting and worthy of thought? Now, let's turn to whales. Do you know what 'the bends' are?"

The manager brightened a bit and said that they were ailments seen in deep sea divers and tunnel construction workers who suffered pains due to nitrogen bubbles collecting around the joints when subjected to rapid changes in pressure. He went on to say that "the bends" were prevented by lowering and raising divers very slowly to allow the nitrogen to dissipate gradually.

"Very good, Ferguson. Now tell me how you would account for the fact that a whale can rapidly dive hundreds of feet and then return to the surface immediately without dying from the bends?"

Ferguson was speechless.

Again the shout, "*Nobody knows how!* The whale knows a trick we don't. Let's talk about ways to find out."

Whoever arranged that curriculum knew his business. As unlikely as Wiener was to play the role of the Prince in *Sleeping Beauty*, he taught this group of intelligent men to look at their world with new eyes, by taking them back to attitudes of childhood. The subsequent weeks of more traditional subjects benefited no end from this bizarre introduction to idea generation. I asked Ferguson if he knew why Wiener used these examples. "Yes. I found out later that at the time of our course he was working on ways to use automation for the administration of anesthesia. This led him to a concern with blood pressure, respiration, and various mixtures of atmospheric gases. When he hit us, he was up to his ears in the subject." This anecdote illustrates another powerful method of idea generation: the pursuit of a solution to another specific problem, just like the Princes of Serendip. We will discuss that aspect a little later, for what often appears to the outsider as pure luck results from ways to sensitize the mind for attention to events and knowledge that would otherwise be ignored as irrelevant.

We sometimes see the approaches of childhood—wonder and curiosity—when a man takes on a job new to him. Whether he is a graduate entering employment, or a new governor of a state, his early days are often the golden period of his innovations. He asks as many questions as an eleven-year-old, listens attentively to everyone, finds zest in everything going on, is unafraid to show his ignorance, and has scores of suggestions for improvements. He finds people eager to help him, and they bring up many of their previously rejected ideas for another try. A spirit of optimism and excitement prevails. It is slowly eroded only by the weight of tradition, disappointing experiences, and caution, which grind down the spirit by excessive concern over procedural minutiae or capitulation to inertial forces. The ultimate degradation can be seen when the initial attitude of exhilarating exploration is completely replaced by one of passive defense of the status quo. Wise leaders always keep some of this childhood fun in their organizations (though they'd dislike the description), for it secures the probing and questioning examination of the present necessary to improve the future. They sometimes do this by transferring burned-out, jaded men to different jobs both to revive them in a new environment and to give their former subordinates a change of air. These leaders also use many devices to keep their people's interest high. One of the best is to make it safe and rewarding to express individual opinions on important issues.

You can observe the counterpart to this in elementary schooling. One teacher is interested only in having played back to her in tests the canned opinions of a great fictional work read by the class. Another shows that she is interested in each child's personal view of the book. The first kills idea production, the second fertilizes it.

Another tendency in childhood, disturbing to adults, is daydreaming or reverie. Yet the greatest creative minds have all admitted to indulging in it throughout their lives. Of course it can be carried to excess, but if it is completely obliterated, no ideas of importance can grow. Reverie or quiet reflection allows images in the mind to rearrange and group themselves in new combinations with a minimum of inhibitions. What we later call inspiration had its source in such moments.

Research on creative individuals shows that they go through several stages in producing a new idea. There are many different labels for these stages, but here is one list: 1. Problem discerned vaguely; 2. Search for additional facts; 3. Sort out facts for gaps and sharpen problem statement; 4. Incubation—frustration, rearranging, and letting subconscious work on the problem. This occurs even when the problem is consciously put aside; 5. Illumination—insight arrives instantaneously due to "seeing" new combinations or new viewpoint; 6. Conscious exposition and test of the insight produced.

Reverie allows incubation to do its job. Almost every great thinker reports that illumination came on walks, at sports, while shaving, on awaking, while listening to music, or otherwise removed from the conscious application of his mind to the problem. Many people suppress the incubation stage because of a Puritanical guilt about "not being busy"—most likely because they don't want others to see them so. They have equated toil with work. Until one gets over this feeling, he will never give his potential for ideas a fair chance to break through the crust of mental confusion and fatigue.

This crust is formed by constant preoccupation with energetic demonstrations of active performance to others. The only ideas such people present are repainted versions of old solutions once used successfully by others, since these can be dredged up by muscle alone. These super-industrious people can be quite useful in the fact-gathering stage, but generally are a nuisance when a new insight or idea is needed. They have completely repressed their creative instincts, and their "innovations" all carry a smell of the antique shop. Whatever facade they erect can usually be penetrated by watching their attitude to a genuine new insight. They invariably dismiss it as "blue sky" on first hearing. When proven, they act as though they discovered it themselves. Sometimes it is not their fault, as in those sad cases where promising graduate students apprentice themselves to a great and eminent professor. Too many years of this and they become feeble imitations of their master, with all of his weaknesses and few of his strengths. They often spend the rest of their lives in redundant elaboration of the great man's ideas, content to bask in his reflected glory. Do not expect new ideas from these unfortunates, but be especially wary of them if your idea questions or contradicts the work of their master.

IDEAS TRIGGERED BY INVOLVEMENT WITH OTHERS

Solutions to many problems lying below the peaks of genius can come by hunting for them in bands. The dialogue between people of diverse backgrounds acts as a substitute for the incubation stage. Their different ways of looking at a problem result in the kind of illumination produced by one individual's imagination or subconscious rearrangements. In general, the more varied the backgrounds available, the greater the chance to "breakthrough" the inhibitions of the present. The history of Operations Research is nothing but the achievements of such groups, where widely diverse skills were concentrated on a common problem.

A classic example came from a frozen food company, which faced an "impossible" problem in coping with the social clashes between migratory farm workers and residents of the local towns. Every obvious solution of better housing, recreational facilities, programs for children, schools, and improved medical care was tried. They all helped a little, but behavior soon regressed. At one crisis meeting, everybody in the company who had the remotest interest was invited. As the gloomy chronicle unfolded, everyone assumed an air of desperation—except one man. He was a climatologist and pointed out that the problem arose because the influx of the workers could not be scheduled to match the maturation of the crops to be picked. That's why they often sat around waiting for the crops to grow, got restless, went into town out of boredom, and got into trouble. He said that the problem would disappear if they could get the crops to grow on schedule!

He was almost hooted down as crazy to suggest that, but the management was desperate enough to let him try. After several failures, he finally found the solution. He "invented" a biological clock by planting a special kind of pea in every plot of the various crops. The pea's growth was the standard to predict with great precision the maturity and peak harvesting of the crop itself. Every factor of rain, sun, soil, and fertilizer affecting the crop was reflected in the growth of the pea plant. By watching *it*, and not the crop, the crop's maturity and the schedule of the workers could coincide.

It worked. The efficiency produced reduced the troublesome mixture of long waits and frantic rush, allowed a steadier pace of work, reduced those trips to town due to previous frustration, and the "impossible" social problem disappeared. There were many other beneficial effects and not one negative. The climatologist at the big meeting played the role in his company's collective consciousness of the uninhibited rearrangement that takes place in the subconscious of an individual. Comic cartoonists often show that one of their characters "gets an idea" by drawing a picture of a turned-on light bulb in the "balloon," which usually carries his statements. Such cartoonists are close to the truth, for the process occurs almost exactly that way.

Another inducement to the generation of ideas from groups comes by creating a permissive atmosphere for apparently wild, irrelevant, or playful suggestions. These suggestions are not usually practical in themselves, but they act as seeds for the others in the group to develop into something useful. The flood of ideas only comes forth if there is no fear of censure, but some people can't stand the apparent disorder and should not participate. They act as dampers on the others' suggestions and suppress the more imaginative. One technique to prevent dampening calls for use of a small bell within reach of everyone in the group. If anyone censures a suggestion rather than building on or constructively modifying it, anyone can ring the bell to stop him. As silly as this may seem, it actually works. I have had the bell rung on me more times than I like to remember.

A strange thing happens to the negative-minded man of adaptive intelligence in such groups for the first time. After having the bell rung on him a few times, he becomes sensitive and resolves not to get caught again. At first he retaliates by being extremely watchful for the negative remarks of others, so that *he* gets a chance to ring the bell. This requires attentive listening. After a while, since he has now listened carefully and has suspended his critical faculty, his constructive participation takes off. Some of the best "idea men" I know went through this pattern. Sessions like this should not last more than an hour for they are exhausting. After the session, the group reverts to "normal" status and summarizes, winnows, criticizes, rejects, and retains the unrefined raw material of the freewheeling session. For this stage, it is best to stay in the same room where blackboards or easels have kept track of the imaginative session's fallout.

I cannot forget one of these sessions. It became so enthusiastic when hot on the trail of a solution that one of the participants could not restrain himself to wait for another pad of paper to be placed on the empty easel. The one blackboard was full, and he was too wrought up to use small sheets, so he seized the chalk and began to draw diagrams *on the wall*. He really had something, and others added their contributions alongside. The whole thing looked like an Italian opera without music. By the time we had the answer, the wall was a mess, everyone felt a little sheepish, but we did have something of value far exceeding the cleaning bill, and we might have lost it. There was also an unexpected benefit. Three days later the building people, on their own initiative, placed new blackboards completely around the room. We had started their idea without meaning to, by giving them a new problem.

One other brake on idea generation is to let considerations of *how* something can be done get in the way of deciding *what* should be done. Unless the objective or problem itself is clear, all the numberless variations of *how* to do it get in the way, and the discussion slithers off into barren controversy over different means. Such controversies are often meaningless, since they can't be related back to an agreed-on *What do we need to do?* Experts are prone to this disability, for they are always long on implementation alternatives, but short on objectives. They are overeager to get things to the point where they can bring their expertise to bear. Objectives require judgment; implementation requires technique.

In this type of idea generation, the temperature often goes high. When new to this approach, the lack of decorum can be embarrassing. Shirtsleeves, smoke, pacing, exclamations, laughter, interruptions, and hijinks remind one of a shop rather than an office. Ordinary rules of social interaction do not apply, for these sessions are more akin to painting a fresco during the

Renaissance than to a meeting of a board of trustees. In my experience it is a mistake to lower the heat in the interest of etiquette. The very heat of discussion, like a piece of red-hot iron, makes it easier to work the raw material and lets everybody land the hardest blow he's capable of. It is not wise to have wide discrepancies in rank of the participants *unless* those of higher rank can forget their advantage and operate on a man-to-man basis. When you do get such secure people they make great contributions. If you blunder and get someone of high rank who insists on using his privilege, it is not safe for the other members to throw themselves into the imaginative, productive mode. The session takes on the daintiness of a quilting bee. When this happens, the leader of the session should adjourn it at the first opportunity and reconvene with one less member.

All of us have acquaintances who are politely known as "men of independent judgment" but who are called "mavericks" by those who don't like them. They are rough-edged folk, dissatisfied with the existing order, but often unable to persuade others because of the antipathy their personalities generate. Sometimes they assume a cynical pose to hide a deeply felt but unpopular belief, yet deep-down are intensely loyal. Others are given to harmless eccentricities in clothing or behavior, which make them unwelcome in certain circles. Many of these good people are prolific generators of raw material for ideas, but lack the patience, skill, or interest required to work it up into usable form. They are always grateful for a listener and are glad to have others use their insights, for their greatest satisfaction is to see the unwanted children of their mind make good. Everyone truly interested in the production of good ideas should value the acquaintance of mavericks. The finest hour of a good presentor comes when he is able to secure recognition for one of these unsung thinkers.

Good ideas come from everywhere. They don't seem to care about their origin, only their viability. Everyone has his own story, each different from the other. Just as Will Rogers said that he never met a man he didn't like, you can never meet someone who can't teach you something. I was once responsible for the design of instructions used by stockholders in filling out documents. My barber was a stockholder in my company before I was born and, when he heard where I worked, made many fine suggestions for improving the instructions. These were almost always used, and he took justifiable pride in his contribution.

A good attitude to assume for idea fertilization is this: What one man can build, another can improve. This is especially hard on those whose lives and energy have been spent in the building, but using it as a starting point separates the innovators from the caretakers. The builder's great accomplishment had to contend with all kinds of pressures, opinions, assumptions, and restraints at the time he did his work, and he was undoubtedly influenced by them. As time goes on, many of these change, and the builder himself, were he around to do it, would be the first to point out an opportunity for improvement. False loyalty to his work may deter diffident successors from making suggestions, but this is misguided. Many great ideas for improvement can come from reexamination of the inarticulate or forgotten premises of an existing philosophy, theory, institution, procedures, or relationships.

Thorstein Veblen observed that immutable conduct and progressively changing conditions result in a logical muddle. Keeping alert for logical muddles is a fine way to trigger inquiries that lead to new ideas. When you hear people recite a list of gripes, or complain that something "doesn't make sense," prick up your ears. This may be the tip-off that leads to an idea for authentic improvement. We live in such a complex world that many succumb to a view that stifles their talent for innovation. It happens like this. As their day begins, they see all the things they must do, and become worried that they will not get them done. They see their job as one of constantly trying to restore things to equilibrium. As events occur and are labeled "problems," action must be taken to restore the status quo. For many, this degenerates to transferring items from the "In" tray to the "Out" tray with maximum speed and minimum disturbance. When they encounter an authentic problem they do not see it as Henry Kaiser did, for he called problems "opportunities in work clothes." Instead they meet it as a disturbance to an already uneasy orderliness, try to solve it with standard solutions, and if these fail, send it to someone else.

The easiest way to get a reputation as an idea generator is to let it be known that you are interested in those things nobody else wants. By tackling them your acquaintances will multiply, you will learn a great deal about the entire organization you work in, and you create a whole corps of scouts who send you the raw material for improvement ideas. Your associates will think you a little crazy at first, but the zest of the unusual and your expansion of knowledge will make up for it. The best illustration I know of the "Status quo" attitude appeared in a letter of explanation for a break-down in handling. After a long discourse on the procedures involved, the letter ended "Of course you must remember that these unusual occurrences occur very infrequently. One could easily get the wrong misconception that the procedures are inadequate." One likely misconception—right or wrong—is to expect the author of such a letter to look on any problem as an invitation to high adventure. Yet most good "idea men" do just that.

Another source of ideas is ponderously called "vulnerability analysis." Where the existence of actual problems sounds the call for a new idea to cope with the disorder of which it is the symptom, vulnerability analysis tries to *anticipate* the problems before they occur. Its approach to life is the opposite of Polyanna's or Dr. Pangloss's. When things are going smoothly, it tries to find the potential weak spots in industries, schools, banks, churches, defenses, processes, cities, or stores—anything that works as a connected system. Some examples might be:

Steelmaking: Enormous amounts of heat are required to melt and reheat the basic product many times from iron ore to finished goods. Any idea that can eliminate repetitive heating and cooling promises great benefits.

Chemicals: Requirements for fresh water are huge, and pollution from waste an increasing problem.

Universities: Constant review of age distribution, competence, coverage, and emphasis on various departments is required to plan for a balance of continuity of excellence and needed improvement.

Extractive Industries: Inventories of reserves, cost comparison of different methods, and exploration of new sources are necessary for survival.

Retailing: Population shifts, patterns for supply and distribution, and changes in taste make this field extremely complex. Ideas are needed in every phase.

It is an interesting exercise to do this for your own area of work in general and your own enterprise or institution in particular. Those with a gift for it will usually find great interest in their ideas, for vulnerability analysis goes to the heart of an operation in an over-all way. It addresses itself to problems that are the concern of everyone in the field, but are often neglected by narrow, specialist functions. There is an old organizational maxim: "Something that is everyone's responsibility becomes no one's responsibility." Vulnerability analysis tries to fill the gap. In its simplest form it asks this question: "Where can we expect the next problem to come from, and where will it hit us?" One of the worst pieces of vulnerability analysis was found in the Maginot Line. Since it was assumed impregnable, none of its guns could fire to the rear of the line. Positions were taken from the rear by encirclement.

Those with a speculative cast of mind often bait their hooks for ideas with questions beginning: "What if . . ." Professional politicians and other leaders seldom answer such questions in public. But they are in an awfully bad way if they don't have men on their staffs who ask all kinds of such questions privately —and then produce good ideas for coping with them. A variation of the "What if" method of provoking ideas comes from asking this question: "What would we do differently if we were putting this whole thing together for the first time?" This is a device to break through the layers of tradition, precedent, and experience. Once exposed, they can be tested for relevance and desirability in the present circumstances. In first-class organizations they usually hold up extremely well, but until reexamined, one can't be sure. The very act of reexamination is itself an idea generator, for it sends signals to all involved that their ideas and suggestions are welcome.

One can safely use this method only with those of constructive temperament. Unfortunately, there are some people burdened with a nihilistic or bitter streak who can ruin an idea session built around this question by exploiting it as a therapeutic outlet for their frustrations. When this starts; stop! Reconvene later without them.

A powerful technique to focus concentration of attention for idea generation comes from "setting up" tasks for yourself or your associates.

Here are a few. Their main purpose is to trigger interest in what otherwise may be a dormant, indifferent, or self-satisfied mood.

Think ahead to the answer you would give to the highest ranking person in your line of work if he asked you this question: "Based on conditions as you know them here, what would *you* do to improve things, were you in my position as leader?" This question forces you—or the people in an idea session—to concentrate on *positive* action rather than compiling a long roll of vague complaints. Everyone has some capacity for this kind of role-playing, and you will often be surprised at those from whom the best ideas come. When the parish priest is invited to think like the Pope, or an assistant professor plays the part of the dean, or the foreman widens his view to that of the chairman of the board, or the head of a bureau takes account of the limited options of a governor, two salutary results occur. The participants *must* extend their vision beyond their own area of concern. This forces them to look at their work from a completely new angle. Such play-acting can produce ideas of immediate value to them after they shed the temporary glory and burdens of the powerful.

The second benefit comes from their surge of appreciation and understanding of the whole effort and their particular contribution to its success or failure. A leader of any kind of organized effort is wise to encourage such sessions. When the people involved in these roles *figure out for themselves* the over-all problems he faces, the leader can diminish his own chore of sermonizing or exhortation. This happens even if they are wrong in certain details because they lack specific pieces of information. If he is ingenious enough, the leader can set up channels to receive the output of the sessions. One quick way is actually to ask the question as he visits the various groups. The jungle telegraph will broadcast his attitude faster than anything he can devise.

Another method of trapping for that increased personal awareness that triggers serendipity is to set down for yourself the seven greatest unsolved problems facing your organization, industry, or institution. Keep them near you and refer to them from time to time. They are the bait to which all kinds of events, advances, and disappointments can be attracted and tested for relevance. Ambassadors succeeding to a new post used to be presented a card by their predecessors as the change took place. On the card were listed the outstanding, current diplomatic problems between the ambassador's own country and the one to which he was assigned. Many carried this on their persons at all times, for it kept them alert for possible solutions whether they were at social functions, private audiences, or international conferences. The goal of every ambassador was to achieve what was called a "clean card." Few, of course, ever did. Their method is exactly the same as your own list, and even if it never becomes "clean," it at least amplifies the chances for success. In dynamic operations, as one item comes off, it is quickly replaced. You can expand your "trap line" by giving your list to other men you know who have a reputation for intelligence and imagination. Ask them to let you know of ideas and developments in their fields that might help solve those problems on your list. They will be pleased at your recognition of their talents, and will usually respond with enthusiasm.

Another way to "set up" a problem for yourself is to undertake to write an article on a subject of interest in your field. Keep two articles in mind, one for fellow practitioners, and one for a "popular" audience. It makes no difference for idea generation whether you ever publish them, but if you *are* serious, it increases your sensitivity. Secure two envelopes or folders in which you place clippings, ideas, or anecdotes which may be of use when you write the article. You will be amazed how the attention you give to everything you see or hear will be heightened. You are alerted to catch any specific information relevant to your articles, and will find yourself reading newspapers or magazines, listening to presentations, looking at television, or perusing reports and books with a new sensitivity.

Similar effects are felt when you agree to deliver a speech or make a presentation. As soon as you have agreed, start labeling another folder, and let your acquaintances know that you are interested in any raw material that may help. This sort of thing breeds rapidly, and you will find yourself a new focal point for all kinds of ideas not even related to your request.

In Chapter 9 I discussed how "marginal men," those persons competent in one field who develop an interest in another, often make great contributions. Try to cultivate this attitude yourself, especially if you are professionally expert. Make excursions and welcome opportunities to participate in the activities of a field in which you have a latent, but unprofessional, interest. You will always get more than you give, for the view of your own field from a vantage point outside it will suggest ideas and applications that could not be seen from the inside. Analogy is a great creative tool and every field is rich in lessons and similarities for another. Jules Michelet, the French historian (1798–1874), summed it up this way as he presented prizes at a graduation exercise:

"Woe be to him who tries to isolate one department of knowledge from the rest. . . All science is one: language, literature and history, physics, mathematics and philosophy; subjects which seem the most remote from one another are in reality connected, or rather they all form a single system." Every time a "marginal man" makes a discovery overlooked by the indigenous specialists of a field, old Michelet's vision gets further support. Become a "marginal man" yourself, and welcome anyone who wishes to become one in your own area. Your idea production will soar if you do. It is the best antidote I know for the poison of narrow, jurisdictional concern, which kills ideas if they are born in the "wrong" place.

A radical approach to idea generation, which requires great nerve, injects the tremendous stimulus of a threat to survival into an operation. This is not for everybody, but when successful, the participants are astounded at their accomplishments. Here is one example of how it was used. A system of record-keeping, which had used nine hundred tons of addressograph plates and manual records for forty years, was to be changed to an electronic computer system. There was grumbling and opposition from some older veterans who were skeptical of its success, and they avoided getting involved. But one day the moment of truth arrived. As the transition operation began, one of the veterans came to the leader of the new system and asked: "What should we do with the addressograph plates as their accounts are converted to the computer?" The leader knew that his questioner had opposed his idea, but that he was an excellent man who could contribute many ideas to help if he would only enlist. Previous attempts to get his support had failed.

The leader leveled his eyes, took a deep breath, and said, "Melt them down. If someone wants to cast some souvenirs from the molten metal, it's all right with me."

The veteran was aghast. He stammered: "But what if this system of yours doesn't work?"

The leader sighed, "If this system of *ours* doesn't work, *you and I* are not going to be the ones who put this whole thing back on the old system."

The veteran left quickly, and was overheard talking excitedly to his cronies, "My God! He's really serious about this thing!"

One week later the veteran had developed a brilliant idea for balancing accounts on the new system that had eluded the computer experts. At the completion of the transition he was promoted, placed in charge of the computer operations, and was a tower of strength until his retirement.

The leader told me that he got the idea for enlisting the veteran's help from the experience of Cortez in Mexico. After landing on the wild coast, some of the men lost courage and wanted to turn back. Cortez made the decision that stopped vacillation and made them concentrate on the real problem: He burned the boats. Risk and threat to survival mobilize intelligence dramatically, but they require a cool hand in charge. This method of provoking ideas should never be used by leaders who are nervous, timid, or uncommitted to the over-all idea itself. Such men encourage flight instead of ingenuity in those they presume to lead. Ship captains who pace the deck moaning "We're all going to drown!" are not good for anybody's morale.

READING AND IDEAS

One of the evils of what has come to be tiresomely known as the information explosion is its relentless tendency to narrow our reading. The pressures to confine ourselves more and more to reading in our primary field of interest must be resisted, if we are serious about generating new ideas. Those supple minds that make the great contributions have always been exercised by many interests. The narrowing specialist who tries to hone his skill by greater and greater concentration deteriorates in effectiveness. Shaw aptly described his terminal condition: He knows more and more about less and less until he knows everything about nothing. Such men are useful only as auxiliaries for better and broader minds, to be called on as one would grab an ice pick for a specific and well-defined task.

The best antidote for this is a wide range of reading. If an expert is really sharp, "outside reading" produces a flood of associations which drench his mind and allow promising and original approaches to sprout in his own field. One of the best comptrollers I know is good enough at geology to teach it in college. He has far more books on geology than on accounting in his home. The best experimental physicist I ever met was a recognized authority on beetles. The most humane and cultured financial officer I know is a national skeet champion and an ardent conservationist. Other acquaintances have similar "paired skills": An expert on financial operations has a profound grasp of Slavic history; an outstanding personnel specialist is learned in Post-Impressionist art; a first-class public relations practitioner is an authority on Mayan archeology; a management consultant's knowledge of geography would put world travelers to shame; a noted economist is a fine wood sculptor; and so on and on. I have little doubt that they are better in their chosen occupations *because of*, not in spite of, their interests and competence in other fields. In fact, it is difficult to find someone in the top drawer of contributors to his profession who does not do wide and lively reading outside it.

A senior editor once told me of the ways he used to keep oriented in our complex world. I have since used them myself and found them so productive of ideas and insights that I set them down here. They are based on one method used by surveyors to establish their positions. This method is called *triangulation,* i.e., three angles. Surveyors take sights to three known objects at some distance from their position, preferably in widely different directions. The place where the three lines of sight intersect determines the position sought. (This is also the basis of celestial navigation; the "known objects" sighted are stars, planets, sun, and moon.)

How does one "take sights" through his reading? Here are the editor's suggestions: 1. Skim an entire daily newspaper. 2. Read a weekly news magazine or review; select different ones from time-to-time. 3. Pick up a trade paper remote from your own field every now and then. 4. Buy different monthly "opinion" periodicals, even if their editorial policy is repugnant to you. 5. Dip into so-called learned journals in other fields. If you grasp only the titles, you're ahead. 6. Scan a book review magazine of some kind. You may stimulate a latent interest. *Buy* some books; don't rely on friends. Use library copies if you can't afford them. 7. Read a foreign periodical frequently. If you know only English, use English, Scottish, Canadian, or Australian magazines. Some others are translated. 8. Reread a fine novel or classic untouched since your youth. You will be surprised at how different it is today. 9. Select a subject or a period in history for a few weeks of concentrated interest. Make it fun, not a chore. Stop when it becomes a bore or overtaxes your powers. Historical patterns help illumine today's events. 10. Do not be afraid of being called a dilettante. You are after stimuli, not professional standing.

After a while, these become almost habitual. Every excursion is like a sightseeing tour taken at your own pace. You will be a rare person indeed if you do not discover unexpected delights or get a new perspective on your own work.

Access to a good general encyclopedia is almost indispensable for quick reference. If you are fortunate enough to have one close by, dip into it as though sampling a plate of hors d'oeuvres. You may trigger an appetite for a heartier meal. Believers in serendipity are always justified by this exercise. If you have a problem on your mind in the incubation stage, you will often discover a connection with pages opened at random. Specialist encyclopedias save an enormous number of false starts and redundant work. Besides, they are fun to leaf through.

MECHANICAL IDEA TRAPS

Ideas flit by at high speed and must be winged to bring them down to earth.

Keep some kind of notepaper within arm's reach at all times. Use napkins or other tissues in emergencies. I once saw an acquaintance write a note to himself on a five-dollar bill in the middle of a symphony concert. He told me later that the idea was one of the best he ever had, for it solved a personnel problem which had been plaguing him for months. For group approaches to idea generation make sure that large paper easels or blackboards are available. Limiting everyone to small-scale pads constricts their thoughts in some strange way. Many don't believe this until they try the expanded approach. Then you can't take it away.

Some people keep "idea files" in which they collect all kinds of materials. They flip through them periodically or when a new problem arises. We all know some of those forlorn people who tell us: "I'm glad that somebody's finally getting smart. I hear that we're going to do what I suggested ten years ago."

Such people really do not deserve much sympathy, even when what they say is true. The person who kept running through his store of untimely ideas, alert and patient for the conditions that would make one of them feasible, deserves our plaudits, not he who shot an idea off like a skyrocket and then forgot it. Ideas are far more abundant than those who know how to care for them in infancy. "Idea files" are the nurseries of improvements.

RECREATION

One cannot engage in the idea business for long before he sees that frontal assaults do not always succeed. Our brains and minds work "in mysterious ways their wonders to perform." Experienced and successful generators of ideas know that they must often fall back and regroup for another try. This is the insight embodied in the sound advice to someone who has to make a serious decision: "Sleep on it. You'll see it much more clearly in the morning."

Recreation is another form of such strategic withdrawal and, when well-chosen, can magnify anyone's potential for idea production. In his most charming essay, Sir Winston Churchill examines the various avenues to recreation, with canny observation on their strengths and weaknesses. Here is a passage from his *Painting as a Pastime,* where he discusses the recreation appropriate for men who deal with things of the mind:

> But reading and booklore in all their forms suffer from one serious defect: they are too nearly akin to the ordinary daily round of the brain-worker to give that element of change and contrast essential to real relief. To restore psychic equilibrium we should call into use those parts of the mind which direct both eye and hand. Many men have found great advantage in practicing a handicraft for pleasure. Joinery, chemistry, book-binding, even brick-laying—if one were interested in them and skillful at them—would give real relief to the over-tired brain.

Sir Winston then goes on to push his own choice of painting. But don't let the title fool you. The first nineteen pages are recommended to anyone who is not satisfied with his present choice of recreation. Churchill did not find his until he was forty, and no one can surpass him as a guide and adviser to all of the possibilities. Recreation requires custom tailoring.

Those who deal in ideas should take care that they get a fit suitable for a long time and are not satisfied merely with the currently fashionable.

I come now to the conclusion of this long and one-sided conversation. If this book has any justification at all, it must be found in the fact that never before have men all over this planet been in greater need for insights, ideas, and practical solutions. These are badly needed, not only to cope with our complex environment, but more importantly to find ways that advance the well-being of the entire human race. I am sure that many such improvement possibilities are scattered, but dormant, throughout our population. Unless these precious ideas can be expressed to others, hammered into useful programs by discussion, and embraced by those affected, we will fall short of what we want and need.

The reader who has stayed this far has proved the possession of one essential quality of a good presentor: persistence in the face of obstacles. I thank you for it, and wish you well, for *your* success is *our* success.

APPENDIX

Checklists

or

Every Man His Own Critic

This appendix splits into two parts. The first is designed like the checklist used by aircraft pilots *before* takeoff. It may be useful in inspection of a proposed presentation to insure that nothing important has been overlooked or taken for granted. The second is intended as an evaluator of the presentations of others. Critical examination of presentations as a member of the audience can furnish valuable lessons for your personal improvement. Those superior raise standards and suggest new approaches; those inferior furnish object lessons on what to avoid.

A. *Preflight Check for a Presentation*

1. Problem-Statement
   What are the two clashing images?
   What exists? What do you want to exist?
   Which of the various forms of statement is best:

Historical Narrative	Blowing the Whistle
Crisis	Adventure
Disappointment	Response to an Order
Opportunity	Revolution
Crossroads	Evolution
Challenge	The Great Dream
	Confession

2. Opening Sentence—Will it excite the interest of the audience?
3. What is the "plan" of development?
   Thesis, Antithesis, Synthesis, etc.
4. Do you have examples or anecdotes?
   a. Which *points* do they illustrate?
5. What devices do you have to get and hold attention?
   a. Is there a balance between Reason, Emotion, and Common Sense?
   b. Can you use assertion, refutation, doubt, and affirmation?
6. Style
   a. Have you made it as brief as possible?
      Is it oversimplified?
      Is it overembellished?
      Are there any tortured passages?
      Are there any embarrassing ones?
   b. Is every point clearly expressed?
   c. What alternations in mood exist?
   d. Is there a mixture of the lofty and commonplace?
   e. Can you use suspense or mystery?
   f. Do you need a recapitulation?
   g. If a multiple presentation, is a leader appointed?
7. Is the tone one of equality, dominance, or submissiveness?
   a. Do *you* really believe in the idea itself?
8. Is the group small or large?
   a. If large, do you have some humor to "break the ice"?
9. What prejudices, fears, or constraints can you expect from this audience?
10. Have you checked the room for distractions? Have you neutralized them?

11. Is the room layout one that encourages discussion?
12. Are visual aids appropriate?
   a. Does each one carry a statement of its significance?
   b. Are the best graphical methods used for statistics?
       (1) If technical, have they been checked for competence by experts?
   c. Is their *size* correct?
   d. Are they related to one another so that someone could extract your message from the set of visuals alone?
   e. Have you considered alternative mechanical methods? (slides, view-graphs, blackboards, etc.)
13. Have you identified the weak points?
14. What cross-examination questions would *you* ask if you were in the audience?
   a. Do you have an answer for each one?
   b. If challenged on your competence, can you reply appropriately?
   c. Have you identified those in your audience who may support you, who may oppose, and who are neutral?
15. Do you state clearly: (1) What you want the audience to do when you are finished? (2) What you wish them to believe?
   a. Does every point made lead to your ending statement in some way?
   b. Docs the audience need to make great leaps to get to your conclusion?
16. Does the presentation use any special vocabularies unfamiliar to your audience?
   a. Havc these been translated into terms intelligible to them?
17. Are unfamiliar techniques employed?
   a. Have these been explained?
   b. Have you established why these are used instead of more familiar methods?
18. Have you considered alternative methods of presenting technical points?
19. If the presentation is a "project" type, have you touched the five areas common to all programs?

    a. Personnel
    b. Intelligence
    c. Operations
    d. Supply
    e. External Relations

20. Have you exposed the ideas involved to the original, inquiring, and skeptical minds among your acquaintances?

B. Evaluation List for Presentations of Others

1. Is the opening interesting?
2. Is the problem stated clearly?
3. Are the points developed to give a well-rounded view of all relevant aspects?
4. Is the *action* or *belief* desired stated clearly?
5. Does the presentor show that he has a vital and passionate interest in the idea presented?
    a. Is he dominant, submissive, or does he treat the audience as equals?
6. Is the style appropriate for the content?
    a. Brevity
    b. Clarity
    c. Variety
    d. Mystery or Suspense
    e. Recapitulation
7. Does the presentor explain or translate technical material well?
8. Are the visuals well designed and related to each other?
9. How well is cross-examination and discussion handled?
    a. Did the presentor anticipate opposing viewpoints?
10. Is the layout of the room distracting, or does it inhibit discussion?
11. Are the examples, anecdotes, or humor relevant to points made and matched to the style selected?
12. Does the presentor's idea appeal to Reason, Emotion, and Common Sense?
13. If a "project" type presentation, does the presentor take note of all relevant factors?

a. Personnel
b. Intelligence
c. Operations
d. Supply
e. External Relations

14. Is the impression created by the presentor one which inspires the confidence of the audience?
    a. Are there any embarrassing points?
    b. Are there any nervous or irritating mannerisms?
    c. Is there a willingness to listen to the suggestions of the audience?
15. Did you learn anything new, or discover new ways to look at the old?
16. Did you see any new approaches which you can use in your own presentations in the future?

This list can also be used to structure your reply when a presentor asks you for a serious appraisal of his performance.

Index

Index

Acton, Lord, 231
Allen, Gracie, 302
Analogy, examples of use of, 89–93
  use of in development, 85–88
Anecdotes, need for careful choice of, 88
  use of in large groups, 147
  use of in small groups, 144
  use of in technological presentations, 257
  see also Analogy
Apriority, method of, 123–24
Aquinas, Thomas, 122
Arab-Israeli War (1967), 20
Ardrey, Robert, 8
Aristotle, 36, 82
Aristotle Contemplating the Bust of Homer (Rembrandt), 6, 7
Attention: as clash between environment and event, 75–76, 76–77
  concept of progress in attracting, 94, 95
  and the emotions, 76
  means to attract, 73–99
  need to take risks in attracting, 77
  role of first sentence in attracting, 118–20
  and sense of development, 77–78, 80
  six questions to be answered to attract, 78–79, 89–90
  sources of distraction, 96–99, 189
  span of in audiences, 86
  structuring of information to preserve, 79–82, 88–89
  see also Development

Audiences, appeal of analogy to, 85–86
  awareness of speaker's personal motivations, 149–50
  capturing attention of, 40–41
  composition of, 6–7
  cross-examination by, 93, 193–220 *passim*
  eagerness of to receive ideas, 15–18, 30, 254
  effect of speaker's insecurity on, 138–39
  effect of style on, 103–4, 118
  effect of technological age on, 16–18
  expectation of entertainment by, 150
  hostile, 15, 155–57
  importance of make-up of individuals in, 139–41
  inclination of to stereotype speaker, 132–33
  interaction between speaker and, 9, 14–15, 132
  large groups, 145–51, 157
  motivations of individuals comprising, 7–8, 139–40
  need for understanding of, 2, 5, 19, 41, 94–96, 110
  need for respect in dealing with, 30–31
  participation of, 153–54
  and question of group psychology, 142–43, 151–53, 200
  reaction of to ambiguous objectives, 45–46, 72

333

Henry M. Boettinger is an internationally known consultant in telecommunications, and former Director of Corporate Planning at AT&T. His lively and imaginative style is characteristic of both his life and writing. A cellist, painter, and electrical engineer who attended Johns Hopkins University, he lives in Cornwall, England, with his accomplished wife, Shirley. Articulate, visionary and practical, he has been called the "communicator's communicator." A Visiting Fellow of Oxford University, and a Fellow of the International Academy of Management, Boettinger is at home in the diverse cultures of science, technology, and the arts, yet speaks the language familiar to persons oriented toward action and achievement.

Moving Mountains